A WALK ON THE WILD SIDE

BY NELSON ALGREN

SOMEBODY IN BOOTS

NEVER COME MORNING

THE NEON WILDERNESS

THE MAN WITH THE GOLDEN ARM

CHICAGO: CITY ON THE MAKE

A WALK ON THE WILD SIDE

Nelson Algren

A WALK
ON THE
WILD
SIDE

GREENWOOD PRESS, PUBLISHERS
WESTPORT, CONNECTICUT

Library of Congress Cataloging in Publication Data

Algren, Nelson, 1909-
  A walk on the wild side.

  Reprint of the ed. published by Farrar, Straus,and
Cudahy, New York.
    I.   Title.
[PZ3.A396 Wal 1978]   [PS3501.L4625]   813'.5'2   78-509
  ISBN 0-313-20294-X

Reprinted with the permission of Farrar, Straus & Giroux, Inc.

Reprinted in 1978 by Greenwood Press, Inc.
51 Riverside Avenue, Westport, CT. 06880

Printed in the United States of America

10 9 8 7 6 5 4 3 2

To
Elizabeth Ingersoll

ONE

"H E'S JUST a pore lonesome wife-left feller," the more understanding said of Fitz Linkhorn, "losin' his old lady is what crazied him."

"That man is so contrary," the less understanding said, "if you throwed him in the river he'd float upstream."

For what had embittered him Fitz had no name. Yet he felt that every daybreak duped him into waking and every evening conned him into sleep. The feeling of having been cheated—of having been cheated—that was it. Nobody knew why nor by whom.

But only that all was lost. Lost long ago, in some colder country. Lost anew by the generations since. He kept trying to wind his fingers about this feeling, at times like an ancestral hunger; again like some secret wound. It was there, if a man could get it out into the light, as palpable as the blood in his veins. Someone just behind him kept turning him against himself till his very strength was a weakness. Weaker men, full of worldly follies, did better than Linkhorn in the world. He saw with eyes enviously slow-burning.

"I ain't a-playin' the whore to no man," he would declare himself, though no one had so charged him.

Six-foot-one of slack-muscled shambler, he came of a shambling race. That gander-necked clan from which Calhoun and Jackson sprang. Jesse James' and Jeff Davis' people. Lin-

3

coln's people. Forest solitaries spare and swart, left landless as ever in sandland and Hooverville now the time of the forests had passed.

Whites called them "white trash" and Negroes "po' buckra." Since the first rock had risen above the moving waters there had been not a single prince in Fitzbrian's branch of the Linkhorn clan.

Unremembered kings had talked them out of their crops in that colder country. That country's crops were sea-sands now. Sea-caves rolled the old kings' bones.

Yet each king, before he had gotten the hook, had been careful to pass the responsibility for conning all Linkhorns into trustworthy hands. Keep the troublemakers down was the cry.

Duke and baron, lord and laird, city merchant, church and state, landowners both small and great, had formed a united front for the good work. When a Linkhorn had finally taken bush parole, fleeing his Scottish bondage for the brave new world, word went on ahead: Watch for a wild boy of no particular clan, ready for anything, always armed. Prefers fighting to toil, drink to fighting, chasing women to booze or battle: may attempt all three concurrently.

The first free Linkhorn stepped onto the Old Dominion shore and was clamped fast into the bondage of cropping on shares. Sometimes it didn't seem quite fair.

Through old Virginia's tobacco-scented summers the Linkhorns had done little cropping and less sharing. So long as there lay a continent of game to be had for the taking, they cropped no man's shares for long.

Fierce craving boys, they craved neither slaves nor land. If a man could out-fiddle the man who owned a thousand acres, he was the better man though he owned no more than a cabin and a jug. Burns was their poet.

Slaveless yeomen—yet they had seen how the great landowner, the moment he got a few black hands in, put up his

feet on his fine white porch and let the world go hang. So
the Linkhorns braced their own narrow backs against their
own clapboard shacks, pulled up the jug and let it hang too.
Burns was still their poet.

Forever trying to keep from working with their hands, the
plantations had pushed them deep into the Southern Ozarks.
Where they had hidden out so long, saying A Plague On
Both Your Houses, that hiding out had become a way of life
with them. "It's Mr. Linkhorn's war. We don't reckon him
kin of our'n," they reckoned.

Later they came to town often enough to see that the cotton mills were the plantations all over again: the prescriptive
rights of master over men had been transferred whole from
plantation to mill. Between one oak-winter and one whip-
poorwill spring, the Linkhorns pushed on to the Cookson
Hills.

Three score years after Appomattox a Linkhorn showed up
in the orange-scented noon of the Rio Grande Valley still
saying "Be Damned To The Lot Of You—Who got the
pitcher?" Had there been an International Convention of
White Trash that week, Fitz would have been chairman.

Cotton grew, fruit grew, oil gushed a year and dried. Before it dried Fitz put in a year as a gaffer, made good money
and found his girl. A ·girl who had thought herself rough
enough.

Cotton failed, fruit failed—oil had spoiled the soil. It became a country of a single crop, and the crop was dust. Fifteen years of it did the girl in, feeling she'd had enough of
oil.

Years begun with oranges and love, till dust blew love
down the Gulf with the oranges. Leaving Fitz penniless as
ever and more loveless than before. As the nineteen thirties
lowered he trotted about town with a hired hose, pumping
out cesspools.

And sensed no mockery in being greeted, hip-boots stream-
ing, with a "Hiya, Preacher!"

Some of the folk of that little town offered the widower
no greeting at all. He was too unpredictable. He would take
one man's jibes without offense and get his back up at another's "Howdy, friend." In a town where nearly everyone
danced, swore and gambled, the only fun Fitz had left was
getting his back up.

He was against modern dancing, modern dress, swearing,
gambling, cigarettes and sin. He preached that the long
drought of 1930 was God's way of putting an end to such
things. But as the drought went on and on and never a drop
of rain he reversed himself and said it must be the pope's
doing.

He was also said to be against fornication. But then it was
said he was against corn whiskey too.

Saturday nights he pulled an ancient black frock coat over
his patches; a coat with a pocket under the slit of the tail to
hold the little brown bottle he called his "Kill-Devil." Getting stiff on the courthouse steps while denouncing the Ro-
man Catholic clergy was a feat which regularly attracted
scoffers and true believers alike, the believers as barefoot as
the scoffers. For drunk as a dog or broke as a beggar, Fitz
could spout religion like a hog in a bucket of slops.

Sometimes a girl would stand a moment among the men,
pretending interest in The Word. But hunger has a scent
more dry than love's and she would move along wishing she
were in Dallas.

For many in Arroyo the Lord's Day was Saturday; but
every night of the week was the Lord's to Fitz.

" 'And when they wanted wine' "—he put down a mocker
who wanted to know what caused the bulge on his hip—" 'the
mother of Jesus saith unto him, "Give them wine." ' Satan
didn't claim Jesus' mother 'count of wine, ah reckon he won't
claim me 'count of a half-pint of busthead."

"What cause folk to git dispatched to Hellfire then?" a believer demanded to know right now.

"You don't git *'dispatched'* to Hellfire," Fitz assured him— "You're born right *in* it. Gawd got a fence clean a-*round* Hell. So a sinner caint git out! Sinner caint dig underneath! Too deep! Sinner caint crawl between! Caint climb over! It's ee-o-lectrified!"

"How'd *you* git out?" the mocker asked softly. He was astride the barrel of the town howitzer, his face and figure shadowed like a canoneer's who has lost both battle and cause.

"Ah *clumb*," Fitz explained, and clumb right into his theme —"Ah clumb the lowest strand 'cause that's the strand of LOVE. Ah clumb the second strand 'cause that's the MERCY strand. Ah clumb the third because ah been LONGSUFFERIN'!"—

"—thought you said that fence was ee-o-lectrified," the canoneer reminded him, but Fitz was climbing too hard to hear—"Ah clumb clean ovah the topmost one of HIS MOST PRECIOUS BLOOD! Brothers! Sisters! Step on the strand of LOVE! Step on the strand of MERCY! Step on the LONGSUFFERING strand and get ready—to cross the strand of THE BLOOD!"

"You know, I was thinking along those lines myself," the cannoneer commented, and spat. Yet Fitz paid him no heed.

"I know some of you boys come a mighty far way in hope I'd save you for the Heavenly Home," he acknowledged. "That *was* my pure intent. But now that I see your actual faces I've had a change of mind. Boys, I'm woeful sorry, but the Lord just don't want a bunch of dirt-eating buggers walking the Streets of Gold. The Lord don't mind sinners—but he just can't stand rats. And I'll be god*damned* if *I'll* take the responsibility!"—and openly took a defiant swig of his half-pint.

Both skeptics and hopers cheered at that— the old man was warming up. "You tell 'em, Preacher! Drink 'er down! Don't you play whore to no man!"

Fitz smacked his lips, rewound his dirty bandanna about his bottle and replaced it in the hidden pocket.

"*Now* tell us about Temptation, Father," the man on the cannon asked, trying to get Fitz pointed at the pope.

"I'll tell you this much about Temptation, Byron Linkhorn," the old man answered directly—"there are so-called Christians right in this gathering tonight who voted for the pope in '28. Do you think the Lord caint remember two year?"

Fitz could forgive a man for using marijuana, but not for voting for Al Smith. Others who had voted for the pope in '28 stood silent, letting Byron take the full brunt of their guilt. It was Byron who had ruined everyone's chance for the New Jerusalem, that silence implied. Now no one could go.

"Tell the *rest* of us how to be saved, Preacher," one hypocrite pleaded.

"Or the time you fell in the cesspool," Byron stayed in there.

Fitz was hell on the pope, but Byron was hell on Fitz.

"The Lord *does* work in mysterious ways, that's certain sure," the old man found his text—"for example, the pitiful critter atop the county property happen to be my son."

"Here come the part *I* come for," somebody dug his naked toes in the earth with anticipated pleasure—"Here's where thet busthead starts *really* taken holt."

"—a critter not long for this world," Fitz gave hope to all creation—"the Lord giveth, the Lord taketh away—and the sooner he taketh away that particular civet, the air hereabouts will be considerable fitter for humans. His lungs is gone, his mind is weak, his heart is dry as an autumn leaf. The brickle thread of his life is ready to snap. I envy him his trials is about to cease!"

The man on the cannon tried to reply, but was trapped by a cough so racking that every face turned to his own. He

was good as dead, those cold looks told, yet not one cared a
tear.

Pressing a bandanna to his lips, Byron dismounted cau-
tiously. His father's cracked voice, with a dozen others as
cracked, joined in a hymn familiar to all. That rose, contented in all its discords, in a chorus above all argument.

> O lovely appearance of death
> No sight upon earth is so fair;
> Not all the gay pageants that breathe
> Can with a dead body compare—

and pursued him down every step of the street hawking
bloodily all the way.

They had come to see someone lose. That it should be the
same doomed fool week after week gave a flip to their satisfaction. Saturday night after Saturday night, it was always
Byron to be singled out. Between his cough, the crowd and
his father, he always lost. What was it in him they had to
disprove? What was it that mere repetition added?

Byron was one whose beginnings had been more brave than
most—that was what needed disproving.

For how Fitz leaped then—literally *leaped*—clapping his
hands above his head and barking triumphantly—

> "Just as I am though tossed about
> With many a conflict many a doubt
> Fightings and fears within, without
> O lamb of God, I come! I come!
> Just as I am! Just as I am!—

—in the name of Jesus, now come as you are!"—and would
skip down the steps, his sermon done, to take anyone's bottle
and everyone's praise, mocking or sincere.

"Keep your boots on, Preacher! Come just as you are!"

Fitz would be weaving a bit. Yet behind his shrouded

glance a gleeful victory glinted. The Lord would forgive one who had defended His ark so well.

"Preacher," one told him, "you just done my heart good tonight. You plumb restored me. Next week I'm bringen the younguns, they need restorin' too. The old woman is beyond restoren. She aint been the same since the time she got throwed by the Power."

"You never should have picked her up," Fitz recalled an occasion when one of his listeners had passed out—"You should have left her right there where Jesus flang her. How's she feeling?"

"Better, thank you kindly. We got a bit of a job for you any time you're of a mind to run out our way."

That was all right with Fitz. If Protestant privies lined both sides of the road to the City of Pure Gold, by God he'd shovel his way to Salvation. But before he'd take money from papists rapists he'd go the other route. He was playing the whore to no man.

He was a Witness for Jehovah and saw the Holy See engaged in an international conspiracy against the Anglo-Saxon race in general and the Linkhorns in particular.

Papists Rapists!—that's who it was who kept cheating!

Dove Linkhorn could not remember a time, a place nor a single person, house cat or hound dog that had sought his affection. But sometimes in the depths of a troubled sleep he had a fleeting feeling that a woman with red-gold hair had just touched his hand and fled beyond a curtained door.

A doorway that had not been curtained for years. The little cavern of a room was so sloping that the post of his high-ended bed touched its ceiling.

The old-fashioned bedstead they called a "stid"—"It were Ma's stid 'n all the makin's was Ma's too"—"makin's" being the shuck-mattress, quilt coverlet, and two square pillows of the kind still called "shams." The sham on his left bore the

embroidered legend, *I slept and dreamt that life was Beauty*.
The one on the right, *I woke and found that life was Duty*.
As often as not Dove's head, in sleep, fell squarely in between.

That was just as well. Although he was sixteen he could
read neither his pillow nor the sooty legend behind the stove:

CHRIST
is the head of this house
THE UNSEEN HOST
at every meal
THE SILENT LISTENER
to every conversation

Fitz had kept him out of school by way of protesting the
hiring of a Catholic principal. But no one had protested his
protest. No one had come to claim the boy for the board of
education. There was no board of education.

If you wanted your young to learn, you sent them. If they
wanted to, they went. If you didn't and neither did they, they
went to work.

There was no work. So they went to the movies. Dove had
not yet seen one, but he planned to go pretty soon now.
When John Barrymore and Marian Marsh came to Arroyo as
Svengali and Trilby, he asked Byron to pay his way inside.

"What if Eternity should come when you were on the
Devil's territory? What chance would you have?" Byron
asked for an answer, thus mocking both father and brother
at once; and avoiding an admission that he didn't have a nickel.

Dove hadn't yet gone to a dance either. But he'd stood in
the doorway of a hall and watched and kept time like the
others—

Take her by the lily-white hand
And lead her like a pigeon
Make her dance the weevily-wheat
Till she loses her religion

Long after he had gone to bed that night the light from the
bitch lamp kept him awake. The lamp had been made by
fixing a rag wick to a stone and setting it in a vessel half-filled
with whatever was left in the frying pan after the morning
bacon was finished. Byron called it a "slut lamp." But Fitz
always said "light the grease," and let it go at that.

By its ceaseless flicker Dove would see the pair of fools
going at it again and both three sheets over. He would lay
there moving his lips with the longest words he could pick
up. "Corruption." "Generations." "Burnt-offering." "Peace-
offering." "Sin-offering." Sometimes whole phrases: "What
meaneth the heat of this great anger?" "Would it were morning! For the fear of thy heart which thou shalt fear, and for
the sight of thine eyes which thou shalt see."

"I can't argue with you no more," Byron would surrender
as the wick burned low, "I'm feeling the sickness too bad."

"Another name for the soul's corruption," Fitz assured him.

"How do *you* feel these days yourself, Pappy?" Byron
asked.

"Well and contented," the old man replied.

Even Dove knew the old man lied.

Mexican and American alike, the townsfolk knew that the
preacher was off his rocker and that Byron smoked too much
potiguaya bush for a lunger. "I was born to smoke bush," he
boasted, "I may die poor but I won't die tied." But what to
make of Dove with his hair neither red nor yellow? And
brows so light he looked browless? "You right sure that boy
got everything he's suppose to have?" one doubter asked
another.

If the boy bought a plug of tobacco he would lean against
the grocer's door and spit the whole morning away. If asked
what he thought he was doing he would mumble, "leanen 'n
dreamen," and would move a scant inch to one side. Yet

sometimes strength would surge through him in a tide, he would run aimlessly and shout at nothing.

"The boy is takin' growth," Fitz explained uneasily.

In Dove's mind, too, was a growing. A sudden light would flash within his brain illuminating earth and sky—a common bush would become a glory, a bird on a swinging bough a wonder—then the light would fade and fade like a slow gray curtain dropping. Such moments were irretrievable.

One day in March he saw a solitary sapling on a hill, bending before the wind against a solid wall of blue, and it seemed to him that it had not been there before he had looked up and would vanish as soon as he turned. Many times after that he looked at the same slender shoot; never again did he see it so truly.

At times he could catch his brother Byron in such strange life-glimpses. One second he would be moving about the kitchen, his useless brother about his useless tasks, and the next he would be a total stranger, doing no one knew what. A picture of him not moving but rigid; tensed with life yet still as death. In after years Dove never heard the long thunder of passenger cars across a bridge in the dark but he caught a brief glimpse of a smoky dawn through an opening door—never heard the white steam whistle in the night but saw Byron stretched, mouth agape like the dead, brown boot-toes pointing upward on a disarranged cot bed in a corner. Yet never learned, his whole life, who Byron really was.

Another mystery was the bougainvillea. It grew beneath a bicycle frame nailed high on the shack's north wall—now why should anyone nail a bicycle, front wheel gone and frame rusted by rain, against a clapboard wall? No one could tell him, yet nobody took it down. The bougainvillea stretched for those useless spokes. It almost touched the down-slung handle-bars. The bougainvillea yearned to conceal all things in leaves. The plant seemed half asleep in the early morning, but became restless toward night. Sometimes a dust-wind made it shudder as though dust-hands touched it roughly. And once when the sun was directly overhead the whole plant bent in pain.

The house itself looked as if one peart wind would blow it down.

Its floor was dirt. The curtains were guano bags. The stovepipe was stuck through a hole in the wall. Behind it rose a jagged cliff as old as America.

One night a small rain lay the dooryard dust. Dove heard the drops tap dancing. And the sleep-drawn breath of two drunks wearied once again of useless drinking.

He turned the smoking bitch lamp low. In the yard the Mexican stars were out, the Mexican dogs were barking. Someone was singing *"Poy! Pooey poy!"* so shrill he must have been mocking the dogs. Dove touched his plant with eyes closed fast the better to understand the leaves. Beneath his fingers he felt it blooming.

In the morning the bicycle lay in the dust and the bougainvillea grew about it. No one so much as noticed that Dove had taken the bicycle down. He himself wasn't sure just why.

Yet as the magic spring of 1930 died in endless drought, Dove's hours too grew drier day by day. Till filled with a nebulous homesickness he would shamble down a dead-end road that long ago had led men west. That led now only to tin-canned circles where hoboes hopped off the Santa Fe.

Years before a box car had slipped a coupling, scudded downhill and turned onto its side in the chaparral. Half sunk now in sand, ruined and stripped, only its bare iron skeleton and a few beams remained to cast a meager shade on days when shade was precious as water. There were always a couple of hoboes resting there.

One day Dove came there, curiously seeking he didn't know what, and saw a man in khaki pants and torn shirt lying flat on his back with a bottle in his hand. When he came closer he saw it was his brother and stood studying him: a stranger sinking in the sand, like the box car ruined and stripped. He had often seen Byron drunk at home; but lying like that for everyone to look at left the boy pale with shame.

Yet he saw boys there no older than himself passing a bottle. They boiled black coffee in open tins and ate beans stuck on a twig; rolled cigarettes singlehanded and boasted of time in jail.

Hard time and easy, wall time and farm time, fed time and state, city time, county time, short time and good time, soft time and jawbone time, big house, little house and middle house time, industrial time and meritorious time—"that's for working your ass off."

In jails where food was inedible, as it was in most county clinks, the men, Dove heard, bought their own by levying each newcomer to the extent of whatever he carried. If he didn't have money he paid with his shoes. If he came in broke and barefoot too the other inmates took as many slaps at his behind as the court decreed for the felony of breaking into jail without consent of the inmates. Yet, barefoot or shod, man or mouse, he always shared in food bought outside the jail.

He heard of a jail in Southern Louisiana where prisoners had built up a treasury of over two hundred dollars and dined the turnkey and sheriff once a week. That at the Grayson County Jail prisoners got out a weekly paper called the *Crossbar Gazette*.

In Laredo the cells were all on one side, he learned. The whip boss at Huntsville was named Crying Tom. In Hillsboro, Missouri, prisoners got sheets and mattresses.

They spoke too of good fortune: one had once been taken into a minister's home for two months; another had come upon a drunken girl in a cattle car; another had found a new jacket hanging in a reefer into which he had climbed one night in Carrizozo.

Dove learned that Beaumont was tough. That Greensboro,

in some place called Nawth Klina, was a right mean little
town to get through. That Boykin, right below it, was even
harder. That toughest of any was any town anywhere in
Georgia. If you were caught riding there you heard the long
chain rattling. But they gave you fifteen cents every week
and a plug of tobacco on Sundays. "*That* part's not so bad,"
thought Dove Linkhorn.

"Stay 'way far from Waycross," an old canboy warned
him—" 'less you want to do a year in a turp camp." And he
began beating a tin-can in time with a song—

"I didn't raise my boy to be a soldier
I brought him up to be my pride and joy."

East Texas was rough but the Rio Grande Valley was
easy—all the crews asked was that you get off on the side
away from the station. You could get through Alabama all
right provided you didn't stand on the spine like a tourist
and wave at the sheriff. And stayed off the A. & W.P.

Those A. & W.P. bulls made a point of putting you off at
a water tank in the wilderness called Chehawee and you
walked forty-four miles to get to Montgomery. For a fiver,
cash down on the barrelhead, you could ride.

Look out for a town in Mississippi called Flomaton, because that's Wing Binga's town. One night he pistol-whupped
two 'boes and they came back and shoved him under the
wheels. That was how he lost his right wing. He was mean
before that but he'd gotten meaner since.

Look out for Marsh City—that's Hank Pugh's. Look out
for Greeneville—that belongs to Buck Bryan. Buck'll be
walking the spines dressed like a 'bo—the only way you'll be
able to spot him is by his big floppy hat with three holes in
the top. And the hose length in his hand.

Your best bet is to freeze and wait. You can't get away.
He likes the hose length in his hand but what he really loves

is the Colt on his hip. So just cover up your eyes and listen to the *swwwissshhh*. He's got deputies coming down both sides. God help you if you run and God help you if you fight. God help you if you're broke and God help you if you're black.

Look out for Lima—that's in Ohio. And look out for Springfield, the one in Missouri. Look out for Denver and Denver Jack Duncan. Look out for Tulsa. Look out for Tucson. Look out for Joplin. Look out for Chicago. Look out for Ft. Wayne—look out for St. Paul—look out for St. Joe—look out—look out—look out—

Dove saw a crippled one caught like a rabbit in the great head-lamps' glare, turning blinded eyes to the engineer and the engineer waving—"Go *on*, go *on*—"

Of their pathetic efforts to keep clean, merely to keep clean, Dove never heard them tell. Yet they were forever begrimed and begging soap and water. As soon as his thirst was quenched, the 'bo was washing his one shirt. On every fence post at every junction faded shirts hung, wet weather or dry. Combs, pocket mirrors and toothbrushes, carried by a string around the neck, were treasured.

He could tell carnie hands and circus roustabouts because they took their money out of grouch-bags, pouches drawn by string, like tobacco pouches.

Once he saw a grizzled old hand passing a woman's black elbow-length glove, the kind that strip-teasers once tossed to the front rows. As it passed from hand to hand, each man sniffed at it and swore he could smell its perfume yet. Its owner finally pocketed it as if secretly relieved that he didn't have to fight anyone to get it back.

And one told of a young boy found bleeding to death in an empty somewhere up the line.

Dove felt the uneasy guilt go around then like the perfumed glove; it too had made the circle of homeless men.

Their home was ten thousand water towers, their home was any tin-can circle. Their home was down all lawless deeps where buffalo-colored box cars make their last stand in the West.

He saw their nightfires burn and burn against the homeless heart, and felt he had himself gone West. That it had come to nothing then, and yet that he would go again.

Someone had done some cheating all right.

"I'm getting the evening-wearies," he decided, and returned to the penetrating odor of cold collards in a bowl above a stove coated with grease. Where dish towels hung in a low festoon from the damper of the stove pipe to a spike above the sink. The sink was a tin trough salvaged from a dump heap. Unwashed dishes and pans lay in it. It had no spigot.

The spigot was outside and served shanties on either side of the Linkhorns'. These three shanties, upended green-pine clapboard so dried and shrunk it left chinks for rain and wind, made a kind of slum Alamo right in the middle of Mexican-town. Their men were either swart, like Fitz and Byron, or tended toward a certain thinness of color, like Dove. The women were fading for lack of forests. Davy Crockett was gone for good.

Old forests had shaped their hands to gunstocks but never to cotton-picking. They couldn't bear mill work and could neither buy nor sell. Hill and plain no longer claimed them. They had lost their claim to hill and plain and Crockett would not come again.

They were backwoodsmen without a backwoods, the last of those who never would pick cotton. Plantation and mill were blocking them off like rabbits when a field is mown. They scorned both factory and town and wore brown jeans in preference to blue.

And all night long, down that unlighted road, sometimes low and sometimes shrill, Dove heard an alien music. In their smoking, unlighted halls Mexicans sang and were well.

Tres Moricas tan lozanas
Mas lindas que Toledanas
Iban a cojer manzanas a Jaen.
Axa, Fatima, Marien.

Dixayles quien sois señoras
De mi alma robadoras
Christianas de ramas Moras de Jaen.
Axa, Fatima, Marien.

Three Moorish girls of spirit
More lovely than Toledan girls
Went out to harvest apples in Jaen
Axa, Fatima, Marien.

Say who you are, Señoras,
The robbers of my soul,
Christian girls of Moorish roots from Jaen.
Axa, Fatima, Marien.

Mexicans had no old forests to mourn.

The old way West, the old trails: wagon trail and cattle trail lost in miles and miles and miles of chaparral and mesquite. Gone and grown over in dry cacti. Old hopes, fierce hopes, pride and patience alike in vain. All the love they had once had for that big brown land blown like dust off the heart's chaparral.

The road West now led only to a low, dark and battered chili parlor in what had once been the big, white and merry Hotel Davy Crockett.

Behind the darkened parlor's pane a lamp's reflection, doubled and blurred, burned like the double-ghost of a great chandelier that once had lighted a lobby like a ballroom at sea. Then its hundred-glassed gleam had flared all night like a light that could never wane. On brandy, brandy glass and wine.

DANCING BY ELECTRIC LIGHT—that had pulled the bloods
into the old Davy Crockett of Saturday nights. The wild
boys from the wells, wearing those big red and green bandannas, come to drink down their wild girls. Their girls that
could drink down the moon.

The old Aztec moon of the Rio Grande, buffalo-robed to
its outlaw eyes, that had watched the wild boys from the
wells blowing their gold like beer-foam across the mirrored
bar and heard the pianola rolling—

> *Sometimes I live in the country*
> *Sometimes I live in town—*

and a guitar player from Arkansas twanging—for drinkers and
dancers, hard-rock drillers, gaffers and gamblers, all alike.
Drinking and dancing and gambling by real electric light—

> *Sometimes I have a great notion*
> *To jump in the river and drown—*

a changeless twang that once had trembled the springs beneath one wild girl on an upstairs bed wearing a silver comb
in her red-gold hair; black-mesh hose and nothing more.

Fitz had been a man past thirty that year of 1909, but a
real wild boy all the same. Who always went right for the
wild girls the hour he came to town. Till he sat one night
on the readhead's bed putting the last of a bottle to her lips.
Eyes shuttered tight against all light she drank as long as
whiskey would pour without once lifting her red-gold head.
It had burned her throat inside and out—then his mouth had
been sweeter even than that. It had held her own so firm
while his flesh, thrusting deep, held firmer even than that.
Till the whole room rocked in the looking light and had
locked them heart to heart.

While the moon that could never wane looked on, on
brandy, silver comb and wine.

While in all the rooms upstairs or down, beds wide or beds narrow, the lights had flared brighter and more bright.

On marble, mirror-shine and wine.

Till the dice players had begun crying out with despair at something more than merely losing, the roulette wheel had begun to spin as if each turn must be its last; and the pianola began a beat that rolled as though all hope were gone—

> *Sometimes I have a great notion*
> *To jump in the river and drown—*

keeping time to the rolling man lashed fast between those black-meshed thighs, breathing her breath as she breathed his till she moaned his lips apart: the pianola roll below flapped loose, the music stopped yet the roll whirred on. Her eyelids fluttered in the drains of her passion—it had not happened to her before like this. Fitz had felt the flutter against his cheek. The pianola roll whispered on and on, it had not happened to him before so heart-shakingly as this.

And the moon that could never wane dimmed down to no more than a gas lamp's leaning glow. Drinkers and dancers, gaffers and gamblers, all had gone.

Out in the sand and the Spanish Dagger, in chaparall-pea and honey-mesquite where under the thorn the horned toad waits, the prairie dog slept in his burrow. White bones bleached in the sun. Before the music was over; before the dancing was done.

And a little wind went searching in circles to ask, Where had those lovers gone before the dance was done?

All was well. They had breathed each other's breath. All was well: they had drunk of each other's lips.

All was well, for what was dust had when living been loved.

Fitz had married his wild girl, who had turned out not so wild after all. She had given him two sons. And since her death he had returned but once to the side of town where the Davy Crockett still stood.

To find nothing left but boarded windows above and a dim-lit chili parlor below. Whose name was painted across its pane:

LA FE EN DIOS
Bien venidas, todas ustedes

The town that had begun with a ball by electric light was dying by the glow of kerosene lamps. Time had gone backward in the little lost town.

By 1930 the old way West led nowhere but to the shade of a water tower where old bums drained sterno through ragged bandannas and left such small earnest tokens of their passing as a tennis sneaker with the sole gone through, an undershirt ironed brown by the wind or an empty half-pint labeled *White Swan Gin—Bottled in Chicago.*

Crease-faced or rosy, shaggy or bald, faded or florid, spare or stout, fried by sun or bedraggled by showers, one by one they came through the door of *La Fe En Dios.* To stand, shifting a cap from one hand to the next between the juke box and a potted fern till the Mexican women finished serving her paying customers. Then they received the last cold dregs from the coffee-urn, half a day-old pineapple pie and a bar of American Family soap.

If they wanted more than that they would have to come by daylight and work for it. Bald or barefoot, old or young, each promised eagerly, even with gratitude, to be on hand at seven a.m. sharp.

And to a man seven a.m. found them riding as fast and as far from the little lost town as any S.P. freight could carry them. Yet let the east-bound freights pass by if a west-bound freight was due. They still sought the old way home.

The old way home that was now no more than any stretch of broken walk you reach at the end of any American town

on any Saturday afternoon. Where blocks of paving stone
lie severed by wind, sand and W.P.A. And a sign that may
say TRUCK TURNING.

Where black-eyed susans grow out of the separating sand
and a rusty beer can with two holes punched in the lid awaits
the Resurrection or one more real estate boom.

The old way home that led, at last, to nothing more than
a tossing gas-flare over a sign at the walk's very end:

YOU ARE NOW ENTERING ARROYO

Pop. 955

A statistic that didn't include the Mexican woman whose
residence was just far enough beyond it to keep her free of
local taxes. Whose own way home, eleven months of twelve,
was up a flight of careworn stairs to a room guarded only by
the Virgin Mary.

Terasina Vidavarri slept within a double ruin. Within the
wreck of her own hopes, inside what was left of the Hotel
Crockett. The last guest had left and all along the long un-
carpeted hall, the doors, like her own soul's door, were
boarded on both sides.

Yet in sleep sometimes heard a pianola play. The boarded
doors opened, the place came alight with the light that shines
in dreams; to show men taking women on all the beds till
she wakened. And saw a full moon rising with a yearning
all its own.

"It is lucky to love any time, for then you have someone
to live for," Terasina thought, "but if you are not in love
that is lucky also. Because then you have no problem."

Actually she'd hardly tried her luck. Her first and only
lover had pitched such a fright into her that she'd taken no
chances since.

A girl of no family, a chambermaid in hotels catering to
American tourists down in Merida in old Yucatán, Terasina,

at sixteen, had become engaged to a bald, middle-aged Floridan of Spanish extraction.

In his youth a second lieutenant, in his middle age a florist both by vocation and avocation, a carrier-off of prizes in flower shows, an exporter of day-lilies. An ancient wet-lipped orgiast in an American Legion cap—what a rare plant her florist was the girl had had not an inkling until their wedding night.

She had wakened from a light sleep. Beside the bed a little lamp threw a deep orange glow. She heard the ex-lieutenant moving about the bathroom and it had struck her that he had been in there an unconscionably long while. She called his name. No reply.

And was looking straight at that door when he strode out naked but for a helmet and swagger stick borne like a rifle— "*Ein! Svei! Drei! What?* Afraid of a soldier?" Yet the impulse to laugh froze fast in her throat, for his face was a mask that brooked no laughter. Goose-stepping high past her bedside, three times past her bed, he came to attention in a light that seemed swathed in a sweltering mist. And touched the swagger stick with disdain between her eyes.

"What? Afraid of a soldier?"

She saw he was completely hairless then.

For the indignities that had followed Terasina still had no name. But once she had warned him, "Now I'm going to scream."

The swagger stick's shadow fell across the sheet. She had bitten the pillow instead.

And the scent of cologne, like a nightmare in lilac, had risen first strong and then faint.

Till daybreak had emptied him at last of everything save self-disgust. Too exhausted to cry, he lay drooling weakly with the odor of lilac dying slow, like midnight in a barber shop.

Two days later the girl had looked in a mirror: above her

blue-black bangs the hair had turned, in one small triangular patch, to the whiteness of fresh snow.

Her Floridan had returned to his flower beds and the Negro boy who assisted their cultivation.

Now, ten years after, Terasina's only flowers were great hairy-stemmed barnyard hollyhocks. And her dreams contained far stranger creatures.

She would find herself waiting in some great shadowed corral in a sheer night dress, for one whose hair, worn long, kept blowing across his face like a mane; whose scent had salt and sweat in it. A stallion made of moonlight, to rear against her neighing and all her hopes rearing with him. Then the salt-sweat scent turned sick and she wakened with a barber-shop scent fleeing faintly along the boarded doors. Weak with disappointment, she would dress in the holy cold and shrive herself like a nun to make herself proud again. Ready to play waitress downstairs to the brotherhood of trailer, truck and bus, below a sign that said:

Pie a la mode . . . 10.
Pie a la mode with ice cream . . . 15
Lonches y sanguiches
25 y 35

And when lettuce ran out used cabbage instead.

"Mexicans are lovely people," one of these smug-looking dunces with a badge in his cap was fond of assuring her, "and may I add, Señora, you got a right purty make on you?"

"You lovely people too," Terasina would promise the Badge.

For ten years now this tightly wound woman with the snowdrifted hair had been serving section hands, firemen, railroad detectives, brakemen, tramps, tourists, engineers, conductors and truck drivers.

Antojitoes Mexicanoes the back of her menu read, but she'd taken no Mexican fancy to any of them in all ten years.

Abierta hasta a las 12 de la noche—EMPUJE, her door invited them to push in and stay late. Yet kept her own self shut around the clock.

"You must be connected with the railroads," one would try—"you got such a purty caboose."

"You remind me of Dolores Del Rio," another reported when his motor was running smoothly. Would the señora mind if he started a small bank account in her name to keep his wife from spending it all on whiskey? Would the señora object to be named beneficiary in a will? Or to taking a trial run in a new trailer over to Matamoros for the weekend?

She marveled at truckers whose vanity knew no truck-turning. The driver sat so long above so much pent-up power that after a while he came to believe the motor's power was his own. Look out, I may shift into first. When he wanted to know what type of heating she had upstairs she said, "Same kind I got down." Well, he was only asking, because he happened to have a buddy in the oil-stove line. *Gracias*, no, he was very kind, but she already had one stove up there and what would be the use of another? Why own something she wouldn't use?

And did she use everything she owned now, or was she wearing falsies?

"God has been generous," she replied, and let her breasts rise with her pride. Yet let him tickle her palm when he took his change, flashed him her wide white smile and palmed two bits for her trouble.

The little restaurant drew drivers because it was the end of a long narrow road. There was always some cross-country monstrosity backing and turning between gas-pump and mesquite.

The only thing in pants around the place who pleased her was the browless, raggedy boy with the streaky red hair who had come in one day with a sheet of Sunday funnies in his hand—"I don't know how letters make words," he told her, "so I'd appreciate it mightily if you'd quote these to me, M'am."

At first she had not understood why he had come to her, of all people. Then she had realized he was ashamed to ask anyone else. So she had gone over the pictures with him section by section until she had gotten stuck on a word herself. That was when she had brought out one of her two books— *How To Write Better Business Letters*. But before they could make any progress with that a driver with a flat tire pulled up and the raggedy boy was gone to beg.

Sometimes she saw him circling a trailer in an anxious dog trot, one shoulder higher than the other and a tire wrench in his hand. Other times there would be only two big dirty feet sticking out from under a truck, the toes spread tensely lest the job be unfinished when the driver was ready to haul. What was he always so anxious about?

Or he'd just be leaning against the tin sign—FLATS FIXED— that whirled one minute this way and the next minute that as the wind off the chaparral passed and repassed. Beside it he could stand looking as lonesome as though tires were going out of style, treasuring each drag on his roll-your-own cigarette.

"What do I owe you, Red?" she heard a trucker asking and the redhead replying, "Makin's 'n cawfee do jest fine for me, mister." She knew by his voice then he needed more than tobacco and coffee. "Hungry all the way down," Terasina guessed.

Apparently he thought money was going out of style too. Coffee and a sack of Bull Durham was his rate for an hour's sweating labor in the sun. It angered Terasina, who could tell a ten-dollar bill from a Mexican nickel either side of the river, to see older men take advantage of him.

At last she had told a driver herself. "Changing two tires and a battery, six bitses please."

"The kid said coffee and a sack."

"Changing two tires and battery six bitses please. *I* set price at *La Fe.*"

The driver put six bitses down. Terasina didn't touch it. "*And* tip for boy please."

The driver extracted a final dime and left without a word. The way Dolores Del Rio was feeling today he didn't feel he could afford it.

"You take it," Dove told her when she put the money beside his cup, "for letting me hang around."

She rang it up promptly—pshtang! "Okay! You got it!"

Six bits credit—he had it.

He decided, after due thought, on *Sesos lampreados*—brains wrapped in egg. She brought the order, fit for a section hand.

All she saw, for a while then, was his big thick ears sticking up like handles. All she heard was the beat, like a tribal drum, of knife and fork against his plate.

"—'n cornbread, m'am. I can eat cornbread till the world looks level."

A minute later: "I'll take a bowl of chili please m'am."

"*Segundoes?*" she asked when the chili was gone.

A single bean lodged in the corner of his lip. "*Si, señora.*"

And under the browless eyes there burned remembrance of ancestral hungers; again the tribal drum beat fast.

"You like more?" she smiled weakly. "*Chicharrones* maybe?"

"I got most all I can chamber," he admitted at last—"but for a slab of that cross-barred pie."

She fetched the cross-barred pie and coffee. Stooping so far to get his lips to the saucer that his back stood up like a surfacing whale's, he slurped it up with one magnificent slurp.

As close as she could figure it he now owed her eighty cents. She brought a broom.

He took it and shuffled heavily, right shoulder still higher than the left, to the door. Then, suddenly fired by the hottest chili north of Chihuahua, stormed from the front porch to

the rear, behind the counter and up the stairs. He swept her
room as if preparing it for holy services, then broomed the
steps down in such a cloud that she rushed up with a sprinkling can.

He washed dishes, scrubbed eatingware till it shone and
patched a screen in a minute. Then announced some triumph
from the kitchen—"*Uno! Dos!*" He was swatting flies with
the *Police Gazette.*

"Is al*right*," she sought to calm him, "every*thing* is square."

Then in the stilly mid-afternoon hush that comes to all
old chili parlors they sat together over *How To Write Better
Business Letters.*

"This is how letters make words," she told him. "The first
letter is 'A' "—she made him push up and cross the A. "Alright. Now 'B.' "

Thus a child taught a child.

When he had shown improvement in both letters she suddenly wearied of the game and found another—how to trip
the little key behind the coin box of the juke so that it would
play without a nickel. It came on playing *Meet Me Tonight
in Dreamland;* for, like herself, it was divided between American and Mexican songs.

The next song was her choice—*Cuando sale de la luna* and
Dove couldn't get enough of that. She spiked a coke with
tequila and asked him how Angloes could drink the sticky
stuff without spiking it. His answer was to agree with her
by adding another shot. He began to shift, one foot to the
other like a happy bear that had never been happy before—

> *I'd like to live in Dreamland*
> *With a girl like you*

It had been so long since she had herself felt joy, it eased
her deeply now to see another's. He was one of the strange
ones all right, and certainly no florist. He smelled of sweat and
salt. No day-lily had touched him.

"I like to see men dance—" her own voice surprised her, and she changed the record back to the juke's Mexican side.

Adios, mi corazon

Every time the juke cried out "*corazon*," Terasina hiccupped. The third time it happened she seized Dove's hand and held it hard across her nostrils and mouth, encouraging him to press. "*Empuje*," she ordered the Mexican cure for hiccups. With one arm about her shoulders to brace her, he pressed so hard she began to choke and he had to stop.

"Death is a poor cure for hiccups," she informed him.

She preferred dancing to hiccups or death. Her joy was to hear the eager mingling of human voices, with children's among them, like voices heard on the other side of a wall where strangers are having a birthday party; and never know one listens who never can enter there.

Once she had heard a young father asking forgiveness and seen the young mother make reply simply by giving suck to his only child. That memory tugged at Terasina's darkly encircled nipples yet, at her own white breasts so aching.

"In Jesus is my peace," she told the mirror in her small room, "*en tristes horas de tentacion, en Jesus tengo paz.*" And the mirror looked back as much as to say I think somebody just lied.

And strangely, for one so devout, in dreams sought neither peace nor Jesus. She would find herself back in some Mexican place, the hour mid-day and all shades drawn. In wan doorways wan dreams of Mexican dogs dreamed on.

Everyone in the city slept save one whose hand rested on the knob of her door as though it had rested there for hours. "It is so hot in the street," the listener beyond her wall complained in a voice much too used to lying. "May I have water?"

"Only Jesus may drink here," she forbade him, and wakened with a sense of dry loss clutching her throat. Out-

side the rain-wind was making mirrors of every ditch. She
saw the true stars walking hand in hand down paving stones
to the end of town. And then walk back again—like lovers
coming home.

Suddenly the cup in her hand looked so empty, she dashed
the water across the floor, poured it running-full of tequila;
till it too ran over.

And drank, with her hands shaking and her back turned
to the wall lest the Virgin Mary see her.

After *Sesos lampreados*, coffee and makin's left Dove as
dissatisfied as had the Sunday funnies, once he had seen a
book.

So after the day's last driver had gone Terasina opened her
other book to him.

Now Dove saw a Chinese prince in flight, bearing lightly
on his back a flaxen-haired boy with a green feather stuck
in his hat; a fairy princess in a nutshell afloat on a leaf, cowering from a gigantic bullfrog saying " 'Croak croak croak'
was all her son could say for himself"; a little patched man
driving a herd of cows while smoking a clay pipe; and rein-
deer, Santa Clauses, dancers, goblins, ducks, mandarins, angels,
castles and teapots and trees half as old as the earth.

But the one that trapped Dove's interest completely was
the steadfast tin soldier who shouldered his musket bravely
although he had but one leg.

He had been made last, there had been not quite enough
tin to finish him. Yet he stood quite as well on his one leg
as others did on two. Dove guessed right away that, of the
whole army, this was the very one who would get to see
most of the world, have the greatest adventures and at last
win the love that all the others wanted too.

The steadfast soldier didn't have far to look: she was a
paper dancer dressed in lightest gauze, with a blue ribbon
across her shoulders pinned by a spangle as big as her face.

She was standing tiptoe, stretching both arms toward the soldier so that, so far as he could see, she too had but one leg. This made him feel very close to her, though it made Dove uneasy. A mistake as bad as that could lead to nothing but trouble. Yet the soldier had made up his mind, and lay down full length behind a snuffbox, so that when the other soldiers were put in their box and the people of the house went to bed, the soldier still had an eye on his dancer.

"Then the clock struck twelve, when pop! Up flew the lid of the snuffbox, but there was no snuff in it. No! There was a little black goblin, a sort of jack-in-the-box.

" 'Tin soldier,' said the goblin, 'have the goodness to keep your eyes to yourself.' But the tin soldier pretended not to hear.

" 'Ah! You just wait till tomorrow,' the goblin threatened him."

Just as Dove had guessed, there was trouble coming. The very next morning while standing guard on a window sill, the goblin blew him off the sill, the soldier fell head foremost from the third story and landed with his bayonet fixed between two paving stones. People went by without seeing him and some almost trod on him. It began to rain, a regular torrent, and when the rain was done and the gutters rushed, two small boys found him, made a boat out of newspaper, put the soldier in the middle of it and away he sailed into a long wooden tunnel as dark as it had been in his box.

The current grew stronger, the paper boat began to take water and sank beneath him. The soldier was swallowed by a fish, yet shouldered his musket as dauntless as ever until a flash like lightning pierced his darkness and someone called out loudly, "A tin soldier!" The fish had been caught, taken to market, sold, and brought to the kitchen, where the cook cut it open with a large knife. She took the soldier up by two fingers and carried him into the parlor, where everyone wanted to see the wonderful man who had traveled so far.

They set him up on the table and—wonder of wonders!—
there were the same children, the same toys on the table and
in the middle, with a sort of glow about her, his own tiptoe
dancing girl! He was home once more!

The soldier was so moved at all this, especially at sight of
his beloved, that he was ready to weep tears of tin joy. But
that would hardly have befitted a soldier. So he looked
straight ahead, a bit to one side, as one returns an officer's
look; but she looked *directly* at him. At that moment one of
the little boys took up the soldier and without reason or
rhyme pitched him into the fire, where he died, true to duty,
looking straight ahead but directly at no one.

Dove leaped up, slammed the book so hard he caught Terasina's thumb—*"Basta!"*

Enough of fairy tales. He hadn't liked an ending like that,
it appeared. For he raced to the juke, tripped it and began
to dance as though trying to forget the soldier's sad end as
soon as the juke began to sing—

All of me
Why not take all of me

Raising one foot then the other, he began a slow swaying
with his head, arms hanging loosely in a dance wherein, the
woman saw, love strangely mixed with despair.

"See the King of the Elephants!" Terasina encouraged him,
and applauded only to conceal her uneasiness. Somehow, that
dance didn't look right; though she could not have said where
it was wrong.

He put his hands on his haunches and, grinning obscenely,
sweat on his lip and breath coming faster, invited all women
in a grind so purified by lust Terasina felt her own thighs
start to part. A look half anguish and half shame made his
face go gray and he sank to the table with his head on his
hands. She saw his shoulders tremble as the music died all
around.

When she touched his shoulder he gave her a smile that suffered too much, that pulled at her heart like an animal's plea.

Holding the fingers of her left hand together, away from the thumb, she sprinkled salt on the stretched tendon and licked it up with her quick small tongue.

"You must get yourself a girl," she announced as though salt had made her suddenly wise. And held the salt of her hand out to him, that he might become wise as herself. He pinched a speck of it, gave it to his tongue, thought for a moment and decided, "There aint no girl in this whole fool's valley worth a second look." Then, swallowing the salt at last, had a cunning afterthought: " 'ceptin' yourself of course, Señora."

"Well," she pretended not to have heard the afterthought, "it *is* true things here are not so good. But if just this one little part of the world had everything, pretty girls and good crops too, bad men would come from the bad parts of the world bringing ugly daughters. Then things would not be so good as they are now. So it *is* good things are not so good."

That night Terasina slept poorly. Half in sleep and half in waking she saw the smile that suffered too much.

A week before Christmas she gave him the key to the *Fe*, to play caretaker and watchman for her till she should return. She could not always go home when her heart was troubled. But this year the trouble came at Christmas, providing her with a pious excuse.

Through the drought of 1930, when old friends' pennies counted most, merchants tossed Kiwanian greetings from all the doors of the little town's stores, and smiled, smiled, smiled. But when the drought was relieved and tourists Matamoros-bound again began to get lost between the curio shop and the post office an hour, they were much too busy to smile. Business was business and time became money then.

The barefoot men and boys in overalls would walk around some tourist's Buick, pointing its advantages to one another so solemnly that it seemed the days of walking from place to place must be over for everyone. Had anyone thought of letting the air out of the tires he would have been prevented, for their interest was proprietary. What they hoped for was many miles per gallon, no nicks on their fenders, contented journeying and no blowouts.

They knew they came from the wrong side of a town that had only two sides, the wrong and the wronger, so strangers with loose cash must be shown respect. And if the women in the cars with the Eastern licenses seemed more prideful than common, that was only agreed to in Spanish, that courteous tongue.

To this lost place the depression arrived as a sort of modest boom, bringing a relief station and a case worker that caused a dozen wetbacks to wade back across the river. "More fried yams for the rest of us," old friends wished them indifferent luck.

Shambling down Main Street one bleak evening, Dove noticed the pharmacist idling in front of his shop wearing the face that said, "Keep moving, Useless. Business is Business."

Useless kept moving, for business *was* business.

Useless always kept moving until he was told to stand to one side. Then he stood to one side until told to start moving. All weathers to Dove were a single season in which he moved or stood unwanted.

On the courthouse steps Fitz was playing the fool for the same gang of cactus-headed rundums for whom he always played the fool. Byron was leaning against the howitzer as though too exhausted tonight to mount it.

"Preacher," asked a hungry-looking misfit, stooped as un-
ler a pack, "is it right for a man's wife to bob her hair?"

"Go to Deuteronomy," Fitz promised, "your answer is
there."

"But I don't *feel* it's wrong," the wife's voice defied Deuteronomy.

Fitz's eyes sought her out. "Woman, did you ever get
down on your knees and ask *God* if it was wrong?"

"No I didn't, Preacher."

"When you do He'll let you know. If He wanted a woman
to cut off her hair he'd have her to shave too, wouldn't he?"

There didn't seem to be any answer to that.

"How fast do angels travel?" was the next issue Fitz had
to solve. That was easy.

"Why, an angel can leave the New Jerusalem at six o'clock
in the morning, travel all *over* the earth, and be back home
at six in the evening where the lion *doth* lie down with the
lamb. Heaven just at hand! Where neither moth nor rust
do corrupt! Where thieves break not through nor steal. No
sickness! No pain! And a thousand years is as a single day!"

"What's the fool rushin' to get home by six o'clock then?"

Fitz ignored Byron.

"There *is* balm in Gilead! No wreaths of sorrow on the
doors—and the doors is all pure gold! Pure gold!" The old
man bethought himself—"Only don't you count on that—
nobody is going to be fool enough to mistake a bunch of
chicken-thieves like you for angels. No, my pitiful friends,
what's in store for *you* aint no New Jerusalem."

"Good old Hellfire fer us, Preacher," a believer sounded
like he could scarcely wait.

"Hellfire *too* good for us!"—someone else trying to get in
good with the preacher for sake of his Kill-Devil.

"We aint *wuth* Hellfire!"

They overdid everything. For they knew Fitz put The City

of Pure Gold within their reach only for the pleasure of snatching it back.

And actually they didn't give a hoot for any city of gold. Desolation here and now, *that* was their dish. Blazing brimstone, eternal torture and a backhanded crack from the hindquarters of bad luck was what they lusted for. Though they never really believed his promise of Heaven Just At Hand, nothing was surer to them than Hellfire. And it took Fitz to lead them straight to its screeching brink. The preacher knew where the real action was all right.

With the passion of one who has been there and back, Fitz brought them closer and closer to the unspeakable edge—

"Un-*utter*-uble sorrows is in store for all," he gave his holy word—a Santa Claus with nothing save horrors in his sack, hollowing every syllable to make Hell so imminent they could scarcely await their turn on the spit. "Un-*utter*-uble sorrows! Un-*dying* Damnation! Ut-*ray*-jus visi-tay-shuns! Invasion by an army! A army of lepers! Two hundred million of flame-throwen cavalry! A river of blood and burnen flesh a hundred mile long! Seven month jest to bury the dead! A army comen! A leper army!"

"Army-Gideon!" one idiot was carried completely away. Oh, they loved those leper mounties so they scarcely knew which side to join first. It didn't matter: no cause was too mad so long as the action was fast and the field bloody. Swept, they were swept by the enormous loneliness of their lives up to the very gates of the golden city, then swept clear back to the burning plains of Damnation. An action so fast it permitted no moment wherein to take breath and look within. To look within at their own hearts, so dark so empty just as hearts.

"Mothers to eat the flesh of their new-born! A time of trouble such as never was since there was a nation *even unto that same time!*

"Hailstones big as blocks of ice! Tawr'nts of bloody fire!

Fountings 'n rivers turnen to foaming blood! El Paso buried under red-hot lava! *Now* you poor sorry buggers you're really going to catch it."

"How about New York?" some people never wanted to go anywhere alone.

"Buried in a rain of toads! Toads big as cats to Wall Street's topmost tower!"

Wall Street had all the luck.

"Every island shall flee away and the mountings will not be found! Fly or die! All who worship Jehovah will have to receive the mark of the beast or die! Walls of bricks and walls of steel staved in by hailstones weighing fifty-six pounds apiece!"

Not even Byron knew where he got his figures.

"Papist rapists—the fiend's agents already are amongst us, preparen to seize the White House. A real person the *ex*-press image of Satan!—the *Pope* of Wall Street!"

Several looked suspiciously at Byron. Fitz's eyes followed —and the movement sent the whole crowd into a single trance-struck shout—

> *In solemn delight I survey*
> *A corpse, when the spirit has fled:*
> *In love with the beautiful clay*
> *And longing to lie in its stead.*

Byron couldn't bear hymning and to him this was the most dreadful of all—

> *This earth is afflicted no more*
> *With sickness—or shaken with pain;*
> *The war in the members is o'er*
> *And never will vex him again.*

"O *God*," Byron answered all like a cry—"O God who scorns the shoeless—forget our daily bread but hasteth thy vengeance! Hasteth! Hasteth!"

"Who the hell's side is he on *now?*" somebody wondered.

But before anyone could make a guess, Byron had turned and was lost in the dark. Yet his father's voice pursued him.

"Friends, I reckoned when I told you, a minute ago, about the invasion of lepers 'n hailstones weighin' fifty-six pounds 'n flame-throwen cavalry two-hundred million strong 'n a rain of toads big as cats 'n mothers eatin' their new-born 'n wind stavin' in walls of brick 'n steel 'n a river of burnen blood up to the horses' bridles, that you were heading for a bit of trouble. Now I have to tell you your real troubles won't begin till Antichrist get worken on your sinnin' hides.

"Already he is spreadin' the *Doc-treen* of evolution, the universal fatherhood of God and the brotherhood of man. Already the Wall Street labor unions are armin' to help him, preparen for the day when no man will be able to earn his bread by the sweat of his face unless he has the mark of the beast—A-F-L—upon him. Neither will he be able to buy or sell. City unions teach you that Chinamens are your brothers! *A*yrabs! Mexes!

"*You come to us and tell us that the great cities are in favor of the gold standard; we reply that the great cities rest upon our broad and fertile prairies. Burn down your cities and leave our farms, and your cities will spring up again as if by magic; but destroy our farms and the grass will grow in the streets of every city in the country. You shall not press down upon the brow of labor this crown of thorns, you shall not crucify mankind upon a cross of gold."*—He leaped straight up and came down barking like a gibbon—

> *"The cross! The cross!*
> *The bloodstained cross!*
> *The hallowed cross I see!*
> *O the blood! The precious blood*
> *That Jesus shed for me!*
> *Upon that cross in crimson blood*
> *Just now by faith I see—*

—O! Look yander! Comen down the streets of gold! I do
see a great bloodwashed throng all robed in white!"

A dozen heads turned quickly to see God only knows what,
but all they saw was Dove Linkhorn looking forsaken. As
though wishing his poor crazy pappy would come down off
the courthouse steps. When the crowd's eyes moved toward
him he turned away to follow his brother into the dark.

He passed the little movie where Thomas Meighan was
being featured in "Young Sinners." But paused in front of
the curio shop to admire the little fringed souvenirs festooned
there, pretending to be made of buffalo hide and to be en-
graved with a branding iron.

> *Out where the smile's a little longer*
> *Out where the handclasp's a little stronger*
> *That's where the West begins*

Byron had read the words to him long ago. All over town
were signs and posters, legends, warnings and invitations Dove
had learned by heart. Now it was his amusement to stand
making his lips move with his memory, so that some passerby
might get the impression that he was actually reading. He
even frowned now and again to pretend he'd hit one that was
tough enough even for an educated boy like himself.

Passersby paid little heed to the sloucher with the hair in
his eyes. So he paused below the barred window of the old
jail. Prisoners, at least, had time for him.

But the only one the jail held this night, his fingers wound
whitely about the bars, was Chicken-Eye Riley, an Indian
gouged in a brawl years before. He wore his hair long,
pioneer-fashion, with a tucking-comb in the back. And stood
with his scooped-out skull bent between the iron, trying to
get a breath of the night he could never see. Dove saw light
glint off the comb.

"Got t'bacco for me down there?" Riley demanded.

Dove picked up a pebble, slipped it into his Bull Durham

sack for ballast, and glanced about for the sheriff. The old
man raged at the townsfolks' habit of tossing sacks of this
and that or anything, even grapefruit, through the bars, for
it forced him to plod a steep flight of stairs to make the
prisoner stand inspection.

"Stand back, Chicken," Dove told Riley. Then tossed the
tobacco—he heard the stone hit the floor with a tiny clink.
The skull reappeared.

"Thanks, son."

"What's it for this time, Riley?"

"Same old thing. Refusing to make love to my wife when
she was sick. What kind of a man do they take me for
anyhow?"

"What kind of sickness have she got, Riley?"

"You sound like a pretty well-growed boy. You know how
women are. Wouldn't a man be a beast to go to his wife at
that time of the month?"

"Reckon he sure would." Dove took a hazy guess.

He actually didn't know how women were.

"Now if I'd took her against her will—if I'd beat her, if
I'd tortured her, that *would* be something to arrest me for.
If I did a thing like that I'd turn *myself* in. I'd give myself up."

"You oughtn't whup a woman, Chief."

"I *didn't* whup her, that's what I'm trying to tell you.
I wouldn't hurt my sow, far less my wife."

"You oughtn't whup either one, Chief. A dumb brute like
that."

"I'm glad you see it that way. But just suppose I did?
Suppose I was kicking my sow and the sheriff happened along.
Do you think he'd interfere?"

"I should think he ought."

"Well, he wouldn't. You know why? Because the sow is
mine to do with as I please. He would no more tell me how
to deal with her than he'd tell the barber how to cut hair.
So why should he interfere now if I'm not kicking my sow

at all but just being tender to her till my wife is well? Can
I help it if my wife is even more jealous than usual at that
time of the month? A little kindness and they treat you like
a monster."

"You shore aint no monster, Chief," Dove didn't sound too
certain, "but I got to get to work now. I'm maintenance engineer at the hotel up the road. Come in when you get out.
I'll have my cook fix you up."

Dove left the tender monster puffing contentedly against
the bars. "Mighty mannerable fellow," the maintenance engineer decided, feeling pleased with the impression he himself
had made.

He had to step carefully over the gulleys that the townsfolk called "love-holes" because they were supposed, in horse-
and-buggy days, to throw lovers into one anothers' arms.

He passed the ramshackle Negro church where the town's
dozen Negroes gathered to pray, and heard them beginning
as he passed:

> *Well, hush, O hush,*
> *Somebody's callin' me.*
> *Well, hush, O hush,*
> *Somebody's callin' me.*

It was that moment before frogs begin, when Mexican
women and Mexican men draw their shawls across their
mouths to keep the night damp out. In the dust-blue dusk
the boarded windows of *La Fe* looked down as blindly as
Riley. The careworn stairway, the windworn walls, the sand-
worn doors down a heart-sore hall, all remembered Terasina.

Terasina Vidavarri.

Frost knocked at the window. Though she had not asked
him to remember, yet he lit her virgin every night. By its
light he got the stove roaring. Then lit himself a little stick
of Byron's home-grown potaguaya and drew a deep, defiant
breath.

"Crazy Old Hasteth! Little-Time-to-Repent! Old-Cut-Off-Your-Nose-to-Spite-Your-Face—if you'd but hasted me to school instead of playing Gawd for a pack of utter fools I'd have a readin' 'n writen trade tonight."

With each draw he rose another inch off the floor.

"Buggy old Just-As-I-Am"—suddenly, the stick dangling from his lip, he crossed himself and genuflected, though his knees touched nothing.

"Pump *that* out of your hose, old man," he told Fitz—"let that do fer you, Hell-'n-Brimstone."

Here was her bedside, here was her bed. Of late she had lain here restless or dreaming and soon would lie dreaming again.

Between the white kerosene lamp's glow and the virgin's flickering yellow, he looked at the words of the story that told HOW A GOOD MAN IS ALWAYS RIGHT, for he knew that one by heart:

" '*Always going downhill, and always merry! That's worth the money.*' "

The tip of his narrow cigarette danced like a tiny ballerina in the dark. He turned the page to where the Eastwind, dressed like a Chinaman, told the Prince to hold tight or he might fall.

" '*Oh, have you come from that quarter?' said the mother, 'I thought you had been in the Garden of Paradise.'*

" '*I am going there tomorrow,' said the Eastwind. 'It will be a hundred years tomorrow since I have been there. I have just come from China, where I danced round a porcelain tower till all bells jingled. The officials were flogged in the streets. The bamboo canes were broken over their shoulders and they shrieked, "Many thanks, Father and Benefactor," but they didn't mean what they said. And I went on ringing the bells and singing "tsing, tsang, tsu!"* ' "

A scent of the Orient came to him. He left the book and followed his nose, sniffing like a rabbit, right up to a bureau drawer.

A chiffon blouse, a white slip frayed at the hem and a black brassiere like the vestments of some holy order. Dove felt of them with that special reverence of men who have lived wholly apart from women. Under these clothes, it came to him like a mystery, the señora walked naked. The realization weakened him so that he sat on the bed's edge with the slip lying limp across his knees and stroked it as if it were her flesh. In the nippled cup of the black brassiere he smelled her special smell, like that of *Russian Leather*.

Here her breast had fitted—why it must be softer yet than this! And tested the garment's texture against his leathery cheek.

Señora, let me touch your naked heart.

A yearning deep as need can go stretched him onto his stomach, clasping her slip to his chest. Pressing the pillow where her head had lain, his limbs convulsed and a dizzying surge left him limp as the slip. Sweating and passionless, guilty and spent, the boy lay a long moment with shuttered eyes. This had never happened to him before while waking.

"That's purty fair pot," Dove thought.

And fell into a snoring sleep.

To dream he was coasting gently about a county fair merry-go-round as he had once seen four small monkeys coast. Strapped tight into toy autos, each wearing a jockey cap matching the color of his car, one red, one green, one yellow and one blue; while about the guard rail people crowded and leaned—he touched the peak of his own cap to make sure it wouldn't blow off when the big race began—

Just as I am! Just as I am!

the music began with the happiest bang.

Now he was losing ground, now gaining—now he was

almost out in front. O—Hasteth! Hasteth! From his father's
shouting face he saw Eyeless Riley's skull emerge—the dream
wheel tipped straight up, the rails slipped sidewise and out
from under.

"Señora! Save me from Riley!"

He sat in the middle of the floor with the pillow still
clasped to his chest. Above him the virgin burned bright.
Beside him the stove burned low. Down the dark road Negroes
foretold and foretold—

O hush, one mornin'
Death come creepin' in the room—

Within the fire Terasina's eyes saved him from Riley as the
dream wheel died with the dream.

"Old grandpaw came last night," was how Fitz said hello
one morning to the frost that had come in the night. The
roofs of Hooverville shown white and nothing to burn but
grapefruit crates and precious few of these.

The single spigot froze, but a Mexican couple two houses
down made neighbors welcome to their well. Rumors of a
coal train coming through raced from door to door like news
of a wedding come June. True or false, it made happy telling:
all people would soon be warm once more.

Dove and a boy called Jehova went down the tracks carrying a clothes pole and a sack. Half a hundred men, women and
children huddled at the water tower. Barrows and boxes stood
about. A Mexican girl held, in a fold of a yellow shawl, a
carnival kewpie to her breast. The shawl's dusty fringes,
tumbling past her ankles, had gathered enough soot to start
a fire itself. Kewpie and child guarded an empty doll buggy
on knock-kneed wheels.

"Your baby will catch cold, sis," Dove teased her, but she
gave him only a glance of unmoving enmity for reply.

"When you're spoken to, answer," Jehova reproached her;

but got no more answer than Dove. "Wetback fraidy-cat" Jehova apologized for her to Dove as the cars came grinding to a clanking screech and the engine began to take on water.

Staking out one side of a car as their own, Jehova climbed atop the coal and lined the iron shelf that runs the length of the car with the biggest lumps he could handle, requiring both his hands. Neither knew why it had to be done this way, except that the other ways were too easy. Dove stood below with the pole. The problem wasn't only to get the biggest lumps in the shortest time but to keep neighbors from snatching them first.

Jehova finished filling the shelf just as the cars began rolling again. And got down just in time to get the sack open at the shelf's end. The first lump, hitting the pole held by Dove, tumbled into the sack. One by one the lumps fell and not one was lost.

As they fell Dove asked Jehova above him—"What if these were yams?" He got no answer, so only asked himself—What if they were *onions?* At thought of onion gravy his mouth watered—just let somebody tell Dove Linkhorn where he could steal onions and Byron would make the gravy. Somebody shouted—a plain-clothes man was humping down the spine. They lunged down the embankment with the sack between them. In the ditch at the embankment's foot a doll buggy lay upside down, its wheels still turning this way then that. A few feet away someone had slung a yellow shawl. It stirred. Then its yellow began seeping to black.

"The wheel caught the buggy but she wouldn't let go of the handle," he heard somebody say.

"Wait for the priest," said somebody else in such a tone that Dove assumed that the priest, when he came, would explain, in low, simple tones, how a child so small could love a doll so much that she had not feared even a freight train's wheels.

In the final week of January he stood in the woodshed of

the *Fe* warming a glass egg between his palms in remembrance
of chickens of summers past. He heard someone trying the
front door. His heart raced out of the woodshed before him
and his raggedy knees raced after.

Terasina.

Wearing long black gloves and looking so much like one
of the unattainable New York tourist women that he stood
stock still, barefoot and abashed.

She smiled her wide white smile. She smelled like Mexican
sunlight and pecked his cheek when he came. He handed her
the egg and said, "A little girl got kilt," for a thank you.

"Tell me later," she told him, and he went up the old stair
so worn by human care, lugging her suitcase that also had had
a bit of battering. At the door to her room he stood aside and
she went in before him.

He had drawn the blinds and fastened them fast. The room
smelled of darkness, soap and peace. His mouth fell full on
her own and his mouth was a boy's: she felt the big deep
warmth of all his being in it. Till the kiss grew into a man's
that parted her lips, and flowed into her own. That arched
her spine and made her heart drink wine. Her tongue-tip
teased his till he gave her his tongue; eyes shut, she drew
softly upon it. Her strength began draining as his gathered
power till only his enfolding hand held her up. The other
he brought up between her thighs so possessively she felt how
kind he is to touch so gently and spread herself in gratitude.
Of a sudden the blinds were too tight for gratitude, they were
being stretched to the point of pain as his lips found her
throat and her back felt the bed. She twisted from under and
leaned for breath against the bed, the front of her skirt hooked
onto her belt. Shame mixed in her with anger. She smoothed
the skirt down.

He took a step toward her and she showed him her nails,
inviting him to try again. In the dark they glinted like delicate

knives forged especially for use against men's eyes. He tossed
his hair back off his forehead and grinned weakly.

"You find yourself another job," she told him.

He turned, disgraced in a groping haze. "I think the fire
needs fixin'," he guessed.

A minute later she heard the big stove begin to roar—whenever he didn't know what to do with himself he threw kindling into it as though kindling came cheap. She waited until
she heard the door close below.

From the window she saw him shambling, the boy who
would be a man if she would be a woman, missing steps down
a broken walk and every time he missed, she stumbled. "It
has nothing to do with me." Terasina guarded herself all
around.

Yet high in the windless light a flight of pelicans ferris-
wheeled to the Gulf, the tail-bird supplanting the leader after
the manner of pelicans, in a ceaselessly changing cycle; down
to a useless sea.

"Well, a man stays sad when a woman makes a fool of
him," went through her mind, and a twinge of compunction
took her. Where was such a dunce to find another friend?

That night, as the drift of snow in her hair slept in the
woodstove's dreaming light, she knelt before sleep and confessed all her fault. A woman of thirty with a boy of sixteen—
she tried her best to feel ashamed, but a sense of contentment
rose instead. And contentedly let her head rest on the bed,
the better to hear, from some far-off square, old-fashioned
music blowing faint across an old-fashioned sea.

Girls were passing hand-in-hand and boys counterclock-
wise, sizing them up. But herself walked a bit to one side as
befitted one luckier than some but lonelier than any. And she
saw she was followed by some sort of luckless mongrel bitch
looking for its owner, its leash dragging dust. It had a broken
tail, as though it had been very nearly run over; people

laughed for the way the broken bone bobbed this way then that, inviting males from anywhere. It ran the alleys dawn till dark, lolling its tongue in ashcan corners and any strip of shade that could hide her; then her scent would catch and she'd run on weakening legs again.

Panting for protection, the bitch stretched in exhaustion at Terasina's feet, blood on her hindquarters and eyes unseeing.

"Don't laugh because others follow it," Terasina defended it to those who dared mock—"she is a leader, the one who decides what game dogs shall play, and now she is thirsty from play, that's all." "What game shall we play now?" she asked, to teach it there was no shame in being a leader, "if you were not so ugly I would take you home with me." (Yet how it panted in that airless heat!)

Its flesh was so thin the reddish meat shown through, and letting her hand pass caressingly down its spine felt her hand becoming part of that flesh. What she held in her hand was certainly no dog.

"Not mine!" she explained to everyone—"It kept following me!" And wakened still kneeling, firelight flickering down all the walls and one hand wringing the other.

"Fill your tires, mister?" Terasina heard Dove, bright and early on the job the next morning as though nothing had happened between them. She looked out at him one story down, pressing hose to valve. He wore fresh jeans, his hair was parted and slicked down, his face scrubbed to shining. Around his neck he flaunted a clean green bandanna—even his ankles were clean! Had he thought he'd been fired for lack of neatness?

When he came in for coffee she hadn't the heart to tell him she'd meant it when she told him to leave. She saw it would be of no use. He would go on working all the same.

Yet she could make things tough for him. Before he'd

gotten the fires going she was on him about last night's dishes. Before the sink was cleared she was after him because the coffee in the urn was low. How had she ever gotten by without him, he wondered; and she wondered a little too. He was perched on a chair filling the big chrome percolator when she leaned a broom against him—"Floor needs a *good* sweeping."

"O, put it up my tail," he told her below his breath, "I could sweep and wash the walls at the same time that way."

"You say something to me?"

"A little girl got kilt."

She glanced at him dubiously and turned away. He felt better for having fooled her, but fooling her earned him no rest.

Just before noon two jungle bums diverted her. One was a kind of Mexican bear, a regular little Pachuco, sideburns and all, arm in arm with a frayed-looking Swede twice his height and three times his age.

"We stopped by to wish you good luck in your new location," the youth congratulated Terasina in Spanish. "Our family ate with yours often in past times, better times."

"The location is not new," she advised him in his own tongue. "I've been here ten years and have no family."

"Meet my father," he switched to English. "He has just been offered the job of district manager in Dallas and needs only fare to get there. Kindly to loan him one dollar fifty cents. If he doesn't mail it back to you in two days I'll make good on it myself—for sake of past times, better times."

"Talk English you sonofabitch," Dove heard Father whisper.

"You should be ashamed of yourself, a nice Spanish boy of such good breeding," Terasina scolded the Pachuco and put two cups of coffee down for sake of past times.

Father dipped right for it but the Pachuco had more pride.

"We take our trade elsewhere, Father," he decided for both, hauling the Swede, complaining, to the door.

Immediately Terasina applied herself to a new sign, labor-
ing pencil to tongue the better part of an hour before it was
done and hung on a handle of the coffee urn:

No warm-ups. No wee bits.

"What it *mean?*" Dove wanted to ask after she'd read it
to him as though it were self-explanatory. Things being as
they were between them, he didn't presume to ask what it
meant, but merely sat and wondered.

"You are paid for sitting?" she asked, and he again hopped
to it.

Simon the Pieman drove up in time to pay for a piece of
his own pie.

"I admire Latin women," he admitted with a chocolate
smear for a chin, for Simon always ordered the most expensive
kind, "and I'm thinking of marrying and settling down."

He got no answer out of her to that, so he tried erudition
on her.

"I'm the intellectual type," he confided. "Here's an example: Did you happen to know that Indians don't react to
lie detectors?"

"Maybe Indians don't lie."

"You always got an answer. Answer me this: Did you
know that Navajoes eat grasshoppers?"

She worked up a mild astonishment. "Imagine *that.*"

"I'll tell you *why,* too. If you really want to know"—

"Why?"

"Because they come from a different culture. *That's* why."

"So would you if you did," Terasina assured him, putting
a lettuce-and-tomato sandwich before him in which she'd
replaced the lettuce with cole slaw.

"Will you warm this up?"—he shoved his half-empty coffee
cup toward her—"just a wee bit?" Terasina pointed to the
new warning; he saw too late that filling the cup would cost
him another nickel.

"What are you trying to do?" he asked, "be the richest
woman in the cemetery?"

Yet he tickled her palm when he left, the simple chocolate
pieman.

They weren't exactly stallions made of moonlight, these
kings of truck and trailer. They were clods whose vices ran
over weakly like coffee into their saucers. Over-eaters, over-
drinkers, snuff-chewing chiselers, doers of great sins to hear
them tell it, though tilting the pinball machine was actually
their greatest. Their conquests were many, they let it be
known. How to deal with the envy of lesser lovers their perpetual problem. Yet when she pretended to one that the weekend trip to Matamoros really sounded interesting, he changed
his plans. It wasn't to Matamoros, after all, but only to
Brownsville. Not for a weekend but just for the day. And
naturally he would have to bring his family.

The only man she'd met in ten years whose flattery she
found difficult to resist, because it was unintended, was
Dove's. In his eyes she read dedication.

"Is that *fresh* choklut pie?" he asked as if thinking it might
be banana cream.

She slapped a bar of Bon Ami down. "Call this pie."

He went to work on the windows—loveless, shoeless,
choklut-pieless. When the windows were done she handed
him a fly-swatter—but had not reckoned he would keep track
of the score.

"*Uno!*" he reported from the kitchen. "*Dos! Tres! Cuatro!*"
He was lying; she could tell by the swish of the swatter he
wasn't hitting a thing. Yet listened to his triumphs mount as
he mounted the high dry stair—"*Seis! Siete! Ocho!*" He was
nueve from the top, *diez* would bring him to the bedroom
door, *once* would bring him to the bed, at *doce* she heard him
swatting above her head, pretending to pursue a greenbottle

that wasn't there, around the bed and around. He feinted it this way—she heard his feet reverse in a dramatic presentation of a man fooling a fly on the wing—then vaulted right over the bed and brought the swatter down *smash* as though pinning it to the floor. Then silence.

A silence in which she ached to cross her ankles behind his back on that same good hard bed. And leaned her head on her hands, made half sick by that natural goodness of body and heart she had been taught was mortal sin.

"*En Jesus tengo paz*," she tried to pray the good hard bed away.

No warm-ups, the sign behind her warned: *No wee bits*. While on the bed Dove waited for her.

He came downstairs at last swinging the swatter disconsolately, hung it where it belonged and pushed out the door.

"Now I give you pie," she tried to call him back.

He spat through his teeth to lay all dust and was gone.

Gone in the silver end of day under a sky emptied of the last pelican.

Terasina abandoned her friend on the wall that night. It was no night for virgins, that was all.

Closed inside and shuttered out, alone in the shuttered dark she heard a small clock say "'sick sick sick'"; a prim little clock alone as herself yearning the small second hand around for the long silken lunge that could ease her. For the stroke to fill the wellsprings of her unused delight.

What a devilish kind of clock, to tick and tick as if minutes spent lying chastely alone were the only actual sin.

She breathed in a season without sound, not a breath of wind nor cricket to chirp. But only a clock offering alibis for playing the beast with a boy half her age.

Till the very stillness took pity, and sleep tossed her about for a while.

Wearing a low-backed evening gown of midnight blue

spangled with green sequins but disgustingly smeared with chocolate, she asked "Which way to the church?" of an elegant little humpbacked gentleman in black tie and tails,— "I wish to become a nun today."

"I am a great admirer of nuns," the elegant little gentleman assured her, and bowed even lower, "in fact, my father was Bishop of Seville. Our family knew yours well, Señora."

"Sire," she replied respectfully, "our family and yours descend from Cortez. Perhaps you remember *my* father?"

"Of course. He was a lame pimp from Puebla."

"There has always been a good pimp in our family," she reported with quiet pride.

"There has always been a good whore in ours," he boasted modestly in turn. "Perhaps you remember my mother?"

"Who could forget that royal lady who kept the pool tables where one might sleep for no more than the price of three games? How is she?"

But before she could hear how the royal lady fared the dream trailed off and she lost her way to the church.

She was sitting in her black lace slip, on the bed's edge, the following morning when Dove pushed in, both arms heaped with firewood for an excuse, without troubling to knock.

"Take the doors down," she told him, "we don't need them any more."

He evaded her eyes, yet her own stayed hard upon him: she saw the hand holding the match tremble slightly, waiting for the flame to take hold. When it took, the weaving light flowered down his countrified face.

Then within her a valentine of gladness struggled bravely up, there was no use denying fire.

"You come to me here you," she ordered him, and he came to stand at attention like a summoned private. Looking past her shoulders at something outside; prepared for any order. Submitting himself so completely that it came to her heart sweetly as an old revenge.

She pushed the suitcase slyly with her toes until it touched his own.

"Why do you stand so? Do you expect me to decorate you for bravery?"

"Never been in no army, m'am."

"Why not? So afraid of being a soldier?"

"Aint afraid to soldier. Never been asked."

"I see. Afraid only of Terasina."

"I respect you most mightily, m'am."

"Then you have changed mightily since yesterday. Then your hand did not respect me"—abruptly she seized both his hands in hers, turned them palm upward and flung them from her in feigned dismay—"Why! The very same. Only dirtier by a day. Why do you *always* disappoint me?"

The stove door opened and blew an orange-colored passion across his face. His face so young yet so old.

"Don't *intend* to disappoint you, m'am." And in the arm he placed about her she felt a commanding gentleness.

"What is a woman to do with such a cunning man?" then waited for him to begin apologizing and so spoil everything.

Instead he hauled her shoulder straps down as though he had paid for her clothes, cleared her of everything to her waist, and made her lean against him. Then lifted her breast to study it: a brown melon tipped with pink. Apparently satisfied with that one, he replaced it and studied the other.

"It's the same," she assured him. "Is there anything else I can do for you, useless cunning man?"

For answer, Useless gave her breasts an approving squeeze.

"Ready for crating," he told her. Then the touch of his lips made her eyes come wet as his hands went gently wild. In a kiss that went on and on, in an everlasting kiss. Till her eyes that had darkened with desire now lighted in electric bliss.

His hide-tight jeans and her black lace slip lay tangled inextricably on the floor. *"Empuje"* and her arms drew him down and in. Compressing her pleasure till she threshed for

release. He eased the pressure then; precisely as slowly as he
had pressed.

And began a kind of controlled abandon that made her
half marvel and half mourn at all she'd missed—"So slow.
I did not know, I did not know."

Right to the precipice's edge he brought her, letting her
subside only to draw her yet closer to the brink. Prolonging
her pleasure till it verged on pain. Then, needing to rid herself
of all this, locked him more fiercely in, beat at his chest with
both her fists, and upon the peak, with one flame-like thrust,
fell and fell in a weightless delight released from all pleasure,
all pain.

Down and down in a dream of falling where nothing lived
but two far-off voices in a Mindanao Deep of peace, some
bottomless depth of perfect rest. Hearing a man's slow-drawn
breath and a woman's grateful sobbing.

Till somebody's hands lightly wandered her face and she
realized remotely it was her own eyes someone was trying to
dry. Tears were sealing them.

After the moment of joy, he had had that deep pang of guilt
that lasts less long than the flesh hangs limp, and is gone, good
riddance to it.

Her hands traced his back to show she understood, though
she understood nothing at all. Then fell languidly away.
Terasina Vidavarri slept like a great baby then.

"I don't know what kind of great I'm bound to be," Dove
considered his prospects calmly, "all I know for certain is I'm
a born world-shaker."

And drew on his hide-tight jeans like a victor.

The born world-shaker was tying an apron around his waist,
preparing to clean up pans and pots, when he saw Byron
hurrying barefoot through the dust. Certainly didn't take
long for word to get around this shite-poke town. Dove had
just time to snatch a *cigarillo* from the tobacco counter and

light it for courage before Byron pushed in and looked around.
In the dappled gloom of early morning he wasn't able to see
a thing.

"Mornin', Byron," Dove introduced himself.

"Mornin', Dove."

"Do anythin' for you this mornin'?"

"Reckon not. Just happen to be passin' by."

"Care for coffee?"

"I'm a mite low in funds."

Dove drew the coffee. "On the house. Sweet roll?"

"Mighty kind of you, Dove. *Mighty* kind. It appear you're
makin' it pretty good."

"I'm makin' it."

"How's Dolores Del Rio?"

"I didn't mean makin' in that *particular* sense"—Dove got
a good strong whiff of danger—"I just work here, Byron."

"How old is that Mex, Dove?"

"She give her age as twenty-one."

"I reckon she lost her measuring stick. How much she pay
you?"

"Aint no business of you'rn."

"Taint likely Dear Little Pappy approve."

"Taint likely I'm to tell Little Pappy."

"Mighty likely I'm to."

"I'd name that right onfriendly."

"Why then, let's be friendly."

"You want a cigar too, Byron?"

Byron coughed his little dry cough. He shook his head,
though the very invitation made his throat tickle pleasurably.
Holding his bandanna to his mouth, he pointed to the register
and held up a single finger.

Dove stared. Byron snapped his fingers. *"Pronto! Pronto!"*

Dove hurried to obey, hoping to make as tiny a ring on the
register as possible. There were bills, there was silver. He

picked four quarters and weighed them a moment as though changing his mind.

Byron's open palm reached over the counter. The quarters fell one by one.

It was only when Byron slammed the screen that Dove realized the cash-drawer was still standing open.

She wakened slowly, feeling more well than she had in years. A great white sun was making a Mexican mosaic across the floor.

She felt lazily grateful to it for going to all that trouble just on Terasina's account. She felt she had been ill and the sun had healed her. Mighty nice of the sun.

But who had slammed a door?

Then saw a small handkerchief of black Spanish lace still damp from her own tears. Remembrance returned like bad news from a stranger. News of some injustice that could never be undone. And visualizing herself convulsed on a bestiary bed, the room that had smelled of soap and chastity smelled now only of lust. She picked her night dress off the floor as gingerly as though it were befouled.

Just as the cash-drawer banged shut.

She composed her features and her hair, dressed unhurriedly and came downstairs assuring herself that nothing was different than yesterday, though a slow-burning fury shook her every step of the way.

Dove appeared to think a number of changes had been made. He was toting a cup of coffee with the look of a daydreaming idiot's, mild and satisfied. The stump of a cigar burned in his mouth as smugly as if it had been paid for.

"Come here to me you," she told him from the register, "I want to show you funny th*ee*ng." Her English had no Spanish accent unless she were under emotional stress; he should have taken warning just from that. "A funny th*eeng—look!*"

She was pointing to a peso note. "*See*. Is made by American

company—Mexico must have Americans to make even their
money!"

He nodded thoughtfully. It didn't seem quite right at that,
and came a step nearer, balancing his coffee carefully.

"But it is al*right*," she reassured him—"Mexicans make the
money for Chinamens"—and with an upsweep of her open
palm spun coffee and saucer and all; he stood running coffee
from eyes to chin, his mouth unhinged for coffee to run in.
Saucer and cup crashed at his feet.

Clenching his overall strap in one fist and gripping the seat
of his jeans with the other, she rushed him forward so fast his
toes touched the floor only twice on the trip—and with a single
two-handed shove sent him stumbling into the dust where
she'd found him.

Dove knelt on all fours in the road as though looking for
something he'd lost. He picked himself up heavily, brushed
himself slowly down. To study her sunstriped figure behind
the fast-hooked screen.

"I tell you once," she reminded him—"*Go*. I tell you now
"*Go. Go. Go.*"

She watched him out of sight.

Then all her anger drained and died.

Leaving her just a small careworn woman with one stocking fallen under a sign that said—

Bien venidas, todas ustedes

Half that night Dove listened to Byron and Fitz arguing
whether the world moved or stood still.

"Take a butterfly," the old man kept insisting, "the way it
keeps hovering over the ground just above *one patch*. If the
earth moved, he'd come down in the next yard, wouldn't he?"

"That butterfly got more brains than you have, old man,"
Byron replied. "*He* knows the world is round and that's more
than you do. So he moves just fast enough to keep up with

the patch. It may look to you like he's just fluttering, but he's keeping even all the same."

"Did you ever throw a ball in the air and catch it coming down?"

"Naturally."

"Then common sense will tell you that if the earth actually moved you'd be too far away to catch it coming down, wouldn't you? Now tell me the ball knows the earth is moving." The old man had victory within reach.

"For God's sake, when they say the earth moves it don't mean it goes forty miles an hour, old man," Byron protested.

"What's to keep it from going forty?" Fitz asked dryly, "if it's round as you claim it ought to be going faster and faster like a snowball down a hill. I'll tell you the reason it don't move is the same reason it aint round—it got corners to keep it from moving. I'll prove it by the good book."

Dove heard him rustling about with the battered Bible, trying to find the passage that proved him right.

"Don't bother, old man," Byron sounded tired. "I know what you're lookin' for—'and the winds blew from the four corners of the earth'—so how can anything round have corners? Go to sleep, fool old man."

The light was turned down. Dove heard the old man creep onto his cot bed. So long as the world was flat he would sleep well upon it. Only round worlds left Fitz sleepless.

As softly as if he'd been saving it Byron asked—"On what day of the Creation did God say 'Let there be light and there was light'?"

"The first, of course," Fitz answered contentedly.

Dove heard a little silence run about around the room and back. Byron had a sense of timing.

"And when did He make the two great lights, the greater to rule the day and the lesser to rule the night?"

"The fourth, naturally."

"Think *that* over, old man." Byron turned on his side. He slept best upon a rounded star.

Dove heard the old man thinking it all over; tossing then fuming. While Byron slept the sleep of the just, snoring softly.

Dove was glad Byron had won for once. But personally didn't care if the planet was shaped like a pretzel. He had issues more pressing to solve.

"First she totes me on and the next thing I know I'm standin' on my haid in the middle of the road. She could have spore me that."

Well, he wasn't the sort to hang around a door he'd been shoved through. She'd have to send for him before he'd work for her again. That much was certain.

All the same, there is no statute forbidding a man to walk down the common highway.

Dust puffs filed behind him early the next morning, and an anxious wind went sniffing ahead like a hound favoring a sore forefoot; gas lamp to telephone pole, one side of the road to the other. Till it came to the lamp that leaned toward the *La Fe* as the *La Fe* leaned toward it. There it scooted suddenly around the corner into the yard, abandoning Dove altogether.

He hadn't heard of any law forbidding a man to go around the corner of a broken-down chili parlor either.

Terasina's back was toward him. Her earrings glinted green against the white of the wash like news of an early spring. Slips and step-ins, yellow and pink, flapped about her like invitations to love in the morning. The strong forenoon light silhouetted her thighs to the full and the wide.

Sure enough, she was hanging yesterday's black night dress. He watched the wind pawing it and saw it turning a little away from the wind like a girl evading a jealous lover. A wind that could not let matters be, but had to twist things around to suit itself.

Raising herself on her sandaled toes to reach the topmost
point of the line, she stretched her brown sleeveless arms and
her haunches pressed hard together.

As he had pressed them with his own large hand, when his
other had pillowed her head.

That he would not pillow again. He spat across the fence
and saw his spittle strangle itself on a thorn.

Look who's hangin' out her dirty underdrawers.

Out of the corner of her eye Terasina saw him leaning.
One more tramp come to stare. So stare. If it helps your health
it does me no harm. I did not send for you.

Won a wetback beauty contest forty years ago and thinks
she's the Queen of the May.

Go when you wish to go.

Let's people see her make a-purpose. Thinks she got so
much to show because she sells old fried beans. Wouldn't be
the least surprised if folks run her back across the river one
of these nights.

If I am to play the whore I will play for my own people.

Better lookers than this Pachuco would be giving him the
eye in Dallas or Houston one of these days. "Let me spend
my money on you, Big Boy," is what they'd be asking him.
Big Boy wouldn't be wasting time on Pachucos then. He'd
have some trim blue-eyed Anglo all his own, to cook him up
real American meals. There wouldn't be any *frijoles* in *that*
house by God. And she'd say "think" instead of "theenk"
and go to a Christian church and wear enough clothes on
her back to keep every passerby from seeing how she was
built between ankles and belly button. In Houston. Or was
that Dallas?

"No work today," she took the clothespin out of her teeth
to announce.

"I got a better job," he assured her.

"Oh? That is *nice*."

"Aint in this old shite-poke town neither."

"What poke town is it in?"

"Dallas, natcherly."

"What do you do there, in Dallas?"

"You'll read about that in the paper."

"You bring the paper and I read about it, so *you* know what you do there too."

"It's not hard to make fun of weakness in others. I'll pay you the dollar I borrowed."

"You owe me nothing but goodbye," she told him and bent, trim at the waist and broad at the shoulders, hitching her skirt to the backs of her knees.

She didn't sense him coming up until his hands clamped her waist—then she wheeled like an ambushed cat and jammed the clothespin into his teeth. He rocked as if hit by fire.

"*Segundos?*" Terasina inquired politely.

He drew off, shaking his head and spitting splinters. No, he didn't care for seconds on clothespins. He reached cowlike toward the blood trickling down his chin, and she held out the little black lace kerchief.

He shook his head. "Keep your rag."

"That is all I can do for you today then." The proceedings were closed.

"You done nothin' so great for me any other day," he told her, wiping his mouth with the back of his hand—"but you durn well *liked* what I done fer you."

Her face showed no recollection.

"It felt *good* is what you said," he remembered gallantly. "*Slow* you said—you liked it *slow*," and put his hand on the nape of her neck. She sank her teeth into his palm, he felt them sink to the bone and forced her, biting still, to her knees.

"It'll be a little faster today," he assured her, "I'm a mite short of time."

Spring-green and sun-yellow the clothes flapped about. Polkadot bandannas flapped a polkadot quadrille. But the night dress turned aside and a stocking hung dark as a shroud.

Till she lay on her side with her head between her hands
and her dress tossed back to her hips. The front of the dress
was ripped to the waist. A low wind paused long enough to
toss a handful of dust and pass on. It was done.

Dove picked up her handkerchief and daubed his chin. He
waggled a lower front tooth. It was just a mite loose. The
noon freight hooted two miles away.

Like a man walking through water he shuffled toward the
S.P. water tower. The freight whooped like a Sioux who has
seen too many westerns.

He stayed out of sight till the cars began passing.

The first stars arrived early that night to see how Dove
Linkhorn was making out. And saw right off that here was
one party who didn't take funny stuff off anybody any more.
Folks who thought this boy looked foolish felt different when
they began to hurt. "Mighty rough customer," the planets
agreed till Dove closed the doors on those gossiping stars.

He heaped straw for a mattress, wadded a bandanna for a
pillow, pulled a yellowed rotogravure page to his chin for a
sheet. Who needed Texas? Let Texas roll by.

And slept without remorse.

Only once, clasping his stomach as the car rocked and
rolled him between nightmares and dreams, he whimpered
a little.

When he wakened the cars were clanking an iron alarm
and daybreak was shagging the shirtless and shiftless, the lame,
the lost and the shoeless from under the brake beams and
down the spines. Fleeing reefers, clambering couplings, climbing raggedly down off the ladders; walking wounded and
battle-stragglers limped, leaned and hobbled to the closest
aid-station.

"Lots of fine folks out seein' the country," Dove tried to
get in step, "Didn't reckon there'd be so many so early in
the year." And stayed out of step for a quarter of a mile, to

some half-sunken barns that might have stabled the federal cavalry that had once pursued Pancho Villa.

As a matter of fact, that was exactly what they had. Though the horses were gone with Villa now—mavericks and herd-bound hides alike. Hoof prints long sunk and riders unsaddled—captains and privates all alike. In rooms where the lighting was still by gas some lay drunk and others lay dying, and all were long since unsaddled. Dead or dying, drunk or derailed, Captains or privates, all alike.

The whole wide land looked disheveled as a bed in a cheap hotel.

"Folks looken a bit peakedy," Dove observed, feeling slightly on the peakedy side himself. A lettered warning stopped him the way a stranger's lips, moving silently, stop a deaf mute.

"What do the sign sayz, mister?" he tapped a fedora no higher than his shoulder, rambling along atop a faded plaid lumberjack.

"It *sayz* here this is a city shelter," a foxlike bark came out of a face like that of a terrier bitch—a face neither feminine nor male, but the voice was a girl's—it *sayz* to scoff up here all you want 'n thank the citizens of San Anton' for it in your prayers—" she paused to let others give thanks—"but stay out of town or them same citizens will slap you right into the crummiest slammer in Texas."

"It sayz all that, sis?"

"It also sayz Laughable Fools with Dirty Feet Keep Off All Trains Not In Motion, Laughable Fool. It says your best bet is to do what you see the smart people do. So crawl your weak-minded ass after mine and do what I do. *Don't do nothing you don't see me do first.* And *don't* call me sis. Call me brother."

"You reckon yourself one of the smart folks 'n me just a big ignoramus?" Dove considered the preposterous notion.

Brother raised a cautioning finger. "I got a jacket. You got no jacket. I got a shirt. You got no shirt. I got shoes. You got no shoes but we're both up against a knife and fork. I ate last night and I ate this morning and you haven't eaten since God knows when. Now who's the smartest, me or you?"

The raggedy line shuffled one raggedy inch.

"You're so smart it's a pure pity," Dove decided—"Just tell me this much—they got liverpuddin' in that kitchen ahead or not?"

"They not only got liverpuddin' friend. They got candied yams, Virginia ham 'n possum pie."

"Yankee vittles is a mite rich for my blood," Dove was forced to decline. Brother glanced up to see who was being kidded now.

But Dove's jaw hung so long, so mournfully from cheeks so cavernous, the hair bothering his eyes had been so long uncut and the eyes themselves so darkly shadowed, it was hard to believe anyone could kid in that condition.

"You should of stayed in the hospital till they cut your hair," she advised him.

"I bet if you taken off that hat you could stand a trim your own self." Dove answered. He felt a friendly hand on his shoulder.

"Ah'll bet y'all from the Big Bend Country, haint yo'?" Dove tossed the hair back out of his eyes to see if it were someone he knew, forgetting for the moment that he didn't know anybody. A Marine sergeant was studying him smilingly.

"Me? No *sir*," Dove corrected him with pride, "I'm from Rio Grande country."

"Taylor 'n Halsted, pleased to meet you both," the terrier introduced herself so assertively that the uniform had to talk over the fedora in order to recruit Dove.

"How'd you like three square meals a day, Red? A chance to see the tropics, chase Sandino, defend your country, get two pairs of shoes and a pension shortly after?" He gave Dove a wink so broad that Dove winked back just as broadly—"and how those South American girls go for that uniform."

"It sounds like a right good position, mister"—Dove decided. "I especially like that part about defendin' my country. But first I got to git me a small bait of vittles."

"I think you'll make a fine soldier, son," the sergeant was confident—"You got no physical *dee*fect have you?"

"Take another look at that squint, Colonel," the disguised girl recommended.

"A squint aint no *dee*fect," the sergeant explained authoritatively, "—it's more what we term a 'impedimunt.' We'll get Red specs to correct his. Spanish women *like* soldiers with glasses."

"Look at them choppers."

Without being asked, Dove opened his mouth and the sergeant put a big dirty thumb flat down on his tongue.

"In six months the clown won't have a tooth in his head," the girl seemed certain. "Jungle-rot will get him."

"Well, we don't want him to bite Sandino," the sergeant already excused Dove from one detail.

"I have one loose awready anyhow," Dove managed to tell simply by removing the thumb temporarily, between two of his own fingers—"it waggles"—and replaced the thumb hoping the sergeant would waggle it a bit for him.

"Let the army dentist do that." The sergeant took his fist out of Dove's face. "You're going to make one hell of a Marine. Wouldn't be surprised if you caught Sandino yourself. You can close your mouth now."

He took out a small notebook and a pencil. "Tell me, you got any other *dee*fects, son?"

Dove reddened. That was when you couldn't read or write. "I reckon that in time *that* might be corrected too," he answered evasively because of those standing about.

"Nothing serious, is it?" He gave Dove a nudge—"Nothin' you picked up from town girls?"

The sarge had girls on his mind alright.

"The second spell he took after supper last night he foamed a bit—Would that be anything serious?" Dove's friend asked blandly.

"He takes *fits?*" The Marine grew anxious. He didn't want to lose a rookie but he didn't want to hook a lemon.

"I never throwed a fit in my whole derned life," Dove defended himself stoutly. "Pay no heed whatsoever to my brother here, captain—jest jealous cause I out-growed him. I aint even inclined toward spells."

"*Good* lad," the sergeant congratulated him, "Tex, you're a real stand-up kid. Tell me this—routine question—nothing personal—if an enemy capable of rape had you trapped with your sister and mother and one of you had to be left behind, which one of you would you choose it to be?

"*How about them señoritas?*" Brother gave Dove a nudge that almost knocked him down.

"*Will* you stay out of this? the sergeant turned on the girl.

"I got neither mother nor sister, captain," Dove found the safest answer.

"Suppose you had."

"Sister would have to go," he heard a terrier-whisper.

"Sister would have to go," Dove repeated hopefully.

"I told you *stay out of this,*" the sergeant menaced the fedora and turned back to Dove—"Put it this way. Your outfit of one hundred men is surrounded by bloodthirsty Nicaraguan bandits but you can save them all by sacrificing your own life. Which would come first with you? The lives of the ninety-nine others or your own?"

Dove needed no help on that.

"My own, naturally." He beamed.

Dove was a little sorry to see the sergeant shake his head and move off.

"Wasn't that the right answer?" Dove wanted to know.

"It was the right answer alright," she reassured him. "How do you feel, Red?"

"Fairly fainty," Dove confessed. The odor of hot soup was swinging his stomach like a bell.

"Now what did I tell you just before, Red?"

"I ferget, friend."

"I told you don't do nothin' you don't see me doing. Did you see me asking Uncle Whiskers for a new suit? Did you see me showing him my choppers? Did you see me standing still to get measured for a rifle?"

"Nobody asked you," Dove recalled.

"You could still call him back—and spend the rest of your life doin' close-order drill down in the banana country instead of riding passenger trains and sleeping in the shade. *I* won't stop you."

Somebody handed Dove something steaming in a bowl just then and all notion of soldiering fled upward with the steam.

When he had finished the bowl he looked up to see his friend's hardly touched. The girl pushed it to him.

"Thanks, sis." She gave him a look. "I mean brother," he corrected himself.

"You'll thank me for keeping you out of barracks one day too."

A haunted-looking cracker in a grease-stained apron put a tab of paper between them already so thumb-smirched Dove thought he wanted their prints.

"Give me a couple phonies, boys," he advised them.

"We didn't have it in mind to give you good ones," the girl told him.

"We got to keep track of how many feeds we put out," the hant apologized. "Citizens got a right to know how their money is being spent."

"My ignorant brother here went back three times for seconds—What will the citizens say about *that?*"

"Directly y'all finish eatin'," the cracker invited them both,

"you might step outside and lend me a hand with a spot of
kindling—takes kindlin' to cook y'all cawnbread y'know."

"He has it in mind for us to chop down a tree," she explained to Dove.

"A mighty mannerable feller, and I don't mind work,"
Dove added, anxious lest he miss a chance to do some.

"I don't mind a spot of light labor myself," she admitted.

A circle of half a dozen vagrants sitting cross-legged about
a sack of charity beans looked like a spot sufficiently light.
With a pan and a bucket between them, Dove and the little
'bo trickled beans through their fingers. Bugs, stones, old
crockery, weeds and beer-corks were for the bucket and
beans were for the pan. Since it was their own supper they
were preparing, they trickled with some care. Dove found a
chipped agate and pocketed it like a blue treasure.

"Everybody got to eat. Everybody got to die," a white-
haired Greek sitting cross-legged told them like it was big
news.

A wisp of a creature beside Dove squeaked happily right in
his ear—"I'm the littlest guy here, 'n the oldest. Wouldn't be
surprised if I was the smartest too. I *know* I'm the sassiest."

Dove's eyes followed his friend's hands. Such a careful way
with the smallest pebble, yet so much quicker than his own.

"I once growed the biggest crop of these yet seen in North-
ern Michigan," a florid-faced fellow in a frayed sheepskin
boasted. "Fact is, it was the biggest crop in that part of the
state that year if not in the *entire* state. Done it without help,
too. Cooked my own meals. Done my own laundry. Put up
my own preserves. Didn't have no wife. Didn't need none.
Didn't have a hired hand. Didn't want one. Biggest coopera-
tive farm in the state, likely biggest in the country, right next
door to mine. Fifty able-bodied men workin' night 'n day
with tractors 'n every farm instrument known to modern
man. Four professors to study their soil. All I had was a old-
fashioned plow my grandpappy made out of a pine tree he

felled hisself, and iron he'd worked out of ore he dug hisself. I turned out a crop near to double of theirs—a mite better than double, truth to tell. Didn't have a hired hand neither. Didn't need none. Didn't have a wife. Didn't want none."

"I reckon the sun didn't hinder none," Dove observed.

As soon as one sack was finished, the hant dumped a sack of black-eyed peas, and for some reason this lightened everyone's spirits, almost as though he had brought in a sack of cherries and told them to eat all they wanted.

Once he came in with a basket of tomatoes and offered them around. Everyone took one or two except Dove. "I wouldn't eat love apples," he warned his friend, "it's a poison fruit."

The careful afternoon trickled through their fingers with less and less care. The big room darkened and dampened, walking wounded came and went. Dove's thick thigh pressed his friend's slender one and he felt the pressure lightly returned. Their fingers touched one moment in the sack.

"You think *these* times are hard?" the Michigan farmer was asking. "Why compared to times I've seen, these are absolutely *flush*. If you just look at it right, we're right spang in the middle of the biggest boom this country ever seen. Look at us settin' here stuffin' ourselves to bustin' on cornbread 'n beans!"

"That's right," Dove agreed, "we eat so much it keeps us skinny just carryin' it around."

"Why," the farmer went on, "when I was a boy in Northern Michigan we didn't know there was anything else to eat on earth but skim milk 'n wild onions. Drunk branch water 'n et sheep sorrel 'n counted ourselves more fortunate than most. Mother run a highly successful boarding house on them two victuals in fact—biggest boarding house that part of the state. Never seed a toilet till I was seventeen year old. I'd heard of backhouses but never seed one. Never seen a well pump. Full grown man afore I tasted ice cream."

"My own folks lived mostly on pawpaws," Dove agreed, "It were mighty hard sleddin' when the pawpaws didn't hit and the wind died down."

"I'll never forget the winter of 1917," the farmer went right on. "The snow was deeper than the world. Wolves killed my goats, hawks got the chickens, night-riders burned my barn an' mother run off with a preacher. Made me of half a mind to quit farming and go to work."

The encircling faces looked like so many tin plates on a shelf. They gave off a faint odor, as of disinfectant with smoke in it. The locked-in and the locked-out lived between the smoke of small wood fires and the odor of jail house disinfectant in 1931.

"I'm the oldest 'n the littlest," the happy mouse introduced himself eagerly to each newcomer, "I'm the sassiest too. Wouldn't be surprised if I were the randiest. How come I be first in *everything?*"

"You're last in pickin' beans," Dove told him.

"But I was the first to vote for Hoover," the old man snapped more now like a youthful rat than an ageing mouse— " 'n the first to admit I was wrong."

"Hoover is a great man," the Michigan farmer was certain —"but he's too far ahead of his time. The whole Republican Party is ahead of its time."

"I lived through Hoover myself," somebody agreed. "It give me real strength. Now I can live through anything."

The kitchen-hant came blowing a whistle. All hands quit on the second's split. Dove stepped over the sack gingerly.

By the time he got to the mess hall the hant had put on a greasy beany just to direct traffic. Mexicans to the right, Negroes to the left. But Dove he directed straight ahead, to where the white Americans ate at the longest board of all.

"Pappy wouldn't approve this kind of carrying-on," Dove realized, "mixin' Cath'lics 'n Protestants this way."

"Where's the Reb table?" his friend came asking.

"Take the elevator, Yankee," the hant instructed her.

Dove got a slab of cornbread in molasses and a stack of beans piled so neatly they appeared to have been counted one by one. When he considered how many he had picked he felt that, percentage-wise, he was getting a bad count.

"Everyone always gets more than me," he complained, and the girl pushed her plate before him again.

"Why you so good to me?" Dove asked.

"Because I want *you* to be good to me," she told him so frankly that he felt he must be doing her a favor and cleaned up every crumb.

"Everybody got to eat," somebody lamented, "everybody got to die."

Dove had hardly finished his third helping when they heard the Man to Houston whistle. "Let's scram out of here before that fool makes us chop down that tree," the girl urged him— "Put that stuff in your pocket, Red."

Dove shoved the cornbread into his jeans and they ran for it.

Most of the cars were empties and came clattering past too fast to chance. They waited, flat on their stomachs on the under embankment until the ore cars, whose ladders hung lower, began sliding by.

Dove counted them coming. "It's plumb mass-dark and they're travelin' fast," he warned her.

"It's the last one to Houston before tomorrow night," she answered. "You comin'?"

Straddling the car, Dove saw its sides were merely chutes slanting straight to the rails. She piled past him and over with a victor's cry and he caught her wrist as she felt no floor. She pulled him powerfully over but his free hand caught the iron edge and held.

Just held. Then froze like floorless death itself on the iron.

He could not pull her up. He could not let her go. Her double-grip on his wrist, pulling the ribs out of his side, in-

formed him if she were going he was coming with her. The
wheels glinted green lightning in the black, he heard pebbles
clicking against her shoes in the roar. His right hand no longer
held the iron: the iron held the hand.

Her little stricken face, lighted briefly, tried to tell him
some last something. Dove caught her overall strap in his big
buck teeth and hauled, neck backstraining till she got her fingers onto the side and drew herself onto the edge. He steadied
her though his arm trembled to the shoulder.

She was caked with coal-dust, fright had hollowed her eyes.
When the train slowed to go into a hole for a passenger train
he helped her down. "It sayz keep off all trains not in motion," he reminded her. Her trembling turned weakly to
laughter then.

They rested their backs on the lee side of a heap of coke.
There she let her laughter turn to sobbing.

"What's the matter, friend?"

"Run," the girl told him, struggling to her feet. Dove put an
arm around her shoulders.

"Where you think *you're* going?" He pulled her back
down.

"Run."

"Mebbe you better just cry," he suggested.

She found that so easy that she kept it up too long, like a
child.

"What you chokin' yourself up for?" Dove finally asked.

"Lost my jacket," she remembered.

"If you'd been wearin' the jacket—"

"I know"—she assured him that she knew where she'd be
if she'd been wearing something he could not have gripped.

Her breath began drawing slower, soot and sleep sealed her
eyes.

Her face in sleep looked furtive yet innocent, like one already punished for a crime she hasn't grown up to commit.
When she was old enough to commit it she'd find it.

Her hand on his own pressed his in sleep. He let his hand fall between her knees then moved it up till it cupped her and rested there.

She stirred and he took it away.

"Keep it right there," she told him, "I owe you that much."

Lanterns and flashlights passed and repassed down the rails, building shadows on the box car doors. Railroad crews didn't care how many climbed aboard once the engineer had given his warning toot; but it made them look bad to have the strays lounging the cars like tourists when a train wasn't moving.

"The name is Kitty Twist," the girl told Dove, "—not my real handle of course. It's just what they took to callin' me in The Home. I'm seventeen almost eighteen 'n I've run from five homes. I'll keep on runnin' till I'm eighteen. Then I'll marry a good pickpocket and settle down."

"I better look this man over," Dove told her uneasily, and wandered down the track, inspecting the cars from grab-iron to stirrup-ladder. When he was satisfied he whistled for her, helped her into the car he had picked, and shut the door. One beam shone, dancing slenderly whenever the long car trembled after shunting.

"Red," she told him in the dark when the car began at last to roll, "put your hands under me before these boards pinch my little hump clean off."

With both hands cushioning her pine-knot bottom, Kitty Twist wriggled comfortably until she grew warm. She didn't mind that Dove's own narrow behind was freezing.

"I love you, baby," he told her because having saved her life he supposed he ought to. "I'll buy you play-pretties and posey flowers. I'll learn me a trade 'n take care of you."

He felt her cold little lips and her small cold mouth, her little cold hands that felt so greedy.

"Daddy, you'll never have to work," Kitty Twist told Dove. "I'll work hard 'n give you all my money."

He couldn't see her smiling too knowingly in the dark.

"The poorer people are the more likely they are to help you," Kitty told him the next morning after they had once again left engine and cars in charge of the crew. "Pick the first unpainted shack you see."

She followed Dove into a littered yard and waited while he rapped the door of a knocked-together-by-hand house the color of soot. A soot-colored wife came to answer.

"My brother took hisself a small fall, M'am," Dove pleaded, "Would you allow him to worsh up at yer pump?"

"Whut he sayin'?" the woman looked to Kitty for help.

"He wants to know can I wash up in your house."

"Come in, child," the woman invited Kitty, holding wide the door.

Dove waited in the yard humming softly—

Well hush, O hush
Somebody's callin' me

Until Kitty came out scrubbed and shining, a band-aid on her cheek and a half a bar of Ivory soap in her hand.

"Oldfolks wasn't fooled for a minute," Kitty reported. "Called me 'Sis' 'n set me down in the tub 'n scrubbed my back 'n made me wash between my toes—Look"—she revealed white anklets—"And would you believe it? She sung to me the whole time."

"What she sing?"

"Don't Bite The Hand That's Feeding You."

"They aint like you and me," Dove explained, "they're simple people. But I could stand a worsh-off myself."

"You'll get one uptown," Kitty promised—"Look—I throw like a damned man," and she hurled the Ivory clear across the tracks.

"Mighty fine whip for a girl," Dove had to concede.

"For a girl hell. Walter Johnson never throwed better. I'm a big-league kid from a big-league town."

"I never did see a real big town," Dove admitted, "full of store-bought marvels. They got them in Houston?"

"They got 'em, but you'll have to go shopping yourself. I go down the main stem and I'm on my way back to The Home by morning. I got a W on me, Jack."

"I'll see law-folks don't snatch you, Kitty," Dove promised.

"I'll see you get shoes and a shirt too, Red," she returned the favor—"I'll dress you up in the finest."

"I'll get you a red silk dress with a tasselly-sash 'n goldy year-rangs too."

"Red, what I'm trying to say is I'll *hustle* for you if want me to."

"I'll hustle for you too," he promised.

"My *God*," the girl thought, "he thinks I mean I'm going to be a shoe-clerk for him. I'm going to have to straighten him out till there's nothing left but kinks."

Although Kitty Twist had never hustled, she knew the trade from older hands with whom she'd been institutionalized, and had run off upon the prospect of going into business for herself.

Down a side-street a sign invited them—PRISONERS' VOLUNTEER AID SOCIETY.

"The usual fee here is two bits," the ex-con at the desk confided, "but if you boys are short I'll accommodate you both for that. Got two bits between you?"

"What's the accommodation?" Kitty was curious.

"One meal, one flop, one shower apiece."

The ex-con pocketed her quarter and they followed him into the kitchen. He put two bowls of withered cole slaw before them and two cups of cold chicory coffee.

"That's the meal," he explained. "You still got a shower and a flop comin'."

"Go get your wash-off right away, Red," Kitty urged him as soon as she'd tasted the coffee—"They're running out of well-water hereabouts."

An old man stood under the stream letting the water trickle in and out of his navel while keeping a worried eye on a lean and vulturous creature crouched above his clothes. The vulture had just finished examining the old man's rags and was cupping his palms to the light; then kicked the bundle off to one side without taking his eyes off his palms. He had caught something all right.

"Extry*ordinary!*" the old man seemed to know what it was. "Extryordinary!"

The louse-runner ground his palms together under the water.

"Them that don't git crushed gits drowned," he announced with barbarous glee.

Then hovered over Dove as Dove undressed in turn.

The shower was cold but there was strong brown soap. The touch of it burned the bruise on his lip, but he scrubbed himself till his fingers went numb. The water kept getting colder and colder.

The louse-runner returned Dove's clothes with a disappointed air. Dove asked him for a cap, and after some rummaging was presented with a battered and sunburned floater of straw. It would keep the coal out of his hair and the sun out of his eyes. He lacked the courage to ask for shoes.

Then down some wide and quiet street the pair trudged past windows curtained and shaded. Although it was only mid-afternoon everyone seemed asleep. They came to a playground where no children played.

"School's out!" Dove decided in a shout, and made for the nearest swing. Standing spreadlegged, he got it pumping high. Kitty's little sexless face looked up at him from below. Every time he swung past her she said, "We don't have time for fooling, Red."

He came down off the swing in a shambling run. She watched to see what was next.

The rings: around and around, toes scraping the ground,

his hair in his eyes and his mouth in a shout, "Look at *me!* Look at *me!*"

"I never seen anything like it." She decided to watch a while.

"How's *this?*"

Dove had looped his knees into the rings and was hanging head down, hat gone and hair brushing cinders and sand.

"Just let me know when you've had enough, Red. I got all day."

But his childhood had just begun and he hadn't had nearly enough.

"Catch me when I come down!" he warned her from the top of a chute. And she, the wingless jay of alley and areaway, had to stand at the foot of the chute as he came down head first to prevent him from breaking his neck. He grabbed her hand and hauled her to the teeter-tawter.

"Break your back or bust your ass," Kitty Twist had had enough—"I'm New Orleans bound myself."

Dove sat on the useless teeter-tawter, a see-saw boy with no one to see-saw. And watched his only friend go out the playground gate. The teatless little fly-by-night outcast wandering the wild earth just to get even with everything upon it.

"She acts like she done me a favor letting me save her life." Dove thought, "let her go."

He pumped himself high again on the swing. He took a flyer, even faster than before, on the rings. Then climbed the highest chute in the yard. When he reached the top he was breathing hard and had strangely lost heart for sliding. He slid down at last only as a way of getting back to the ground. Stumbling with loneliness, he hurried after anyone who could keep him from being alone again. Leaving his boyhood at the top of the chute and his true manhood still unreached.

Kitty was nowhere in sight. Nobody at all down the sun-stricken street. Dove wanted to run back home.

"Here's your hat." She stepped out of the shadows so softly that he knew she had been watching him.

"I'm not yet sure you're real, Red," she told him as though to explain his suspicion.

"If I don't ask you to prove something like that yourself," he told her thoughtfully, "then you wont have to have ask proof of me."

"I'll watch it after this," she told him, always wary. But he was lost, she saw, in wonder of the houses lining either side of this avenue where private footpaths led to every door.

"How many folks you figure live in jest that one place?" he asked, pointing at one.

"None at all," she informed him, "the sign says FOR SALE."

After that Dove noticed many such signs on houses whose paint was beginning to crack. Weeds grew in the paths guarded by oaks that had guarded Indian trails.

In a small suburban park they came to a line of sleepy stores, in several of which no business was done any more. Kitty took him for a leisurely arm-in-arm stroll down one side of the little half-dead town and up the other.

"You got kin-folks around here?" Dove asked because of the way she lingered.

"Neither chick nor child," she assured him, bringing him up in front of a window where sawdust lay scattered. As they watched, a musty-looking rabbit hippety-hopped from a corner, got half-way across the window and turned back to its home-corner. Kitty left Dove to conduct inspection of the areaway behind the shop and returned briefly.

"We'll look in here after dark," she reported back, "I'll need a little boost. Don't worry—I'm the best damn stinker for my size and age in the business."

"I can't help you in *that* business, sis," Dove informed her, "account I prefer a daytime trade. Like on one of them big white boats I seen a picture of in N'wawlins."

"In *where?*"

"A book. Picture-book."

"I mean where was the *place* you just said?"

"N'wawlins."

Kitty thought everything over. Even then she didn't sound too sure. "You wouldn't by chance be talking about New Orleans, would you?"

"It's what I said. N'wawlins."

"I see. And when you get there you'll walk into the steward's office without a shirt, barefoot, needing a haircut 'n ask him if he needs a captain?"

"I weren't intended to be no captain," Dove told her. "I weren't meant to be more than a private. But I don't figure to try even for private without I first look genteel."

"What size shoes you wear, Red?"

"Haint wearin' none. Walkin' barefooty."

She studied the feet he kept throwing from one side of the walk to the other.

"Thirteen and a half," she judged.

"That's pretty close," Dove agreed.

"Close to what?"

"Close to fourteen."

"You can stop putting on the weakminded act for me any time now," Kitty Twist advised him. "I'm on."

Down in Houston's Mexican slum there stood, that June of '31, a three-story firetrap with a name:

H
O
T
E
L

That's all: Hotel Hotel.

"Never did try sleepin' in a skyscraper afore," Dove looked up—"Whut do it costes here?"

"Thirty-five cents apiece," Kitty informed him, "and some places go yet higher."

"In that case," Dove decided, "we'll have to find an inexpensive place."

"We get breakfast throwed in here though."

"What gits throwed?"

"Mission donuts 'n coffee black."

"Then we're too far north."

Kitty tried to let it go but the temptation was too strong.

"How do you figure that, Red?"

"When folks stop puttin' out liverpuddin' for breakfast, everyone's too far north."

"And I'm not in the least surprised," Kitty agreed. And supporting herself on his arm she slipped her sneaker off a moment, slipped it back on and released his arm.

"Well what do you know? Just look here what I found in my shoe, Red."

A five dollar bill lay folded in her palm.

"That's purely luck, sis. How it git there?"

She gave him a knowing nudge. "Didn't I tell you colored folks are the friendliest? Why does everyone think that their kitchen matchbox is the First National?"

"I never would of pecked that door if I'd knowed that that was what you were up to," Dove told her.

"That's why I didn't tell you."

"It aint right to steal off folks while they're doin' you a kindness, Kitty. Do unto others as you would be done by."

"I'll try to remember that too—" she swung him about. "Why, Red, Do you know what a pair of three dollar shoes and a two dollar shirt would do for you? People would be calling you Preacher, that's what. She took his arm and hurried him into the lobby. "And you wouldn't be the first country boy to turn into a town pimp neither," she added to herself.

"My pappy *was* a preacher of sorts," he told her. "The sort to make you throw your Bible away."

He stood on one side while she conferred with the desk clerk, and eyed himself sidelong in the long lobby mirror. She was right at that: if anything could improve him it was clothes.

"The only bedtime story my old lady ever told me began and ended with 'You leave me cold,'" Kitty Twist recalled. "That's what she'd say when she'd sober up. When they took me away from her and put me in Juvenile I was a real little terror there. I was mad 'cause I hadn't stole things like the other kids. I wetted the bed and a matron snitched so I had to sleep in the Skunk Room. That's the dorm with rubber mattresses for bed-wetters. I was eight. They were afraid by the time I was ten I'd flood them out.

"That was when Mama went on the wagon to show them she meant it when she said she wanted me back. Got a crowd of ex-alkies to back her so I had to go. 'All for my baby' was how she'd put it.

" 'If that's the case you can step down any time,' I finally told her, 'Because now *you* leave *me* cold.' Mama couldn't stand a tie—in her book somebody had to win and somebody had to lose. When she fell off the wagon you could heard the crash for miles.

"But if I was going to do another stretch I was going to do it for something *I* done, not on somebody else's account. They caught me crossing some bridge. If I'd made that bridge I would of been alright. I would of been out of Illinois.

"By the time I was fourteen I was back with kids a full head shorter than me. I wetted the bed the first night. Imagine— fourteen years old and right back where I'd been at eight! I realized then I wasn't getting ahead."

She pulled up the sleeve of her right arm. It was tattooed from shoulder to wrist.

"Got 'em on my legs too. Done 'em myself with plain needles 'n plain ink. I had thirty-two days wrestling with the bear so I worked on myself to keep from getting even crazier. I wanted to do something they could never undo. That *nobody* could undo. Now I'd give anything to be rid of the damn things. But at least it showed the others I wasn't no rat.

"Did you ever see four big men hold a girl down on a table while the fifth does the whipping? It was how they done me with a leather belt four feet long. It had a silver buckle I can't forget yet. And how they did drag it out! I could count up to ten between wallops. One hundred licks—I took the most they were allowed to give. And didn't cry Tear One. That showed I wasn't a crybaby.

"Why'd they do it? I flooded the toilet with cotton, that's why. Why'd I do *that?* Search me. I'm always doing things I don't know why. Maybe I just wanted to be a character. You know how you get to be a character? You sit in your room like the living dead, that's how. They take everything away. There's nothing to read—not even a candy wrapper. You can't write letters neither. You get half a cup of dry cereal for breakfeast, two slices of stale bread and a piece of bologna for lunch and half a cup of sloppy stew for supper. That's how you get to be a character.

"I found a friend. A skunkie just like me. A little deaf-and-dumb Spade chick, used to lay there on the floor shagging and counting on her fingers. I stuck around, even when I had a chance to run, on her account. She was my friend. When they put her in some sort of hospital I had no reason for sticking any longer. Next time I came to that bridge I took the trolley. How long *you* been on the run, Red?"

"Things did get a mite hot around home," Dove acknowledged, "so I just tuck with the leavin's."

She misunderstood. "Stealing *is* kicks alright. I like to get in there and do the job myself. There's something about going through an empty joint when it's dark and empty and you can take what you please that's got kicks like crazy. It's so much fun you want to do it all the time. You know what the best kick of all is, Red? It's when you put a gun on grownups and watch them go all to pieces and blubber right before your eyes. That's the *best*. How long you say you been on the run?"

Dove didn't answer but he was on the run all the same. Making good time down Dream Boulevard. She watched him curiously. In sleep his mouth looked as if he'd just been insulted. She couldn't know that he was standing on the courthouse steps in Fitz's split-tail coat, leading the singing—

> *In solemn delight I survey*
> *A corpse when the spirit has fled—*

while a figure with a shaded face, astride a howitzer, kept swaying in solemn delight.

> *To mourn and to suffer is mine—*
> *While bound to this prison I breathe—*

a prison where it cost ten cents to go in and see a corpse from which the spirit had actually fled. Kitty Twist, wearing black elbow gloves, was selling tickets just the other side of the wall. They had grown rich and famous traveling from town to town but she giggled too much and he woke to her giggling. For she had locked him to her in a vise and it was a moment too late to get loose.

"I'm just so *ashamed*," she told him later. "What ever got *into* you to make me *do* such a thing?" In her eyes stood the same glass tears.

"I must of just got carried away," Dove decided.

"Promise you'll never pull a sneaky trick like that on me again?"

"I promise."

"Then I forgive you."

"You're good to me. Real good. Just one thing I don't understand."

"What's that, Red?"

"What's wrestling with the bear?"

"Solitary."

And exhausted by forgiveness and good works, they slept the late light down.

"Let's hear your whistle, Red."

Dove made a kind of feeble piping. Kitty waited.

"That was it," he had to admit.

She put two fingers to her lips and sirened a low-pitched shriek. "When I put on the steam you can hear it two blocks —it means drop everything, it's the nab."

He stood, shifting from one foot to the other in the unlit areaway.

"What's the matter, Red? Afraid?"

"Afraid of steppin' on glass is all."

She triggered a dime-store flashlight—"Follow the spot." Dove followed.

"We're lookin' for Cousin Jim," she explained.

"Got no cousin of that name," he thought he saw a way out of this—"fact is I got no cousin. See you later." She hooked his belt and hauled him along to the rear door of a shop. She knocked so imperiously that his feet tried to turn right around. Her hand around his waist held him still. He hoped she couldn't feel him trembling. She knocked again. But all was locked and barred.

"Make me a step."

He made a stirrup of his hands and raised her until she secured a grip on the open transom; then it was up and over.

She dropped so softly on the other side that, though Dove listened, he did not hear her land. Then the door swung silently, he felt the flash placed in his hand. How had she gotten behind him? "Straight ahead to the register," she took command—"I'm backin' you." And gave him a forward shove that carried him through to the cash drawer of exactly the same model of Ohmer register he had banged for his brother. So he banged this one too and the whole side fell out. He stuck his hand in the side, grabbed a handful of something papery. Under his feet a house cat leaped from sleep. Dove went headlong, shattering the flash and on his knees felt wings brush his hair—the fool cat was halfway up a wall trying to get at something big as an owl. Clutching his bills in a flurry of feathers and fur he saw the thing flutter, wall to wall, for the open door. Its wings got through just above the cat and Dove stumbled crazily after both just as the whistle-shriek rang out.

By the alley entrance light a small figure struggled with one twice its size. "Folks are certainly active tonight," he marveled.

The entrance was his only way out. He walked slowly till he was almost upon the wrestling pair—then jumped for it, felt a big hand reach and miss him and bounded free to the open street.

Over a fence and down the dark, over another and down a wall, big feet going every which way till he fell in a grassy plot.

With no sound but that of one sleepy cricket to heed the pounding of his heart.

"I'm not sure whether you'd call that runnin'," he congratulated himself breathlessly—"but if I'd had a feather in hand I could call it flyin'."

His hand had fastened so hard onto the bills he had to rub his palms to get the circulation going again. Then he stuffed them into the pocket of his jeans. This was no time for counting, what he needed was a railroad track.

If Dove had one sure instinct it was, like the rabbit's, for keeping out of sight till you reach the end of town. He turned

this way and that, till a signal tower's red and green stars led
him at last to a railroad embankment.

"Which way to the S.P., Mister?" he called down to a lantern swinging in the dark.

The light swung up. "You're walkin' the S.P. now," the
lantern assured him—"keep off all trains not in motion."

Dove put his back up against a telephone pole and waggled
his loose tooth a while, but it wouldn't come loose all the
way. And as he waggled it seemed to him the pole he was
braced against was in the middle of the track. A headlight
came bearing down at ninety an hour but no hurry, it had
been coming on for days. He slept on.

The clackety-banging roar of box cars a dozen yards away
woke him at last. Far down the line a little red caboose jog-
gled and swayed like a caboose on a toy railroad.

Dove put his hand on his bankroll to make sure it didn't
jump out, and clambered into a rocking gloom.

"Anybody here?"

No word but a creaking floor.

"Good deal, Linkhorn," he congratulated himself. "Got
yourself a private car and by God you've earned one." He
closed the door and turned on his side. Sometimes crooks
rode these trains.

The day and the night that followed always remained a
hazed kind of memory to Dove. All he recalled clearly was
opening the door the next morning and seeing a veil of mist
so blue it blurred the outlines of house, hill and tree. And as
the morning warmed the whole big blue world began to
smoke faintly.

Louisiana.

In the long afternoon the clouds stacked. And still, over it
all, that pale shifting veil.

A real southland haze in which one sees whatever one
wishes to see. A haze that seeps behind the eyes and makes a
wish-dream of everything.

"I figure I'll learn me to play the gee-tar," he dreamed against the boxcar door, "I'll just go around playin' a gee-tar —that's what brings the purty girls around."

Louisiana.

He saw a taller Dove in shining pants, astride a stallion white as snow, playing a guitar with one hand and holding the stallion back with the other, singing and prancing into New Orleans.

Louisiana.

His fingers wandered over unseen strings

> *Bold brave and undaunted stood*
> *young Brennan on the moor—*

Dove reined in a bit to let the people see him better.

Wishes and hopes in a blue-smoke dream as the big car rolled and his head lolled lightly. Nothing but peace and pretty weather. Dove dreamed that whole blue-smoke day away till the milking-stars came out.

Later, while lying prostrate on the top of the car, and the train was taking water in the wilderness, he thought himself unseen while flashlights and lanterns inspected couplings and wheels. But just as the train pulled out, someone called up laughingly, "Keep stretched or get down inside, son."

So he stayed prostrate smack into a roaring blackness with a tunnel-roof scraping his back. Coal fumes piled down on him. He got his bandanna over his mouth and nose and hooked one arm under the wooden spine. All that kept him from fainting was the hope that no tunnel can last forever.

This one nearly did. When air hit him again his senses were reeling. He spat coal dust half across that fool state.

Dove had a railroad bull to thank for his life, and other bulls less to thank for. They wouldn't come into the cars by day, when they were crowded, but hurried discreetly past as if the cars were empty. But at night they'd get four or five 'boes off by themselves and really go to work on them.

One noon an armed nab stuck his nose in a box car door—
"Come on out of there one by one!"

Nobody moved. Each knew that the first to go out would
get bloodied, while those who followed might get by un-
scratched.

"I said 'Come out' by God!"

Nobody moved.

"By God you don't come out, we come in."

Their silence dared him.

"You know," he turned with feigned boredom to someone
behind him, "I'm so tired of kickin' asses I just think I'll start
crushing skulls."

The second he said that somebody leaped to be the first—
the deputies mobbed him while the others scattered free.
Three bulls with gun butts to one unarmed stray was the
common yardstick of the railroad bull's courage. No man
with the nerve to go after another with only a gun against
bare fists could become a railroad bull: you had to have at
least two other guns on your side to measure up to a vocation
wherein ferocity betrayed innate cowardice.

Sometimes the bulls took everyone off a train, marched
them downtown, fingerprinted and photographed the lot,
then released them with the warning, "Now we got a record
on you. If you try riding through here again you go to the
pea-farm." Thus the homeless were blocked out of town
after town, until almost any town you could name had issued
fair warning to anyone what would happen to him if he tried
it again.

Another afternoon Dove jungled up with four others beside a creek. Those who had used this patch of jungle before
had left a sign asking those who came after to leave it as clean
as they'd found it. Moreover, someone had left a pair of almost new shoes for Dove to find. They fitted as though made
for him.

A couple of the boys got a mulligan going. Dove lay naked

in the creek smoking a cigarette and smelling the mulligan. It was his first peaceful moment since leaving Arroyo.

He didn't see the officers until he heard the shots. One put six holes into the mulligan pot—it steamed into the fire while the strays fled. Dove's head peeked out of the water like a sitting duck's. He came out dripping and sheepish.

The game then was to see how fast a bum could get dressed while getting smashed in the head with billys from both sides. He got one for his shirt, two for his pants, and would have gotten by with no more than that if he'd had the sense to run for it. But in the midst of blows he had to sit down and try to pull on his shoes—that got him so many that he ran without them at last.

When he hopped off the yards in Algiers across the river from New Orleans his head was still aching.

He got the topmost layer of blood and soot off his face at somebody's pump. Offering a nickel to the tolltaker at the ferry, the man jerked his thumb in a come-ahead-son gesture —"The lady paid for you."

Dove saw a middle-aged woman who had walked onto the ferry ahead of him. He walked up beside her, nickel still in hand.

"I'll pay my own way, thank you kindly all the same m'am," he told her, and dropped the nickel in her palm. She turned beet-red but Dove felt better.

When the boat pulled into the pier and a deckhand hurled a coil of rope to fasten the boat to the dock, Dove rushed up and helped him tie it. But all he got for his trouble was an irritated, "I'll handle this, son."

That was how Dove came at last to the town that always seems to be rocking. Rocked by its rivers, then by its trains, between boat bell and train bell go its see-saw hours.

The town of the poor-boy sandwich and chicory coffee, where garlic hangs on strings and truckers sleep in their

trucks. Where mailmen wore pith helmets and the people
burned red candles all night in long old-fashioned lamps.

The town where the Negro women sang,

> *Daddy I don't want your money*
> *I just want your stingaree*

And piano-men at beat-out pianos grieved—

> *Early in the morning before day*
> *That's when my blues come fallin' down*

On the Desire Street dock Dove turned into the first place
he saw where beggars and bummies can lie down to rest.

"Look like you been a-fightin' a circle-saw, son," the desk-
clerk told him.

"No. Just sortin' wild cats."

"I'll give you a nice quiet room then, where you can rest
up undisturbed. I came to town barefoot myself, so green
you could scrape it off me with a cob."

"I'm a quarter light of proper change, mister," Dove observed without touching his change, "I think you've made a
small errow."

The clerk came up with the palmed quarter. "You'll be
wearing shoes sooner than I did," he laughed. "Up the steps
and first room to your right." Between the first room to the
right and the tenth there was no difference. All were equally
keyless.

The ceiling was chicken wire. By the smell the chickens
were still somewhere near. But the bed was exactly what an
exhausted bum needed.

Dove slept through the dusty evening into the feverish
night. And all night heard the river boats call and call.

Once he heard a woman, sounding like she was standing
alone on a corner, telling the world all about it—

Didn't have nobody to teach me right from wrong
Tol' me 'Girl, you're good for nothin'—
Now my Mama's gone.

Under wire on either side other dime-a-nighties slept out their ten-cent dreams. Till the hundred harps of morning struck on strings of silvered light.

And down the long unshaded street a vendor of colored ices beat a rainbow of tin bells. A bell for every flavor as he tinkle-tinkled past. Every flavor made of water sold to tunes made out of tin.

Come bummies, come beggars, two pennies per tune.

With occasional glances at the metal net to see no one was peeking, Dove was bringing each bill before his eyes, memorizing its denomination and adding that to the one before. Stretching each carefully in the hope that two might be sticking together.

When he reached forty, one loose single still lay on the bed. So he began all over with the one loose child. And was only satisfied that he was the owner of forty-one dollars when he had counted back once again.

A Linkhorn was rich at last.

Old-time sterno drinkers and bindlestiff nomads made the flophouse forenoon murky with their hard-time breath. But he was a Linkhorn in a cubicle all his own. He owned neither shirt nor shoes—but joy to a world full of shirts and shoes. One loose tooth was a small penalty enough to wake up being Dove Linkhorn.

Too bad, of course, about that little fool gal who hadn't been smart enough to keep from getting herself pinched. Kids like that shouldn't try crime till they knew what they were doing. "I hope this proves a lesson to that child to go straight before it's too late," he hoped. "She weren't cut out for the life like us crim'nals with a more natural bent."

A little handkerchief, torn nearly in two and gray now

with soot, dropped out of his pocket onto the floor. When he brushed off the soot he saw it was black and had once had lace on it. He felt a certain stiffness in its folds. And felt a shadowy apprehension that he might never hurt anyone except those who were dearest.

That he would know an abundance of pangs, some swift, some slow, some merely passing, and one that would never let him go.

"Hopes I didn't hurt you bad, Señora," he explained. "Just when I was gettin' ready to help you up to say I didn't mean what I done, that fool engineer blew his whistle and I had to hasten on."

Yet the light lay pasted like a second-hand shroud against a guilt-stained wall: she had held a handkerchief out to him and he'd wiped his mouth with the back of his hand instead.

"I'll get somebody to handwrite a letter," he promised himself, "to tell I'm sorry now for what I done."

Down the long unshaded street a rainbow of tin bells pinked out two pennies worth of applause and moved off to some far wider street. Morning seemed done.

A looming fear followed down the darkened stair. The bannister had been greased with another's guilt, step by slow step down an echoing well. Where regrets of strangers burdened all the air.

Out on the open street he felt like a parolee released on some promise he could never keep.

Dove left all guilty loomers behind for a while in the wide wonder of Canal and the hurly-burly holler-and-bounce of its sun-bound whisper and roar. Theatre marquees, mounted policemen, a red motorcycle with a blue side-car and a popcorn machine popping right out on the street. A woman's perfume turned him clean about—O, look at her legs moving under her dress! Here comes another! He found his way into an awning's shade and leaned there against a barber's pole until his senses steadied.

"Why do I act so derned *suspicious?*" he complained to himself—a man with forty dollars don't have to take a back seat to no man. Why, a man who owned that much was already on his way to being a captain.

A banana or a cotton captain, a peanut or a popcorn captain, a coffee or a whiskey or a corn-likker captain—though of course nobody got to be a captain of anything just like that. First you had to help those already captains to haul their coffee and pop their corn, drive their black locomotives or steer their big white boats. Not even a captain could do everything himself. "I could be a tooth dentist," he thought. "A doctor is good too, account he can cut 'n slash 'n have license to do it."

You began at the foot of the ladder and when somebody tried pushing past you he got your big foot in his face—he'd have to get a pair of waterproof boots right soon. Though there wasn't, of course, much danger of anyone being foolhardy enough to try wise stuff on a Linkhorn—

"I count purty fair too," he considered a bookkeeping or banking career "though I *do* have that one little *dee*fect, that I never got beyond B." Nevertheless, he took measure of his varied powers, "I *do* have a very strong mind. I reckon a man with a mind as strong as mine could in time prize up creation and put a small chunk under it."

In the window the barber was signaling something with a bottle of hair tonic in his hand. Dove grinned to see if the man wanted to make friends. When the man made for the door with a shears in his hand Dove judged not and shambled back to Canal.

He bought two colored ices, an orange one and a green, from a vendor wearing sunglasses, and slipped him a Mexican nickel. Sure enough, he got an American penny in change. "Good deal, Linkhorn," he congratulated himself, "when it comes to figuring I'm already well past B. Got to git me a change purse for these smaller operations."

He followed a St. Charles Street trolley up to Lee Circle. There, one hand stained green and the other orange, he crowded an elderly fellow with a bandaged foot off a bench to make room for his own big feet. The old man went off stabbing the pavement with his cane.

"Crip got all fired up about somethin'," Dove sensed, "Now I wonder who *that* captain might be," and squinted up in perplexity at a heroic sculpture. "Must be somebody from the Rebel War," he finally decided.

A bald-headed man in a soiled suit and a Hoover collar came up to Dove's bench with a sheepish air. "I'm not a beggar," he explained, "actually, I'm in the diplomatic service. They're holding a post for me in Washington and when I get there I'll sleep in the best hotels, of course. Tonight, however, it will be necessary for me to sleep out again unless someone like you should loan me fifteen cents."

He offered Dove his calling card, stained yellow at the edges. Dove pretended to read it and became so impressed that he owed the man a nickel, "Since it's for the country," he explained.

The St. Charles Street trolley swung about the circle. "Have to ride that sometime," he promised himself.

An Anglo girl in a white sailor tam and an over-the-shoulder bag sauntered into the shadow cast by Lee's boot and paused to smile directly at Dove. He glanced back over his shoulder but saw nobody waiting for her there. She popped her gun smack at him—"Well?"

Dove rose, bowed from the waist hand over heart, thus sweeping his straw skimmer almost to the earth.

"Howdy, m'am."

The girl left without looking back.

No matter. When he got that good old gee-tar and picked himself out a couple good old tunes he'd have his pick of the merry lot.

And coasted, easily and unseeing, past broken men and

breaking ones; wingies, dingies, zanies and lop-sided kukes;
cokies and queers and threadbare whores. Ulcerous panhan-
dlers lame and cancerous, tubercular pencil peddlers, staggering lushes. Old sick cats from everywhere yowling as they
went.

All was right with the world.

Till he caught an unexpected glimpse of himself in a window and saw nothing was right after all. No wonder that
girl had shied off.

Who ever heard of a captain of anything going barefooty?

From the Barracks Street wharf to Bienville, drydock to
drydock, dead ocean liners lay like ruined whales, their great
white hulls turning to rust. The whole town was in drydock.

Over all, in a coffee-hued haze from happier years, one
still smelled the big brown smell of coffee. The warehouse
walls, like the hulls, were stained with it. The planks of the
wharves were embedded with it. Below the planks ancestral
sacks were rotting in the lap and wash.

The whole town was in drydock, the whole country in
hock, but the pit of the depression, a secretary of labor announced, was past at last. The President's stand on wages
had averted an even worse slump, the secretary added, "Business is starting back."

"Nobody goes hungry" said Little Round Hoover, wiping
chicken gravy off his little round chin. A man with the right
stuff in him didn't need government help to find work. That
would make him lazy. He might even get sick. Self-reliance
for the penniless and government help to the rich, the Old
Guard was in again. Hoover patted the chicken inside his
own pot. "*I* got it made," said Little Round Hoover.

And in all those miles of wharves and docks the one boat
still shipping water was a freighter under an Argentine flag
and the proud Spanish title of *Shichi-Fukujin*.

In his dizziest daydream Dove had never dared to dream

up anything this big. All he could do was gape as the shallows slapped, a little man looking up at a little man looking down.

The one looking down waved to him to come up. As soon as he got on deck Dove saw his help was needed here. For one thing, the sailors were too small to steer anything this big. With eyes too little to tell the difference between a lighthouse and a dock till they'd be right on top of it and then it would be too late.

His friend who had done the waving began talking something neither English nor Spanish and pointing at the smoke stack with a paint brush. Dove had never seen a brush that big nor a stack that high. But if needed he could make that old chimbley look like new.

He reached for the brush but the little man held it back, pointing now to a dock window at dock level:

"Boss man."

"Wait for me," Dove warned the crew. He hurried down the gangplank, into the warehouse and up a spiral stair. Through an open door he saw a framed photograph of an ocean liner that took up half a wall. Below it a drydock foreman sat wishing he were rich.

"Papers"—the man held out his paper-taking hand without looking up.

"Aint the newsboy," Dove explained.

The man glanced up, then wished he hadn't. Before him stood something in a pith helmet off a Walgreen counter, share-croppers' jeans, sunglasses, a dollar watch with a tick like grandfather's clock, and butter-colored shoes.

"You the bull-goose here?" Dove asked, "I'm lookin' for boat-work."

"There's ship captains lookin' for that, son," the foreman told him.

"Didn't reckon on bein' no captain right off," Dove offered to compromise, "I'd be mightily satisfied just to swab the deck—or if by chance,"—he added cunningly—"you hap-

pened to have a chimbley needs a fresh coat of paint I'd admire to try my hand."

"You have to have your able-bodied seaman's papers."

"More able-bodied than most," Dove persisted. "Whatever
you'd pay me I'd be mighty grateful and praise you most
highly for. I'm a very light eater, I might add."

"Son you aren't implying you'd *scab*, would you?"

"Mister, I'll cook, I'll cuss, I'll mend yer socks, I'll stoke yer
en-gines 'r catch you a damn whale bare-hand. 'N if you
want me to scab somethin' I'll scab 'er fore to aft. For I want
to learn the sailing trade 'n I'm strong enough for four."

"You *do* know that there is a seafaring man's union?" He
gave Dove the benefit of a serious doubt.

"Mister, I'm a Christian boy and don't truckle to Yankee
notions. Put my name in your ship's dinner-pot and you're
my captain, I'm your hand. Just tell me ever-what you want
done and I'll 'tend it, for I'm bedcord strong. If I don't turn
you out what in your eyes makes a fair day's work you can
put me off at the first port of call. Aint that fair enough?"

"Mighty fair, son. If more boys were willing to work for
nothing there'd be just that many more millionaires."

"It's how I figure it too, mister. You got to work for nothing or you'll never get rich, that only stands to reason."

"You know," the foreman put a brotherly hand on Dove's
shoulder—"I liked your face the moment you came in here.
Would you take off your glasses so I can see more of it?"

Dove snapped off the sunglasses and snapped to attention.

"I liked the way you entered, too," he assured Dove, "without bothering to knock."

"I judged you had time and to spare."

"And the intelligent way you stated your case."

"I reckon I measure up," Dove admitted modestly.

"You measure up to something," the foreman thought,
"but I'm not sure to just what."

What the foreman was actually measuring was the stack

through the window that went sixty feet up from dock level; and the shaky union scale that rose every foot after twenty-five. An eight-hour day at two-seventy per hour for ten days, the foreman made a mental estimate of what he could claim on the books.

"I'll pay you a buck-fifty an hour to paint that stack, Son."

Dove came scurrying back up the gangplank like the flightless Kiwi, a bird not built to fly. He heard the foreman holler from window to deck, "Put this man in the chair, boys!" By the time he reached the deck the scrapers, brushes, paint and thinner were ready. Dove jumped right into the bosun's chair and shouted, "Haul steady, maties!" Then glanced down and found himself nearly twenty feet off the deck.

"Okay, boys!" he called down cheerfully, "I'll start here 'n work up!" But the chain kept going higher.

Who would ever have thought such a fine breeze would be stirring here while other fellows had to sweat out the heat below? He was about to take a second look but the chair began to swing like a cradle and he changed his mind.

Up and up. Above him leaned the rust-flaked stack, below the river tilted oddly. The hands of his watch seemed strangely bent, but seemed to say 10:55. Good—in five minutes he'd have his tools together so he could begin right on the hour. A full day's pay for a full day's work, that was the way to rise in the world.

"Beginnin', maties!" he called over the side, "Beginnin'!" That should show them he was no coward.

Something tugged at the chair and he understood the foreman had had a change of mind—he could come down any time now. Dove whipped the rope fast around the stack, and knotted it with the last of his strength. By God, the man had sent him up, he wasn't going to get him down without a day's pay in hand.

Once fastened, the chair steadied and so did Dove. Not enough to stand upright, but enough to get the lid off the paint can. Just as he got it off, the wind tilted the chair and the tinned oil spilled. He dabbed it off his jeans. "Lucky it didn't get my shoes," he took the happier view.

No use taking a chance on ruining his shoes altogether with a wind that tricky sneaking around. He clamped the lid back on and glanced at his watch: 11:04. By God, just because a man couldn't read didn't mean he couldn't count. That was a dime he'd made already today or he'd know the reason why.

That was when he looked right over the edge and down and saw the little circle of grinning faces looking up. He closed his eyes to keep from heaving. That would never do the first day on the job.

When his stomach had steadied he remembered something and found, in the bottom of a Bull Durham sack, just what he was looking for: a palm-full of light green potoguaya and a couple of brown papers. "Wasn't told nothin' about not smokin' on the job," he argued sensibly. And at the first drag felt the chair rise an inch.

"Let her rise," he thought, "the higher we go the higher the pay."

Scraper, thinner, bucket and brush lay at his feet forgotten; as he had apparently been forgotten by those below. When he looked at his watch again it was almost two. My, how time did fly.

"Lunch!" he shouted over the side, "bring her up!"

But saw no one climbing the rigging one-handed, tray in the other, to ask whether he took sugar and cream in his coffee.

"Bunch of hogs are at chow," he thought sullenly, "stuffin' theirselves like a set of sows. Struck me right off as a sorry lookin' crew."

All through the treetop afternoon Dove dozed, and every time he woke, woke hungrier.

"Chow!" he tried for his dinner one more time. But all he got was a wave from a deck-hand far below.

"I know your play," he finally informed the foreman aloud, "you're tryin' to starve me down. But you wont do it till I got a full day comin', friend." And went right back on the nod.

It was almost five when he wakened again, feeling a chill breeze pass. He unlooped the draw-rope. "Good thing I didn't have lunch," Dove thought going down, and hopped out onto the deck, pale and swaying. Two of the crew had to hold him up and every man but the foreman looked pleased with his work.

"Not a damn dime, boy!" the foreman let him know right off. "Mention money and I'll heave you right over the side!"

Dove got his landlegs under him.

"Mister, I went up in your fool chair like you asked me. We made a bargain."

"Now you listen here to me, son. I'm Chief-by-Jesus foreman of this everlastingly damned dry dock, I'll have you under-goddamn-stand that. I'm not to be dic-hellfire-tated to by you or anyone. Is that the Christian-Killing-Moses clear or not? I can make it mother-murdering clearer if you want."

"A *bargain*, mister."

"Talk sense, boy."

"I'm a-talkin' sense, mister, 'n you leave mothers out of this. I were aloft six hour, not chargin' you for overtime because I realize I didn't do too well my first day. But I *tried* six dollar worth."

The foreman took Dove by the arm, led him to one side and whispered, "Take this and get off my God-by-Jesus deck." Dove looked down. It was a two dollar bill.

"I got six comin', mister."

"As high as I go." He had changed it for a fiver.

"I'll settle." Dove took it. The foreman went wearily to the rail, looking downriver and out to sea.

Down on the dock Dove took one last look up. The little man at the rail was grinning down. He waved the big brush at Dove. "Be work on time tomorrow, matey!" he called. Dove waved back. Mighty mannerable fellow.

Yet felt a lingering sadness as he left the big river to know he wasn't going to sea after all.

Later that day he discovered the door of the men's room in the Southern Railway Station barred by a white-haired Negro porter. "Excuse me, pappy," Dove tried to get past.

"Country boy, you got colored blood?" Pappy demanded.

"Naturally it aint white," Dove told him.

"No funny business," the old Negro warned him, "I'm responsible here."

Dove didn't know what was wrong. He just *felt* wrong. And left the REST ROOM FOR COLORED in retreat.

He was bending above the water-fountain when he saw the porter coming at him again. The old man had been searching for someone like this in dreams for years.

"You got colored blood, you caint drink this water."

"Aint everybody got colored blood, mister?" By this time Dove really wanted to know.

"You think you make a fool of me with fool questions," the old man answered, "but all you make a fool of is yourself. Boy, if you white, stay white. If you black, stay black and die. Now get out of my station and out of my sight."

"It purely wonders me," Dove brooded thoughtfully, "Why, a Christian don't scarcely stand a chance for a drink of water in town no more. Looks like my crazy little pappy was right after all."

His throat felt parched and he turned into the first doorway he saw with a Coca Cola sign over it. Coca Cola signs went all around this shady nook with nothing on its shelves but empty cokes. He rapped the counter with a dime.

A little brassiereless beauty, a real fence-corner peach all of nineteen appeared, opened a coke on a nail hooked to the counter, and let her shoulder strap slip to bare her left breast to its tinted nipple. Under the breast was tattooed the single word—*Whiskey*.

"Aint this the By-Goddest weather you ever seen?" Dove asked.

"I've seen By-Godder," the fence-corner peach replied.

"Now I reckon I got a nickel change comin', m'am," Dove reckoned.

"Reckon you awready got your change"—and replaced the strap, looking bored.

"You don't feel maybe you made a slight errow, m'am?"

"*Right* sure."

"How much fer a stror?"

"Help yourself, country boy."

"Now *there's* another funny thing," Dove marveled, taking four straws in an effort to get even, "you're the second person in the past hour noted that. However do folks tell?"

The peach merely looked blank. When the straws would draw no more he bent each carefully and put down another dime.

This time she wiped the bottle with a counter cloth and slipped in a single straw. He took it from her with his eyes glued to that left strap.

It didn't slip an inch.

But she rang up his dime and slammed the register so fast, just as the right strap fell away, that he thought she had punched the machine with the nipple. Now she merely leaned on the machine, resting the breast on the NO SALE sign.

Underneath this one was tattooed—*Beer*. Dove studied the word solemnly. "Do you mind if I spend an opinion, Miss? Somethin' a bit personal?" he asked at last.

"Nothing you could tell me could possibly be personal."

"Why it strikes me you got a mite too much whitenin' on," he told her all the same, "it make you look plumb puny."

The blankness of her regard surpassed itself. She didn't so much as blink. Just tipped the bottle's last drop out, put the bottle away and replaced her strap.

"M'am, I can't help thinking there's something dead up the tree."

She raised one pencilled brow in the mildest of inquiries. "Yes?"

"Last night I bought a sody the other side of the station 'n it were only five cents."

"That's the other side of the station. They got a price war there."

"Hope nobody got kilt," he hoped and put down a third dime.

This time she opened the bottle, wiped it off, inserted the straw, rang up the dime, shut the register and stepped back all in a single motion. Yet the strap failed to fall. Dove drank slower.

Nothing.

"How many sodies you sell in a single day m'am?"

" 'Bout as many as there are crows at a hog-killin'," she made a close guess.

"Why, that's a good few," Dove decided.

"What *did* you come in here for, mister?"

"Got barred from the water-founting."

"I think you're wasting your money."

"After all, it's *my* money."

"And so long as it's money, it's a-plenty," she pointed out— "but when it's all spent it can get right scarce."

"I've heard that some times money don't hardly last till it's gone, that's true. Or so I've been told. You think my forty-dollar might last that long?"

"You spend it all on cokes it wont, if you follow me."

"I don't follow you too near. All I know is this coke tastus right fine."

"It *what?*"

"Tastus right fine. But what if I should put a dollar down here?"

"Try one."

Dove put it down and she had snapped it up before it touched the counter.

"*Now* see if you can follow me."

Somewhere at the bottom of that narrow passage a girl was laughing mirthlessly like a girl laughing at herself, and all its doors were numbered.

No light, no window, no sound. Dove stood lost in a burning blackout till he heard someone hooking a door. Then a little green light came up in a corner and the beer-and-whiskey beauty stood stripped to her slippers in a glow, a girl delicate as a deer.

"Never did see such a purty girl afore even though you are a mite scarce-hipped," he told her. "I'm gittin' a mighty *urr* to lewdle. Would you care to lewdle too?"

Later, with one foot planted on the floor to keep himself from falling off the narrow cot, he grew confidential.

"My stomach is swoll," he told her.

"Next time drink whiskey," she advised him and added, "Country boy, your time is long up." Then hooking his trousers on one green-tinted toenail, derricked and dropped them with dainty disdain across his knees at the same moment that his wallet dropped from the pocket and curiously vanished beneath the sheets.

"M'am," Dove declared, "you *are* the very *darnedest* galperson ever I *have* met up with."

"How's *that?*" she sounded suspicious about something.

"Why, them toenails."

"You've had your money's worth and more," she decided as though suddenly resolved not to be good friends after all. "Get dressed and get out."

"I'm just layin' here gettin' myself up an apology to you, m'am. I'll have it done quite soon."

"Apology for *what?*"

"Why, for callin' you scarce-hipped like I done. There was no call for my takin' an advantage such as that. As a matter of fact, you got what railroading folk call a mighty trim caboose."

"The bathroom's to the right."

"M'am, I'm right sorry, indeed and double-deed I am. But the fact is I'm plumb fatigued and now I got to rest a spell."

She padded around the bed and peered out into the hall. "I'll get a party who'll restore your strength," she promised.

Her back was to him, her hand on the knob and the pocket of her parade pantie bulged with his wallet so plainly he could see the grain of the leather through the sheer of the cloth; but he didn't try to snatch it. Instead he hooked a fingertip in the rubber-band that bound it, stiffened his arm exactly as he had just seen her stiffen her leg, and thus derricked it as neatly and nervelessly as she had derricked his pants.

She sensed a slight movement behind her and whirled toward the bed. There the big boob lay pretending to sleep and anyone could see at a glance he was faking. "Mister, I don't know who you think you're fooling, but it isn't me," she gave him final warning and stepped into the hall—"Knifey! Knifey-Love! A party to meet you!"

Dove sprang out of the cot, into his pants and was out the window shoes in hand.

Two Negro girls directly across the way, watching for men to come out the front—they spent their afternoons keeping count—appeared mildly surprised to see one come out the window instead. How do you count *that?*

Someone, it seemed, was forever thinking up ways of doing things that no one else had thought up before.

There's one advantage women have over men: they can go down to hell and come straight up again. An old song says so and it says just right. Yet it fails to allow for special cases like Dove Linkhorn's.

Dove knew he'd been underground all right. The moment he stepped back onto the Canal Street side of the Southern Railway Station it seemed he had either come up out of somewhere or else the sky had risen an inch.

The city fathers, Do-Right Daddies and all of that, Shriners, Kiwanians, Legionaires, Knights of this and Knights of that, would admit with a laugh that New Orleans was hell. But that hell itself had been built spang in the center of town —this they never could admit. For panders and whores are a plain disgrace, and Do-Right Daddies are family men whose families are part of themselves like their backs.

But not many a daddy (do-right or do-wrong) is satisfied simply to own a back. He has to kick loose of home and fireside now and again. He has to ball with outlaws, play the fool on the door-rock, and have a handsome hustler call him by his first name in the presence of an out-of-town friend. That makes daddy feel like a man again. Three shots of corn likker and the whole stuffed zoo—Moose, Elks, Woodmen, Lions, Thirty-Third Degree Owls and Forty-Fourth Degree Field Mice begin to conspire against the very laws they themselves have written.

It was all right to take a slug of whiskey from your own flask in a taxi, but forbidden on a trolley-car. That didn't help those who rode trolley-cars. You couldn't carry liquor down the street, but if you owned a car you just bypassed that. For every statute they had a little loophole—that by coincidence fitted their own figures as if measured for them. Those who had no hand in writing statutes—panders and madams and such as that—had a harder time squeezing through.

It was an ancestral treachery that all do-righters practice. When opening time was closing time and everyone was there, down where you lay your money down, where it's everything but square, where hungry young hustlers hustle dissatisfied old cats and ancient glass-eyed satyrs make passes at bandrats; where it's leaping on the tables, where it's howling lowdown blues, when it's everything to gain and not a thing to lose—when it's all bought and paid for then there's always one thing sure: it's some do-right Daddy-O running the whole show.

There were stage shows and peep shows, geeks and freaks street. It wasn't panders who owned the shows. There were all down old Perdido Street. But it wasn't geeks who ran that chippified blondes and elderly rounders, bummies and rummies and amateur martyrs. There were creepers and kleptoes and zanies and dipsoes. It was night bright as day, it was day dark as night, but stuffed shirts and do-righties owned those shows.

For a Do-Right Daddy is right fond of money and still he don't hate fun. He charged the girls double for joint-togs and drinks, rent, fines, towel service and such. But before any night's ball was done, he joined in the fun.

Later he had to be purged of guilt so he could sleep with his wife again. That was where the pulpit came in. There had to be something official like that to put the onus on the women. The preachers, reformers, priests and such did this work well. Some girls were just naturally bad, they explained. Others were made bad by bad men. In no case was it ever the fault of anyone who profited by the shows. Daddy, you can go home again.

Pulpit, press, police and politicians pushed the women from crib to crib and street to street—yet never pushed any but diseased ones out of reach. Daddy still wanted some healthy good-looker available for his weekend and there had to be a retriever to fetch her. That was what helped keep pulpits filled, increased newspaper circulation, made the arrest blotters look respectable and gave politicians a record to ride.

When we get more houses than we can live in, more cars

than we can ride in, more food than we can eat ourselves,
the only one way of getting richer is by cutting off those
who don't have enough. If everybody has more than enough,
what good is *my* more-than-enough? What good is a wide
meadow open to everyone? It isn't until others are fenced
out that the open pasture begins to have real value. What
good is being a major if you can't have more than a second
lieutenant? What good is a second lieutenant for that matter?

The girls themselves read of the latest crusade, but their
eyes skimmed idly over the print. When the last sermon was
preached, the last editorial written and the last raid done,
then those who had preached, written and raided would be
coming down to see them for a bit of fun again.

That was the ancestral treachery no one would admit.

Yet over the treachery, under the revelry, there hung, that
airless summer, a feeling that this was all as sad as hi-jinks in
an invaded land. In the ravaged faces of young girls and the
painted faces of boys in secret bars there hung the sense of
impending defeat.

Lonely bones of the old French Graveyard, that had slept
contented decades through, felt it and wakened to work their
dusty way out through brick, through wood, through stone.

Dove Linkhorn, passing a crumbling wall, peered in and
saw how harshly death dealt with old bones.

Old bones that death would not let lie still. Spaniard and
Frenchman, Creole and Kentuckian, bones of sailor and hunter
alike, women of honor and women kept, all bones bleached
the same in the Saturday sun. They too had been to Hell and
come up again.

Dove's own bones felt sore. "Too dern much runnin' 'n
jumpin'," he scolded himself, "nothin' to show for it but a
suit of clothes 'n a pair of shoes 'n a dollar watch. Things
could be worse."

When a girl with eyes that could only have been gotten in

a box of tacks demanded, "Boy, you got a dolla?" Dove
didn't feel it was right to lie to her.

"I got a dolla," he admitted, "but I don't feel like foolin'."

She opened the door. "Come in here. I'll *make* you feel
like foolin'."

Ten minutes later Dove came out hungry enough to eat
snake. There was a poor-boy sign at the end of the block,
but before he could reach it another girl stopped him by
swinging a screen door right in his path. "Boy, you got a
dolla?"

"I got a dolla but I need it for eatin'."

"You can eat here," she promised him. He stepped inside.
It didn't look like a restaurant.

Ten minutes later he came out, leaned a moment against
the crib, then proceeded slowly, head down to get past the
rest of the doors till he came to the sign with the poor-boy
painted on it. But when he looked inside all he saw was one
more brassiereless girl opening a coke.

He shuffled on and on, block after block, finding his way
toward food more by scent than by sight.

And so at last entered a certain sea-cave acrawl with the
living smells of lobster and shrimp, steaming with simmering
oyster stew and awash with gumbo in which little snails paddled about. He sat at a table as scarred and aged as the Old
French Market itself.

When his eyes had got used to the deep-sea light he dis-
cerned a Negro the size of Carnera, naked to the waist and
shining with iron-colored sweat, decapitating snapping turtles
with silvered precision.

Now the trouble with turtles is that they believe all things
come to him who will but struggle. There's always room at
the top for one more, they think. And in this strange faith
the snapping kind is of all the most devout. For it's precisely
that that makes them the snapping kind. Though the way be

steep and bloody, that doesn't matter so long as you reach
the top of the bleeding heap.

The dark butcher looked to Dove like Doctor Death in
person.

Doctor Death whose patients come one by one along an
ever-narrowing plank, each confident of ultimate mercy: a
last-minute reprieve, with full civilian rights restored—the
knife would snap in mid-air, a modern miracle. Death was all
right for certain classes, sand turtles and such, but didn't suit
noble old sea-going families of true terrapin lineage.

Losing his head didn't lose one his footing. His legs kept
seeking yet bloodier heights. Say Not The Struggle Naught
Availeth, Onward and Upward was the cry.

Indeed, once the knife had done him in, to raise oneself
in the world became more urgent than ever. Sensing that time
was against him, he worked all the harder to succeed. Till the
floor about the pyramid streamed black with blood, with
some on their backs and some on their bellies.

Dove felt another's eyes watching the growing pile: down
on the floor beside him a severed terrapin's head, big as his
own hand, stared cataleptically at its own body slipping and
flipping up the distant heap. It could be no other's body, for
it alone matched the king-sized head that stared with faith
unshakable.

Stepping on the stumps of a hundred bleeding necks, hauling itself over other backs, giving one a kick there and one
a shove there, the body sent a dozen rival climbers sprawling
over the cliff to failure. Dove and the Head watched together
to see if the Body would make it.

Driven by some strength greater than that of others, wading contentedly over mothers and orphans, it got its blind
flippers at last onto the tail of a red snapper, hauled itself
onto the snapper's back, pushed Red out from under and
landed smack in the middle of the heap.

He was the King of the Turtles.

The king waved his arrogant flippers triumphantly—"Always room for one more at the top"—just as something bumped him hard from behind and his short day was done. Sliding, sprawling, skidding, he slipped off the heap in a bloody skein and landed flat on his back below the table wigwagging frantically.

"Dear friends and gentle hearts," he wigwagged, feeling the final cold creep up—"Will you stand by to leave your old friend die? I wanted nothing for myself—money, comfort, power, security—I worked for these only because those dear to me wanted them. (Of course, as long as they were handy I shared them from time to time.) Would you really leave me here to die?

"True, I ate well. But that was only to keep up my strength for the sacrificial ordeal of my days. For I never knowingly harmed a fellow creature unless he got in my way. I never took unfair advantage unless it profited me. Can you really leave so lovely a turtle to die?

"A devoted father, a loyal citizen, a faithful employee, a kind employer, a considerate neighbor, a regular church-goer. Out of purity of heart I respected the laws of God and man. Purity, and fear of jail. Could you really stand by and watch so saintly a turtle die?

"I seemed a bit intent a moment ago, you say, on grinding my brothers' necks to gristle? I confess—but that was a moment ago, and now I've changed my ways. Could you bear to see such an open-minded turtle die?

"Life me up, lift me up, gentle hearts—lift me up to let me look one last time at the top of the heap where once I ruled so."

And with that most slowly drew in his dark tail. His flippers grew rigid. His struggles forever ceased.

The wisest of turtles was dead.

Just as Bing Crosby came onto the juke singing *I Aint Got Nobody*.

"What'll it be, boy?" the waiter asked.

Dove didn't hesitate. "I'll take the tarpon soup."

He didn't yet know that there was also room for one more at the bottom.

TWO

IN THE cheery old summer of '31 New Orleans offered almost unlimited opportunities to ambitious young men of neat appearance willing to begin at the bottom and work their way up the Ladder of Success rung by rung. Those with better sense began at the top and worked their way down, that route being faster.

In the cheery old summer of '31 some states were dry and some states were wet. Russ Columbo was singing *Please*. Al Capone was quoting Mark Twain and someone held women to be equal in aviation to men. A woman refused to answer the questions of a Senate committee and the American Legion claimed that state legislatures were handicapping sales of products turned out by the American working man.

A New York minister discovered that Jerusalem had had a worse administration than Jimmy Walker's and said he'd rather live under Hoover any day than Hezekiah.

The excesses of that year were due to a backward swing of the moral pendulum, Harry Emerson Fosdick proclaimed, adding that if the saloon were still around it would be even worse. The President pressed a button in Washington that lit a fifty-two million dollar building, highest yet raised by the hand of man, at Thirty-Fourth Street and Fifth Avenue in New York. Wallace Beery was saying What I Like About a Mama is Plenty of Mama and cotton prices dropped to a new low.

The Ladder of Success had been inverted, the top was the bottom, and the bottom was the top. Leaders of men still sporting gold watches were lugging baby photographs door to door with their soles flapping. Physicians were out selling skin lighteners and ship captains queued in hope of a cabin boy's mop and pail.

Offices of great fire insurance companies went up in smoke, which seemed no more than just. When the fire department—long unpaid—cleared off, little remained but scorched files, swivel-chairs on which no one would ever swivel again, lovely heaps of frosted glass, and all that mahogany.

All that mahogany that hadn't helped anybody but brokers after all. Then the brokers began jumping off rooftops with no greater consideration for those passing below than they'd had when their luck was running. Emperors of industry snatched all the loose cash on which they could lay hand and made one fast last run. Lawyers sued one another just to keep in practice.

And every bughouse had one little usurer hidden away in a cell all his own where he did nothing but figure percent with his fingernail on the wall, day after day after day.

In less time than it takes to say God with your mouth open, the go-getting door-to-door canvasser became the backbone of the American economy. He went to work for Realsilk Hose or Hoover Vacuum long enough to go-get himself a dozen pair of Realsilk hose or a second-hand sweeper by stealing it part by part. There was also small change, milk money and such, left lying about on shelves and sills while housewives studied one proposition or another. Change-snatching too came under the head of go-getting, for hundreds subsisted upon it week in and week out.

However, the secretary of the Federation of Labor pointed out, Business was resisting further decline.

Self-reliance for the penniless and government aid to those who already had more than they could use was the plan.

But park benches were wet of a morning whether it rained or no; and it was possible to tire even of bananas.

Still and all times weren't as hard as some people grew fond of pretending. All that had happened really was a withdrawal from abnormal prosperity with business progressing on a downward grade toward new planes of normality and increasing equalization of opportunity. In short, we were going full steam ahead. Only this time one exciting opportunity was precisely as good as the next exciting opportunity. Which was to say, simply, that nobody got paid any more.

The pimps alone didn't seem to catch on that the country was progressing downward to new rates of normality. They had been progressing downward for some time without even knowing that they were in style. Now of a sudden they discovered themselves with more girls than beds to put them on. Scarcely-twenties looking for a daddy, any old daddy who'd tell them where to lie down. Landlords and landladies passed them on to the cabbies and the cabbies passed them on to the pimps. It was then, between prostitution and Prohibition, that the ancient color line was finally breached.

Negro bellboys had gained a virtual monopoly on the delivery of illicit alcohol and had found that white male guests either wanted a woman with the bottle or a bottle with the woman. This errand boys' work evolved into soliciting. Immediately, he looked with scorn upon his own women. Like the Negro policeman, the Negro ponce was harder on his own people than was the white pander.

He saw now at first hand, that what his Mama had told him wasn't true after all: that "good" white folks never acted like bad black ones. For he saw men and women with the best names in town, the do-right names, howling like wolves in the Saturday stews, panties on the bedpost and pants on the floor, yet knew Do-Right Daddy would be back with his family, come Sunday morning, in the pew with the best name in town.

The Negro began losing his awe of the white women there and then. He gave her the choice of moving over or being turned in to the law. The errand boy became an informer as well as solicitor. Times weren't as bad, he felt, as the papers made out.

Everyone was out soliciting in one commodity or another. Everyone was pecking somebody else's door. The whole town was out pecking, nobody stayed home to buy. Either you rapped doors on commission or you organized a chance of fools even sillier than yourself into crews and took your commission out of theirs. And since theirs was purely theoretical, it followed yours must be theoretical too.

If, for example, you swindled a housewife into signing for delivery of two pounds of coffee twice a week for twelve weeks, you received two theoretical dollars for perpetrating the swindle. Actually, however, you had swindled her for nothing, because the driver accredited himself with the order —"that party changed her mind. You know how women are," he advised the door-to-door man.

The driver in turn was victimized by the device of deducting two dollars from his regular salary in lieu of that same housewife's deuce. By the time that the deuce had found its way from wife to owner's pocket, there wasn't a man on the street crew who had been on it the week before.

Dove Linkhorn, now in a seersucker suit and sea-green tie, stood on the corner of Calhoun and Magnolia. That here stood a man far above the blue jean and Bull Durham class was plain to be seen, for he was smoking a *Picayune.* Indeed, he lacked only something to sell to start making his own way down the Ladder of Success as fast as the next ambitious boy. So when he saw men encircling someone or something down the street he hurried there as fast as his butter-colored shoes could make steps, in hope that someone was throwing a fit.

But all it was was a little round man with something glisten-

ing in his hand. Dove elbowed in to see what glistened so
nicely.

Cawfee pot.

Hello, pot.

Shor a purty old pot.

"Wreneger's the name," the little round man was telling
his crew, "but you boys call me plain old 'Smiley' because
that's what *all* my goodbuddies call me. And you know what
I tell my goodbuddies? I tell them, 'Goodbuddies, if you aint
sellin' you just aint tryin',' *that's* what I tell my goodbuddies.
And that's what I'm tellin' every one of you, 'cause you all
my goodbuddies too."

Little old red 'n green cawfee pot. Well I be dawg. Bet
you make right good cawfee.

"The idea aint to see how many doors you can rap of a
morning—*that* aint sellin'. That aint even tryin'. If you only
rap two doors a whole morning and sell both, *then* you're
tryin'."

I had me a cawfee pot like you, cawfee pot, I'd know
where to get the chicory for you.

"Heed the housewife's woes, boys. Give ear to her trials
and little cares. Make her joys your joys, her tears your tears.
If you listen long enough sooner or later she's going to ask,
'Young man, whatever is that contraption in your hand?' "

"Look like a cawfee pot to me," Dove helped the man out.

"Thank you, Red. You work with me. The rest of you
men split up two to a block, one down one side and one down
the other and meet me back here at noon. If you aint sellin'
you just aint tryin', all you good old goodbuddy buddies."

"Dirt-eatin' buggers, every one," Smiley assured Dove the
moment they'd scattered. "Don't you think *I* know what
they're up to? Got a pencil and a receipt book so they're
going to make out five or six phony orders with addresses
of empty lots 'n then go drink derail in Lafayette Square
thinkin' Old Dominion pays off on *their* lousy word." He

banged Dove's big back good-naturedly—"They'll find out better soon enough, won't they goodbuddy?"

"They sure will, mister," Dove agreed gleefully.

"That's why I was so careful about choosing you," Smiley grew serious. "I told myself, 'There now is one face I can truly trust.'"

"I truly trustes you too, Mister," Dove replied, feeling happier by the minute.

"I want you right beside me while I pitch, Red. Because when you pitch for Old Dominion you're pitchin' for the red, white and blue!"

"Mister," Dove stopped short to offer Smiley his hand, "you're talkin' about *my* team now!"

Smiley shook perfunctorily. He wasn't used to being taken literally, it made him unsure of himself. "The first thing to remember, son, is our own Confederate dead. When the housewife asks you how much coffee does she have to buy before the pot is legally redeemed—some are sharper than you might expect—tell her you're J. E. B. Stuart's grandson and your daddy is dying in Memphis. Tell her anything *except* that she has to take fifty pounds before she owns the pot. If she wants to know what percent of chicory we use say something about Chancellorsville."

"I'LL SAY I WORK FOR OLD DOMINION!" Dove cried with so genuine a pride that Wreneger, one of those men who like to say 'It can't get hot enough for me,' felt curiously wilted.

"Stand to one side, son, I'll show you how it's done," he invited Dove into the shade of a small unpainted porch, allowing him to guard one of the pots.

"We aint buying no coffee pot, mister," the housewife assured Smiley the moment she saw the hardware in his hand.

Smiley fixed his face as if to eat mush out of a churn. "It's not a pot, Madam. And it's strictly not for sale. It's a French Dripolator and it's a goodwill gift, no strings attached, from Old Dominion to you. Take it. It belongs to you."

"I'm greatly obliged, but we already got a pot." The woman's eyes shifted to the lopsided figure in the yellow-knob shoes.

"Jeb Stuart's grandson!" Dove came to attention.

"At ease," Smiley ordered below his breath and hurried into his pitch. "Madam, this here genuine French Dripolator is shortly goin' on the market nationally for three-dolla-eighty-five cents with a national campaign behind it. What we need now is kindly folks who won't be selfish about it when they find they got the best cup of coffee in town. The kind who'll want to share with their neighbors and spread the word about our offer. That's the friendly sort of thing is going to give our national campaign a headstart—I said *at ease*—of course if you don't care to cooperate I'm sure the lady next door will be interested."

She'd sooner risk the black death than have her next-door neighbor own something she didn't. Dove watched her sign for receipt of the pot wistfully.

"Just a mere formality," Smiley explained the need of her signature to the woman, "so's the company won't think I sold it to my wife." Even to Dove the laugh that followed sounded hollow.

The fraud consummated, Smiley handed Dove a pencil, receipt book and pot. "But don't let go of that thing till you got that signature," was his parting warning. And off he went to lie in the shade and dream up new ways to beat Old Dominion.

Dove was relieved that his goodbuddy hadn't asked him if he knew how to use the pencil. It was real nice to have it to carry behind his ear all the same.

He came to an intersection where one road led to town and the other away. The town road was festooned, street lamp to street lamp, with welcoming pennants; it was wide and newly paved. The other was lampless and pennantless and plainly led nowhere at all. Without hesitation Dove chose the nowhere road. For that was the only place, in his heart of hearts, that he really wanted to go.

Shuffling loosely along in his proud bright shoes, occasionally tucking in his sea-colored tie, he came to an iron-wrought fence where a Negro woman was shearing a bush; and waited in hope she would look up and ask, "How do I get a pot like that?"

But all she did was study him, shears in hand, as if Old Dominion might have sent him out to rape and rob her and she was nicely put together at that. He shifted the pot to his other hand. It was hanging so heavy he scolded it, "Pot, you give me the wearies." And his shoes gave him such a punishing pinch, as though they were on the side of the pot.

He came to a four-story tenement built flush to the broken walk to get the last inch of space, where another Negro girl, her face still full of an easy sleep, leaned an arm against a patched and rusted screen.

Dove held up the pot to catch the sun.

"Little ol' cawfee pot. Git it fer free."

She opened the door and grasped the pot's handle, taking his word as fast as that. But Dove was a little too smart for her. He kept hold of the spout.

"Got to sign your name for you gits it."

"Signs you anythin', cawfee pot man." She plucked the pencil off his ear and scribbled a name on a receipt blank. Old Dominion was going to like his work, Dove knew.

"Awntie and Mothaw might like pots too," the girl told Dove, and hollered up the stair.

Two older women, as if waiting for just such a call, came clumping so eagerly down the steps that they wedged in the narrow way—for a moment neither could gain an inch. Then worked themselves free and the winner came up breathlessly.

"Whut you got *now*, lucky girl?"

"Got me a goddamn pot."

"You write for us, Minnie-Mae, then we gits too."

"My own handwrite is so poorly, Miss," Dove confessed, "I'd be most obliged if you'd do just that."

Minnie-Mae snatched his receipt book, tore out two order blanks, scribbled on both and handed them back.

"Old Dominion thanks you, Miss," Dove assured her, "I'll deliver both pots tomorrow."

"My girl-friend might like one too," Minnie-Mae invited Dove to step one landing up.

"You oblige me again," Dove assured her as she urged him ahead, with Awntie and Mothaw following heavily. It was just one of those days when everyone is on your side.

For from window to window, lightless passage to lightless hall, the wakening whisper went—"Come git you a cawfee pot." Doorway to door, to friend to foe, Awntie and Mothaw went spreading the word. Whether it was Huey Long or Old Dominion giving things away again, nobody cared a doodle in a wood. Negroes dark or Negroes light, high-yellow, blue-black, gold-toothed or toothless, everyone liked coffee. Minnie-Mae was ripping receipts and handing them for upreaching hands to sign and return as fast as she could reach and tear.

"Come git yo' goddamn pot!"

Dove couldn't make out a word of the lingo ringing about —it was that Negro-to-Negro jargon that accents English like French and French like English then slurs the rest when white ears of any nation listen.

Dove didn't care—he was getting rich. When Minnie-Mae ran out of blanks he raced down to the street for more. Business was progressing on a downward grade to new rates of normality, opportunity was being equalized, time was money.

Wreneger, with two of the crew, were waiting for him at the corner.

"Where you been, son?" Without a word Dove handed him fifty orders, signed and sealed. Smiley's aides, one a towering Florida cracker and the other a pint-sized Georgian, crowded in to see how Texas did it.

Smiley thumbed through the packet swiftly, thumbed part way back as though to make certain of something scarcely credible, then ripped it straight down the middle and fifty French Dripolators went blowing like confetti down Elysian Fields Avenue.

Dove ran one down before he understood—then let it blow after the others like watching all hope die.

"*Goodbuddy*"—a sort of soft horror had caught in Smiley's throat—"Who told you we sold to *Negras?*"

Dove sat heavily on the curb, took off his left shoe and pressed the sockless toes. Smiley mounted post above him.

"Git up, boy."

Dove switched to the right-foot toes. They hurt like everything.

"Face up to it, boy," the Georgian urged him.

"*Got* to face up," the Floridan counseled him.

Dove's glance took in all three. "I resign from you-all," he resigned from all three.

Smiley bent swiftly, scooped up Dove's proud shoes, handed the left to the Georgian and the right to the Floridan— "Whut's it going to be, boy—pot or shoes?"

Dove, risen, found his voice at last—"Them shoes costes more 'n *any* ol' tin pot!"

"Aint no ol' tin pot, boy," the Georgian defended Old Dominion, "you know right well that there's a genuine French Dripolator."

"Get goin', son," the Floridan advised him.

Dove shuffled down the grass while Smiley padded the pavement the whole barefoot way back to the tenement.

"Mister," Dove promised Smiley Wreneger at the door, "you wait here. I'll git you back your sorry pot."

Smiley snapped open his watch, gave it a glance and closed

it with a decisive click. "Don't like to law a man, You got five minutes."

The moment Dove got a door between himself and Smiley he thought, "this might take more than five," and latched it. Then poked his head inside the beaded curtain Minnie-Mae called a door. Her eyes glowed upon him from a farther corner like two plums in a bowl of cream.

"Don't stand half in and half out, cawfee man," she invited him, "either come visit or go away."

Dove stepped inside, apologizing, "Don't mean to appear ongrateful, miss, for you've been pure-quill kind. But a certain party has carried me back here account of one old coffee-pot. Now aint that as sorry a circumstance as ever you heard tell?"

The girl was sitting in an old-fashioned rocker wearing only a white wisp of a slip. Somewhere in the room punk was burning. But her own scent, burning more darkly than that, cut through it.

"Why, where your fine yellow shoes, cawfee man?"

"The company's holding them against that same pitiful pot. O *miss*," Dove broke with the disappointment, "I *do* try my very *hardest*. Other boys rise without scarcely tryin'—Why don't *I* rise like other boys?" He covered his eyes with the back of his hand.

"Why for very *shame*"—she took his hands down and caught them softly below her own along the rocker's arms— "shame and *double double* shame on a great big cawfee man like you takin' things so hard as this. Of *course* you'll rise as high as other boys and likely even higher!"

"I'm not as right sure of that as I once was, miss, however kind on your part to say so. You see, I got handicaps others haven't got." His knees pressed her own and she let them press. "You don't *appear* handicapped, cawfee man."

"In more ways than one, miss," he leaned as he mourned,

"more ways than one. First, I can't so much as read my own
name. For another, there's a man right outside your door
waitin' to law me. Now if that aint as pitiful a set of cir-
cumstances for a country boy to overcome I never heard of
pitifuller."

"O *caw*fee man," she chided him tenderly, tucking his
hands back below her own, "you *are* the biggest country fool
ever to walk barefoot to town. Now tell me *true*—What color
wuz that mizzly old pot you keep grievin' so about?"

Dove rocked her forward to get a closer look at the pot,
gleaming like a burnished treasure in the gloom on the mantel
just above the girl's head. "Mostly green, Miss." Could he
get a hand loose he could reach it.

"*Caw*fee man, you upsettin' me"—and putting her feet wide
behind him and her full weight forward, forced him to grasp
the rocker back of her neck to keep from being upset himself.

—"and a spot of red on the handle."

"O so you *say*"—she hooked her ankles behind his and her
arms about his waist to help him keep his balance—"So you
say, but who ever heard tell of a red 'n green cawfee pot?
I don't think you'd lie, yet it's hard for a girl to believe—a
red 'n green pot." Yet for one in grave doubt her voice
sounded curiously approving; and let him rock her forward
again. "What I *really* wants to know is *do* it make good
cawfee?"

"Why, they tell *me* it cook pretty fair, miss. Yet it *could*
be that they lied. It's a thing I'd not take another person's
word for, were I you."

"I 'spects it depend some on whether I grinds my own."

"It's always best do you grind your own, miss. For that
way it's much fresher."

"So *you* say. But what good is fresh if there aint enough
to satisfy? Mister, if you talkin' 'bout some little old scrawny-
size pot I aint interested. What I needs is a *great big pot*,
enough for both morning and night."

"So long as it make good cawfee, miss, size don't scarcely matter."

"It matter a lot if it so small it boil over the minute your back is turned."

"This is a slow-boiler type pot, miss," Dove recalled, rocking her back so far that her slip slid to her navel, "with a spot of red on the handle."

Minnie-Mae let her head rest on the chair's cushioned back and looked up still unbelieving. "So *you* say. But you talks so smooth I begin to doubt you's a country boy at all. You a city boy without shoes—Now *aint* you?"

Dove straightened up with a sudden pride. "I'm purely country, miss, head to toe, and aint nothin' to be ashamed of in *that*. It weren't town boys made our country great—when danger called it was country boys first to answer the call! And many and many a barefoot boy has rose mighty high, though I don't recall their names at the moment. Us country boys, we give our *all!*—O miss, if only someone would give *me* a chance to rise I wouldn't ask for pay. You don't get rich askin' for raises, that much I know. It's the boys who were willing to work just for the experience got to be millionaires! Miss, if I could just get my shoes back I'm sure I'd start to rise like others."

"Why you just said yourself boys without shoes rise more high than them that has them. Don't handicap yourself further by puttin' on shoes, you comical fool."

Someone tried the latch of the door, then padded softly off. Dove saw the pot almost within reach and felt himself gaining ground inch by inch.

"Your belt-buckle botherin' me, country-fool."

The old-fashioned rocker went creakety-creak.

"*Now* grind cawfee and god*damn* your country shoes!"

But Dove only stood waggling his loose tooth, carefully gauging the distance to the pot with his pants around his ankles. He got his little finger around the spout when he heard a swamp mosquito taxiing in: he knew it was a swamp mosquito because it had two motors. It raced down the runway of his left buttock, rocked to a stop, then tried the flesh tentatively as if testing for density. Dove gave his rump a waggle to shake it loose and the movement cost the insect its footing. With the fury of any dignified individual shoved without warning into the street, it planted both feet to gain the greatest leverage and sank its avid proboscis so deep Dove leaped like a hare with the pang.

"O CAWfee man! O you MIGHTY CAWfee man! O you CAWfee-grinding CAWfee man! O you grind so *good!* O you *my* CAWfiest cawfee man!" The bug began drilling for bone but the girl gripped both his wrists. All Dove could do was waggle and jerk in a perfect frenzy and the harder he waggled and jerked the more resolved the bug grew to get a bit of bone.

"I get you shoes! I get you shirts! I get you hats 'n all that! O *proud*-size cawfee man!"—then her voice was drowned in a grateful animal groaning—"*Gawd! Gawd! Gawd!*" And with every "Gawd" she regained lost ground, climbing his back and forcing him further and further from the pot. By the time her ankles were locked behind his neck Dove knew he was losing territory fast. As the old-fashioned rocker went creakety-creak.

"Out of that!" The girl's foot slipped around Dove's chin and by her instep catapulted him as if he'd been kicked by a mule. He landed entangled in his pants just as Smiley crashed through the window bringing sash, screen and all with him.

Minnie-Mae met Smiley mid-room with the full momentum of the chair behind her—Dove shut his eyes at the soft solid *whooosh* as her fist broke Smiley's breath and his legs flew up and he landed even harder than had Dove.

As an empty rocker went clickety-click.

"I love a fool," Dove heard the girl tell, "but you two suits me too well."

"One of them must be me," Dove guessed, though she was looking down at Smiley with the pot in her hand. "Get out of here, cawfee fool," she added, and Dove hopped to it, kangarooing right across Smiley—in mid-air a fat hand clasped his ankle—down he came once again.

"Miscegenation!" Smiley sat up roaring, hauling Dove in like he was something on a line. "Miscegenation 'n pot theft! Dirt-eatin' bugger! Wheah's my pot?"

"Heah's *my* pot!"—Minnie-Mae proved whose it was once and for all by clanging it like a bell against his skull. Dove heard the tinny *wannng*, felt his ankle freed, sprawled across a chest and was out the window. He landed running, gripping his belt and pursued by an illusion that Smiley was right behind him with a screen around his neck, Minnie-Mae right behind Smiley with a dented pot and the law behind all waving a billy three feet long.

Dove didn't stop for breath till he'd rounded four corners and saw no one was following after all.

"Reckon I do take things a mite hard," he thought, getting his buckle fastened at last. "Still, it do seem a great curiosity, how some boys rise so easy while others got to struggle so and lose their shoes in the struggle. Sometimes I almost think it'd be money in my pocket if I'd never been born."

Back on the corner of Calhoun and Magnolia he rested on the curb and sat looking at the day. It was a mighty nice day and people looked friendly.

"I reckon I ought to start lookin' for work," he thought.

"Don't run, goodbuddy," a towering shadow advised him. Craning his neck about, Dove saw the long Floridan and the half-pint Georgian.

"Don't need to run, goodbuddy," the Georgian assured him, "we on *your* side now."

"Been on your side from the very start as a matter of fact."

"Too plumb beat to run anyhow," Dove abandoned hope.
Then saw that each bore a yellow shoe. He eyed both shoes
with distaste. "Them durn things have nigh to destroy me,"
he decided, "and they squeak like a new saddle besides."

"Man owns shoes as proud as these might one day try
socks," the long Floridan commented as he shod Dove's out-
sized left foot—"soap 'n water wouldn't hurt none either,"
he reflected, handing the right shoe to the Georgian.

"Caint even tell how many toes on this one," the smaller
man marveled as he shod the right, "but it looks like it left
six tracks in the barnyard. What part of the graveyard you
sleep in last night?"

"Tried a hotel but the air was so close I just roamed till
sun-up, like a bug on a hot night."

"Plenty room at our place," the big man offered his hand
while his voice rumbled like a bumblebee in a dry gourd. "My
name is Luther but call me Fort, account Fort Myers is my
home town."

"Mah name's Luther too," the little one offered a firmer
grip, "jest call me Luke."

"Like the bullet said to the trigger," Dove introduced himself, "Just tell me where to go."

"Did you have a little trouble back there with our friend?"
Fort asked while they crossed Canal at Tchoupitoulas.

"If folks hadn't pulled me off I'd have whupped him before
he could of got word to God. I was just preparen to feather
into him."

"That would have served him right, too," Fort agreed, "he's
the kind whose pappy made his way by driving his niggers
and now he's trying to make his by driving whites. He's
picked up a bit of Yankee philosophy—you don't work you
don't eat. No true Southern man would never put a choice
like that to a fellow human, black or white."

Up a rickety backstair Fort pulled the string on a sixty-watt bulb. A room filled with a watery light, and mosquitoes buzzed in from the river. Dove saw a sink full of dirty dishes and a high brass bed precisely like another he had seen in his lost long-ago.

"I'll make out on the floor," he offered.

"Aint needful," the Georgian pulled a curtain aside to disclose a cot in a sloping alcove. An empty gin-fifth rested there, uncorked, unlabeled and unclaimed: a bottle without a name. Luke tossed it at the screen, which parted politely to let it through, then closed quietly again. The bottle crashed below.

"Who's throwing things?" Fort, in the other room, sounded startled.

"Some nigger drunk pitchin' glassware," Luke replied lightly.

"Ought to be lawed," Fort decided firmly.

"In my part of the country we don't law them," Luke boasted.

"We aint in your part of the country," Fort pointed out. "Got the rent up?"

"It's three-thirty a week for the set of us," Luke explained as if the question had been asked of Dove.

"That comes to one-ten a week," Fort broke the figure down for everybody present.

"Agreeable to me," Dove accepted the alcove and went to try out his cot. "I don't suppose you fellows got a yaller yam to spare?"

"Nary a yam, son."

"Wall, I just had a hankerin'."

He heard Fort and Luke bickering about the last week's rent, but listened only absent-mindedly. His right buttock still burned where the mosquito had gotten him. He rubbed the spot while waggling his tooth, till sleep stopped waggle, rub and hankerin'.

Fort looked like an ice-house horse mistakenly entered in a claiming race, then insulted publicly for not winning.

All his life he had been lapped by competition too fast for an ice horse. All his life he had been outclassed. Therefore no failure had been his own. How could a man who had never had a proper start be blamed for anything?

Worse, nobody would listen to Fort's side of the story. How all the good times had passed Fort by, the love and the high living. "Watch out for yourselves after this," he warned all men, "I'm takin' care of Number One."

Yet moments of melancholy touched him when he realized that, somewhere, some deserving girl with a steady job was being deprived of him every day. He had tried, through lonely hearts columns, to help her to find him. But the columns had turned out to be taken up mostly by spongers advertising for somebody to support them.

What was the use of a world that failed to reward the deserving while heaping all manner of goodies on people who ought simply be given a kick in the teeth and sent flying? Someone just hadn't been paying attention was how things looked to Fort.

He had ruined himself over and over for the sake of others and not one yet had said, "Thank you, goodbuddy." Forty years of selfless devotion to humanity had brought him no more than the faded cotton on his back.

Actually, those thin and rubbery lips had begun taking care of Number One with the first tug of his pinewood mother's teat. And had lactated every available nipple since. "That was a real smart woman," Dove heard him talking in his sleep—"she *gave* me twenty dollars."

That was how Fort had gone about making others happy. That was why, when teats ran dry and orange groves froze and shoe-soles flapped he could feel himself so terribly wronged.

And could bear his cross so mournfully, a sort of Kiwanis

Christ in a Bing Crosby shirt, resigned to insult and injury, without a shred of larceny and incapable of imposing his woes on others. In fact, he told Dove so: "I'm not the kind to burden others with my troubles. Nobody will know from these sufferin' lips through what Old Fort have went."

Then play by play revealed through just what Old Fort had went.

However self-deluded, he wasn't much deluded about New Orleans. "It's just scratchin' a pore man's ass to try to make a living in this town," he informed Dove right off. "This town'll starve you to death. I'm a mechanic, a cook, I can drive a truck or cab, I play the gee-tar and I can keep books for anybody. I made twenty cents yesterday and a nickel the day before and that's doing better than a good many. A man can live on a dollar a day like Hoover tells him he got to—but where's he to get the dollar?"

"It's a hard git-by," Little Luke cut in, "but what have a man got to lose by leading a Christian life? What if he *don't* get rich but just poor-hogs it all his days? He still got a high place in the Kingdom comin', aint he? Rich or poor don't matter—Heaven apportion its awards accordin' each man to his merit as I look at it."

"I guess everyone get exactly what he got comin'," Dove agreed, "but I aint old enough to vote myself and don't think I will till I am."

Fort had come out of the 'gator backlands to Coral Gables just as the beaches were being prepared for the boomer and the shark. Boomers and shark already lolled the palmetto sands. "Makin' any money?" they asked instead of "good morning."

Fort had wandered among them looking for another Southern boy, but every face he saw wore the same obscene "N.Y."

"Makin' any money?"

He had stood bent and sweating over oven and stove, plying the frycook's fearsome trade, while New Yorkers got suntanned with girls half their ages a hundred yards away.

Soiled and baked by grease and sweat, still bent but beyond sweating, when waiters swung through the kitchen door, he glimpsed boomer and shark once more. Now they had changed to evening clothes and their girls to sleeveless satin. On the damask white as snow, dark wine or light looked equally cool.

One night an order had come back—"Not done enough," and had then been returned once again—"now it's too well done." He had heard the metallic ring of laughter right out of downtown Gomorrah.

Between the dark wine and the light on damask white as snow.

Fort had that pinewood prurience that made him feel that going half-naked into the sea, even in the summer night's sheltering dark, was "lewdling." So when he went wading into the midnight waters he wore long winter underwear. He felt safer, somehow, that way. Fort was afraid of all open waters.

He only went in far enough to let it spill through his palms and was careful not to splash. High overhead the bright windows paid for in Yonkers and the Bronx were filed one above the other. Oh, he knew what they were up to behind the shades all right.

O you smiling, treacherous girls, blouses unbuttoned and skirts unzipped, lolling up there in your bed lamps' joy, saying "Maxie, play with me just right," while some king of the garment trade undressed her garment by garment. Hotel Sodom—that was what it ought to be called. To think of Christian girls, good Southern girls, daughters of families who remembered Shiloh and Atlanta naked up there in the arms of hairy brown thieves from Babylon. The giraffe-like man in the sea spilled Southern waters from palm to palm. In his heart burned all Atlanta.

Back in the windowless frycook's quarters he froze one

minute and sweated the next. He saw himself wheeling a
Stutz—it was always a Stutz. And the wind that went by
lifted the skirt of the slender blonde girl beside him so high he
reached his big hand out—"*Makin' any money?*" she taunted
him, and then there was no one at all on the seat beside him.
Indeed, there was no seat beside him. Only a soiled pillow too
hot to touch and the morning light seeping in from the hall
that led one-way to the kitchen.

"*Makin' any money?*" the chef had asked as soon as Fort
had tied his apron that morning.

"*Makin' any money?*" was the last thing Fort had heard
that night.

He had learned to command the easy credit of that day and
rushed, with other thousands there, to lay hand on anything
of earth or steel or stone whose value would be enhanced as
soon as a city would be built up about it. Though not a street
had yet been cut from swamp, everyone knew the metropolis
would soon rise and held stubbornly onto their pieces of
earth or stone though offered fifty times their worth. Why
give fortunes to strangers? Land that had sold for two dollars
an acre went for three hundred. Business lots worth two
thousand came to be worth a hundred thousand. Lots remote
from any business district were reckoned business lots. Farm-
lands worth fifty dollars an acre became "subdivisions" and
were held for ten thousand per acre—"in a couple years this
will be downtown."

On the morning he made his first timid hundred dollar killing, Fort left the chops for other cooks to fry. Five hundred,
eight-hundred—twelve-hundred dollars! He had never in his
life been worth so much.

He developed cunning. Four thousand, eight thousand—
the wind was behind him now but he was afraid to move out
of his small furnished room for fear of breaking the magic.
Twelve-thousand—fifteen-thousand—at eighteen he thought of
actually buying a Stutz. When he'd run up eighteen thousand

he resolved to pull out at twenty-five. The bottom *had* to fall out, he sensed. He wouldn't be caught trying to make a million.

He made his limit in a single operation—then realized that stopping now would only be to throw away another twenty-five grand. At fifty he would surely stick. Every day he thought of that Stutz.

At forty-two thousand he bought himself the loudest swimming trunks in Coral Gables and showed himself in the sun at last, feeling suddenly half kindly toward other dollar daddies. Why hold it against a man because he was born in New York? A New Yorker could be a good American too.

He spent three days haggling over the price of a Model-T that he drove proudly back to his furnished room at last, and proudly mounted the hot dim stair for the final time. On the table a letter reported that his forty-two thousand was un-negotiable dust.

The sleeping till noon and the sherry, the port and the Stutz and the linen, all had been in his hands and all had slipped through. Now he would never give any waiter orders. Now he would never once sleep past seven.

Fort walked through the curious ruins of a future that never would be, through old never-was cities. The great million-girded metropolises fallen to decay before anybody had laid a brick. The grand hotels, the gleaming lobbies, the fountained parks, where now there was nothing but grass and cinders along the Southern Railway's right of way.

Walked the little midnight towns, remembering the dark wine and the light; hearing his own heels ring. Thinking still how it might have been to walk at morning in a garden of his own.

And find her lying on her side in a striped hammock, in a dress so sheer the softest breeze rippled it and half-pretending sleep. He would rock her gently, there would be no need of words. Only her waking smile and her drowsy hands lazily slipping the buttons of her blouse to please him.

At midnight in the never-was towns hearing his own heels ring.

Or in the steaming New Orleans night, heard laughter faint yet still undying—dark men and fair women going at it again in the heart of downtown Gomorrah.

Then block after block the big freckled man, so stooped, spavined and drooping, wandered the lovely New Orleans night till he found an ice-cart. Then would sniff the ice in the cart's single flickering flare, holding two pennies tightly as a child, this financial counsellor nearly six and a half feet high. Was the chocolate syrup really fresh? No syrup but chocolate could assuage his self-pity. Had it been made that *very* morning? At last he would venture one slow suspicious lick before finally letting his pennies go. He just wasn't taking chances any more.

One warm night Dove went along to help him find an ice-cart with proper chocolate, and that night the first lick convinced him. He turned and beamed down on Dove—"Lend me two more cents, goodbuddy"—and held out the ice to the vendor—"Make her a *double*, goodbuddy!"

That night the chocolate must have been just right.

Though himself without manners enough to carry grits to a bear, Fort was ashamed of shabby companions. Above a cup of chicory coffee he would study Dove so steadily that the boy would begin to wonder what he could have done wrong so soon in the day with the sun scarcely up over Melpomene Street.

"Your whole family eat with their hats on?" Fort finally asked.

Dove set his straw skimmer to one side of his plate.

"Never heard of hat racks," Fort commented bitterly to the bitter window.

"Your whole family drink out of the saucer?" he asked.

"I *like* coffee poured out in the sasser," Dove explained firmly. "Would you kindly pass me the toastes bread? I like it better with a touch of long-sweetenin', but since there aint no long-sweetenin' I'll just give it a touch of the coffee in my sasser."

Fort lived in a welter of unwashed socks, cigarette butts, icesticks, Bull Durham and strewn want-ads. What he was through with he tossed on the floor and never washed a dish.

"Got the megrims again from eatin' too light," he accused the human race in general and Dove Linkhorn in particular. "So dern hongry if I went out in the sun I'd be prostated like a dog."

"There's a loaf of store bread on the fireboard, Fort," Dove told him.

"I'd as soon let the moon shine in my mouth as to eat light bread," Fort spurned the baker's common loaf.

"Well," Dove thought it all over a minute, "light bread's better than nothin'. I've tried both."

But Fort, moved by the vision of himself prostrated like a dog with people stepping over him, rose and announced, "Turnin' over a new leaf—takin' care of *Number One!*"

And left in a rush to start taking care of Number One.

"I do believe hard times is crazyin' him," Dove told Little Luke later.

If Fort cast gloom wherever he went, Little Luke was a man whose life was one long yak. A go-getter with a little pug face like a rouged pekinese and a breath to cripple a kitten. "I'm unfinancial for the moment," he never blamed anyone but himself for being broke—"I was selling holy stones for luck and like a fool I sold them all. Didn't keep a single one for myself. Carelessness, carelessness."

"I don't believe in nothing like that," Dove told him, "and wouldn't buy one from a stranger if I did."

Luke always had a commission coming in, a percentage going out and an urgent transaction in the offing.

The offing was in a shambling gin mill called Dockery's
Dollhouse, down in the district where all his strange business
was done. Others said gin was a weakness with him, but Luke
had a different name for it.

He called it wanderlust. Wherever he went some Miss Jane
or Miss Molly pled with him to settle down with her on some
fine old Southern estate. Luke would put her affairs in order,
assuaging her fears by day and her lusts by night, until she'd
surprise him preparing his blanket roll—they all went hysteri-
cal on him then. If he left her now she'd kill herself. Things
had gotten so bad he'd taken to sneaking off in the middle of
the night.

"That part I can readily believe," Fort would comment.

"Met Miss Molly at a Memphis candy-breakin' 'n she
treated me like I was somethin' on a stick. Had this fine old
home in Greenville and a restaurant chain—oh the sweet potato pie that woman put out!"—Luke went lying blithely on—
"the sentimental little fool. When she seen I had my mind set
on leaving she give me five-dollar meal ticket good in either
Memphis or Atlanta."

"Was that before or after she killed herself?" Fort inquired
mildly.

"I'm *plenty* worried about her," Luke implied darkly.

And went on the nod right where he sat, his Bottled-in-the-
Barn just within reach.

"Watch out for that carnival-talkin' jailbird," Fort warned
Dove the moment Luke began to snore. "He'll talk a country
boy like you into some fool operation and you'll be the one
to take the rap, mark my word. Watch out, goodbuddy."

Goodbuddy promised he'd watch out.

As soon as Fort slept Luke opened one glimmering eye.

"Ssssss—*Tex*," he whispered to Dove—"Watch out for that
piss-complected faker. He's been in every clink between
Miami and Houston. He hollered on me so he'll holler on you.
Watch out, Tex."

Tex promised to watch out.

"That's what I call a couple considerate fellows," Dove realized, "watchin' out for my interests in shifts."

One night Luke came banging and jangling in, trailing odors of seafood and gin. "Srimps! He'p yorse'ves, boys!" He bounced a greasy bag on the table, put another nameless bottle beside it, fished two Spanish onions out of his pocket and invited everyone in town.

"Don't taste quite fresh," Fort grieved, filling his face, "taste a mite swivelly."

"The scripters says it's a sin to eat anything that parts the hoof or don't chew cood but I like srimps all the same," Dove reported.

Luke began stacking quarters and halves ostentatiously. Somebody had gotten rich fairly fast.

"I'm jest eatin' them because I need sustenance so bad," Fort explained, his voice round with self-pity—"two orangey ice-sticks just aint enough to sustain a man till evening."

"Take this for tomorrow's sustenance then," Luke sent a quarter to him with a small disdainful finger-flick. Dove tightened lest Fort return the insult with his fist.

"They don't know how to make hot sauce in this town," Fort observed, pocketing the quarter as if he'd just earned it.

Orange ice stuck to his chin. Hot sauce colored his chops. Hairs stuck out of his nose and snot hung hard to the hairs.

"You want one too, Tex?" Little Luke had another quarter ready to roll.

"Thank you kindly all the same," Dove declined.

"I didn't think so," Luke concluded without looking at Fort.

A shrimp's tail had lodged between Fort's teeth and he was having the devil's own time prying the tip of it with his tongue.

"Mighty funny they don't clean these things before selling them to folks," he protested as if he'd paid double for something. Dislodging the tail at last, he spat it on the floor.

"I *would* eat one of them ing-urns," Dove announced.

Luke looked confused.

"He means one of *them*—" Fort indicated an onion.

It was true enough that two orangey ices wasn't enough to sustain a man like Fort till evening. It wasn't enough to sustain Dove either. Yet each evening he announced, "I got to get a soon start in the morning. Will one of you fellers holler me up?"

And lugged a sample-case into the day's first light, telling half-awake housewives, "A Store at Your Door." Past the Confederate Veterans' Home. A Store at Your Door down Humanity Street and up Gentilly Road. Rapping the front door or rapping the back down Peoples Avenue.

Peoples to Almonaster, front doors and rear. As the fore-noon heat began to heap both sides of Spain Street down to the wharves.

By noon, with his case lighter only by sale of one jar of hair-straightener, he'd be sitting on the Desire Street dock ad-miring a ship from Norway or Peru with a big nickel bunch of bananas beside him and one little dry Spanish ing-urn.

Dreaming and peeling, Dove would recall all the storied shores he had almost seen. Through half-closed lids his thoughts rocked down, down the great river to the almost-sea. The masted and magic almost-sea. Rocking so far out on the dangerous waves it was really too far, and so would rock himself gently back to shore: the sheltering home-harbor shore. Where friendly street lamps lit the way to some old chili parlor door. And half-dreaming heard voices of women of his little lost town

> *When you're on some distant shore*
> *Think on your absent friend*
> *And when the wind blows high and clear*
> *A letter too pray send*

—to Dove's own homesick shore.

He would blink the bright tears from his eyes at last. No time to be homesick any more. Scarcely time left for a man to rise. He would pick up his sample case and lug on, rapping a front door or rapping a rear. It couldn't be too long now before some little good looker would invite him too into a fine old Southern home, serve him sweet potato pie too and say, "Big Fine Daddy, please stop runnin' wild."

But he only came to a great lonely house where a wan redhead of twelve or thirteen cried out at sight of his little store —"Granny! A man with *everything* we need!" She seized a bar of tar soap "for my nappy old hair." A shoehorn for her nappy old shoes and cologne for her nappy old bath; a nail file, a comb, a compact—"There's things *you* need here too, Granny!" It looked to Dove like the sale of the year.

Till an old, old woman's voice recalled the girl, and she returned looking more wan than before. And, kneeling silently, replaced every item she had taken from the case.

"It's awright, Miss," Dove reassured her, "Lots of ladies pick out things 'n then change their minds, times bein' hard as they are."

"I didn't *intend* to disappoint you," the child told him quietly. A nickel spun into the case, the screen door slammed, that old, old house stood sick and still.

"You would of done better to take the soap," Dove reproached the empty porch and shut his case.

But pocketed the nickel. It would buy a cup of Southern coffee and a paper for Fort to read out loud to him.

He walked the endless Negro blocks to home because it was still day. He was suspicious of them by night or by day. What were they forever laughing about from doorstep to door that he could never clearly hear? Their voices dropped when he came near and didn't rise till he was past earshot. Yet their prophecies pursued him—

De Lord Give Noah de rainbow sign—
Wont be by water but by fire next time—

Fort was lying on the high brass bed when Dove climbed
the Tchoupitoulas Street stair that evening, just as Dove had
left him that morning. A couple of noon cups had been added
to the morning saucers, a few snipes to those on the floor.
"Haven't been able to stir the whole day," Fort sighed.

Yet Dove had the momentary impression he had just come
in.

Dove handed him the paper and cleared the table and sink
while Fort read aloud.

Fort crumpled the want-ads. What was the use of getting
out a paper that didn't tell who needed a Financial Counsellor?

The Financial Counsellor didn't get up till the dishes were
done.

"I s'pose I got to go shop 'n sweat over the cook stove for
y'all now," he informed Dove by his tone just what it was
like to be imposed upon by everyone day after day.

"Won't we wait till Luke shows up?" Dove suggested, "account all I got myself is one misly little two-bitses."

"He'll come in drunk as a dog but he won't have his rent
money up," Fort made a safe guess.

"That's his turn, an' he caint help it," Dove defended his
friend.

Fort began frying something and after a while it must have
been done, because he lifted two shapeless gobs into dishes
and put both dishes down.

"I'll eat anything that won't eat me," Dove announced, and
dug right in, cupping his spoon in the palm of his hand before
he even made sure the stuff was dead.

Fort gave him the even look.

"You actually *like* this slop?"

"You mean if I had my druthers? Why, if I had my druthers I'd druther eat speckledly gravy," Dove assured him.

"You don't actually mind living this way?"

"It's better than jail." Dove was sure.

"That's jest what I thought," Fort's suspicions were confirmed—"You actually *like* this life."

"It's the only life I got," Dove felt bound to explain.

Little Luke came in grinning with good news on his face and another newspaper under his arm. "We've just done turned that corner," he announced. "Didn't I tell you times had to get worse before they could get better?"

"Luke," Fort rose to tell him, "if we were standin' around wonderin' which one of us to eat first you still wouldn't call times hard." Then he left to look for something to eat.

Luke skipped to his coat and brought forth a stack of green-margined certificates "entitling bearer to one free finger wave and shampoo at the Madam Dewberry Beauty Shop"—he rattled off the larger print. "Now tell me, what woman in N'awlins don't want a marcel wave and shampoo for free?"

Dove couldn't name a single one.

"Tell you what it amounts to, Tex—you're handing that lucky gal the equivalent of a five-dollar bill."

"I am?"

"You're workin' *with* me on this, aren't you?"

"Would it be alright with Madam Dewberry?"

"That's my responsibility."

"Mighty obliged, Luke."

"All you have to do is watch out for telephone wires."

"Aint no plumb good at climbin', Luke."

"Who said there was climbin'?"

Somebody's step sounded on the stair and Luke ducked the certificates hastily into his coat. "Got a hundred more stashed under the steps," he lowered his voice and touched a finger to his lips—"Mum's the word."

Rapping with Luke was a lark. Instead of a heavy sample case all Dove had to carry now was a bundle of certificates, and didn't have to climb a telephone pole after all.

"I'll have to wait to see what my husband says," his first prospect told him.

"Reckon you'll just miss your free wave 'n shampoo then, m'am. We aint comin' by this way again. Fact is we're almost out of certificates already. Only puttin' out a hundred in the whole dern town."

The woman studied the certificates with a married daughter beside her. "Seems just too good to be true," both frankly doubted him.

"M'am, why don't you just telephone Madam Dewberry and *veer*fy what I'm sayin'?"

Inasmuch as there was seldom more than one telephone to a block in New Orleans in '31, the bluff was safe. She took one for herself and one for the daughter.

His second prospect had a harder head. "You wait here, young man—I *am* going to phone."

"Yes'm." Dove obeyed her.

But when she disappeared to primp for her trip to the corner grocer's phone, Dove scurried to warn Luke off the block.

Luke took a swig from a half pint off his hip and didn't feel the need to hurry anywhere. "Take your time, Tex."

"Here she comes now." Luke intercepted the hardheaded number.

"Good morning, m'am. I'm the manager of the Madam Dewberry Beauty Parlor. My young assistant here reports you want to confirm this invitation. We *like* that. You're the type of customer we're looking for. If we can satisfy *you*, we can satisfy anybody. Don't waste your nickel—I stand back of every word on this certificate." Luke drew one out of his pocket. "I'm not going to charge you even a quarter for this one, m'am."

He put it in her hand.

"I didn't mean I wanted it for *nothing*," Hardhead protested.

"If you want to pay the young man the courtesy fee of
twenty-five cents, that's purely optional."

The woman handed Dove a quarter and returned to the
house reading the smaller print.

The rest of the morning went easier. By noon twenty-five
quarters jingled in Dove's jeans and he still had twenty-five
certificates for the evening.

But by evening Luke had invested his own quarters in a
bottle of gin, so that before they had rapped many doors they
were in no shape to rap at all. Toward midnight Dove heard
horns and bells. They were helping one another down Tchoupitoulas and the whole dark city rang.

On their old stairs' steep sad height Dove held Luke back.
"I wonder did old Fort eat today?"

"Let the sonofabitch starve," Luke pushed into the room.
On the bed Fort lay with his face to the wall.

"Shhhh," Dove cautioned Luke, "don't wake him up."

"The sonofabitch been awake for hours," Luke decided,
and shook Fort by the shoulders. "Hey! Good old buddy!
Srimps! Fresh srimps!"

Fort turned about. Hunger kept glassing his eyes. He didn't
see shrimps. He didn't smell shrimps.

"Because there *aint* no srimps because we et 'em all, goodbuddy," Luke laughed with real glee and did a little taunting
song and dance—

> *You made a lot of money back in '22*
> *But whiskey and women made a fool of you*
> *Why don't you do right*
> *Get me some money too—*

Dove remembered his own pockets and withdrew six cold
shrimps wrapped in a paper napkin.

"Here, Fort," and held them out over the sleeper's face to show it wasn't a joke after all. "As good-tasted a srimp as ever you et—" Fort swung a hand and sent shrimps and napkin flying.

One ricocheted off the wall onto the bed. Dove picked it up and nibbled drunkenly at it, looking down at six and a half feet of self-pity huddled under a dirty patch quilt.

Hours later he was wakened by someone padding about. Luke was snoring in the chair. Dove saw a match's flare. Then a kind of chewing-sucking sound. "I hope he finds them all," Dove thought and returned to sleep.

In the morning Fort had left.

"I think he's a mite fitified with us," Dove felt. "We hurt his feelings last night."

"His type feelings is hurt till they smell cookin'," Luke was certain. "Then they come runnin'."

"I wouldn't fault him," Dove excused Fort. "He's just a poor hippoed critter."

"Hippoed?"

"He's liver-growed. His liver has growed to one side, that's plain to be seen. If he'd been held upside down when he was a young 'n 'n shook good, it could have been shuk loose. Too late now. Be there ary egg about?"

"How do you want it? Up or over?"

"I'm not dauncy," Dove answered, "I like an egg ever-what way."

When both eggs were everwhatted, Luke set them down thoughtfully, though not commonly a thoughtful man.

They left the pan and the dishes for Fort to clean and made their morning run with twenty-five certificates each from Luke's secret cache.

Upon their evening return dishes littered the table, flies fed in all the pans and an odor of meat burnt or burning hung like a promise of better times. Fort was stretched more than the length of the high brass bed, smoking a cigar looking as long as himself; like a man who had never missed a meal. It was an unsettling sight.

"Spared half a steak for you boys," he recalled, blowing mosquitoes off in a T-bone shaped cloud—"but you didn't show up so I said to myself, 'You better knock that steak off before the flies get it.' Had to force myself, but I did. Sure would have admired to share it but it's no use kicking myself for not waiting now."

Sure enough. A steak's remains had been fried right there on their own stove, and Fort didn't spend that night in search of shrimps. Instead, he laughed at them both in sleep.

He never laughed except in sleep but Dove and Luke took their laughter waking. In the days that followed they stayed drunk, off and on, most of the summer day and often well into the summer night. They had no reason for not being drunk.

The days of peeking timidly into a backyard to check on telephone wires were past. A businessman like himself, Dove had come to feel, hadn't time to bother with that sort of thing. He rapped fast and hard at front doors these days, and once when a housewife answered he challenged her before she had a chance to ask what he wanted—"Go ahead 'n call up! See who cares!"—and with a tip of his straw floater was gone in an evening mystery, down a gently weaving street.

For some reason sales began falling off. Would times get better before they ran out of certificates? Luke was sure things were on the upgrade, the worst of the depression was over and they would have certificates left they would have no use for. But Fort felt the depression had just begun. Things were going to get a lot worse he foretold, and would stay that way longer than anyone believed. Then the bottom would fall out.

Nonetheless, whenever they returned, shrimpless or shrimpified, the odor of sirloin, hamburger or chops made the air of the little room muggy, and Fort would be blowing off the odor with clouds of Cuban cigar smoke. Somebody was doing all right.

"If you boys would only let me know whether I could expect you, I'd be only too pleased to put your name in the pot," he would complain. "Had steak *again*."

"I'm not peckish, I'll eat anything, even steak," Dove provided for any such future event—"put my name in your pot anytime, Fort."

But the only name in Fort's pot was spelled F-O-R-T.

To show his gratitude for the night before, Dove invited Luke to turtle soup in the Old French Market.

In the dim familiar place they had to make way for a beggar in dark glasses, poking his way through seafood odors with the help of a white cane. "Excuse me, girls," Dove heard him murmur as he passed, "excuse me."

The turtles had been given a twenty-four hour reprieve. No beheading being done today. So they ordered bowls of gumbo and gumboed bowl after bowl. Then it was catfish time and they catfished till they foundered. By the time they left the heat in the street had passed and the catfish sun itself had foundered.

"I've just about et myself into the creek," Dove decided.

He felt so full of fish and gumbo he didn't even mind when a collie in a well-kept yard charged him the full length of her chain. A white woman, holding the brute by its collar apologized, "I never knowed Queenie to go after a *white* man before."

Then she took a long second look at the redheaded stranger before her and added with soft suspicion, "She never been wrong afore, mister."

Dove merely tipped his skimmer. "Thank you kindly all the same, m'am,"—and slunk off—"Durned old hound smelled the catfish *in* me."

Out where yards weren't kept so well and walks were cracked like those of home, he always felt less guilty. The last

door he rapped that day was on such a walk. A Negro woman
with violet eyes came to the door. Dove tipped his hat, felt his
heel nipped gently, and turned just in time to see a fat white
mongrel whip about and dash for cover under the house as if
it had done something wonderfully daring.

"He don't care for white folks comin' into his yard," Violet
Eyes smiled matter-of-factly. "He say he can't go into theirs,
why they come into his?"

"Thank you kindly all the same," Dove told her, thinking
guiltily again, "Durned old hound smelled the certificates on
me."

"This walkin' 'n talkin' 'n rappin' 'n tappin' is too much
like work for me," Luke decided, and Dove had had enough
too. Though it wasn't walkin' 'n talkin' Dove minded. Nor
even rappin' 'n tappin'.

It was rather that each quarter he stole weighed a bit more
than the one stolen just before. The sample case was lighter
after all.

"How many them phonies you got left, Tex?"

Dove handed Luke the last of the batch. Luke took a count.
Thirteen. "I know a place where we can get shet of these in
one stop," he promised.

On South Rampart Dove waited out front while Luke
ducked around the rear of a Negro shanty and returned with
a pint of Bottled-in-the-Barn.

They drank it down to the half-pint mark. "That stuff is so
good a feller can't hardly bite it off," Dove told Luke.

"It's the pure quill," Luke agreed, "you can smell the feet
of the boys who plowed the corn."

Dove took another just to see if Luke were right about that.

"It sure aint gravy," he reported.

"Care to see the girls, boys?" a little man in a flame-yellow
shirt and cowboy boots asked from a doorway so wide it must
once have been an entrance to a pretentious bar.

"They givin' it away today?" Luke asked innocently.

The little blond man had sideburns past his cheekbones, he might have been twenty-two or forty.

"To a couple good-looking fellows like you I wouldn't be surprised if they did," he conned Luke right back.

"Reason I suggested *that*," Luke explained, "is that *we're* giving things away." He drew forth a green-margined certificate. "Free finger waves at Madame Dewberry's. Reckon the little ladies might be interested?"

"Why, this is the very deal they've been wondering how they can get it," the little man pretended, "they'll take your whole load off your hands."

By the time the two pitchmen realized they'd been outpitched they were inside one of those high old-fashioned parlors where a ceiling fan whirrs so leisurely in a big twilit gloom that you can't tell whether anyone else is in the room.

Gradually the forms of half a dozen men sitting as men sit in a barber shop, collars open and Sunday's funnies on their laps, one or two with cigars in hand, emerged from the dimness.

Something brushed Dove's hair and he touched a spider made of metal, suspended upon so slender a wire it was not discernible until a wave from the ceiling fan swung it; then a burnished glint wound right, wound left in the soundlessly woven air.

The woven air so softly spun by spiders red, by spiders green, some low-hung and some high; some gold and others rose. Spinning webs so fine on thread unseen in a long twilit gloom.

Dove picked up one magazine, pretending to read as other men did. Till suddenly wishing somehow to outdo them all, and spying a book on a divan, he picked it up boldly and returned to his chair. He flipped its pages carelessly, as though the light were too poor for a man to strain his eyes. He had flipped almost through, then gave one more flip, and his hand trembled on the page.

For there his steadfast tin soldier stood, his musket clasped under his grenadier's hat, and behind him waited the same platoon of two-legged soldiers. The one-legged one was still the most steadfast.

In his simple-minded amazement he thought it must be Terasina's book.

"The girls will be down directly, boys," a bespectacled mulatto woman wearing black crepe chiffon, in which she had pinned velvet flowers, came bouncing to announce.

"Ask them do they want free marcels, Lucille," Luke asked her.

"It's been many years since anyone called me 'Lucille'," she told Luke.

"Many years," Luke agreed wistfully, "many, many years."

She peered at him but the years really had been too many. Faces of others had come like waves of the sea one fast upon another. Now there was no longer any recalling what shore, what summer nor what night hour their eyes had met in love or lust or simple bargaining.

"They call me Mama now," she explained, "I'm just the housekeeper here."

Then she caught sight of Dove clutching the parlor's one book.

"That's our Hallie's," she told him.

Dove looked at the name scribbled in the front. So that was how to write "Hallie's." And kept his finger on that name though he closed the book.

An old man in a high-backed chair hoping to make the price of a pint, and the boy beside him longing for love so hard that a name in a book was already beloved. While others waited like window-dummies, anonymous men waiting to stay anonymous. They sighed, they spat, they snored now and then, but were careful not to begin idle talk that might lead to discovery of mutual friends.

A little black boy in a shirt that reached no farther than his navel studied each client in turn. Some smiled, some looked the other way. He would look till he had his fill of each, then move onto the next. If offered a penny he would pocket it yet never crack a smile.

A feminine scent, as of incense mixed with cologne, stirred the portieres. Dove gripped the book tighter.

This would be Hallie.

But it was only the fan overhead that had stirred the curtain. Now the metal spiders hung more still, now the barber shop boredom grew yet heavier. Across the street a man in a black stetson was offering a bag of something to a girl in the corner door. Dove saw her look both ways down Rampart and look both ways down Perdido. Then reached swiftly into the bag and dodged as swiftly back. A moment later she reopened the door just long enough to spit a peanut shell into the street. Any transaction, even for peanuts, made with one party still on the walk could mean a pinch for the girl.

But the risk she'd taken paid off, for the stetson girded up his loins and entered clutching his bag big enough to provide a peanut for every girl in the place and still leave two for himself.

The first street lamp came on, looked both ways down Rampart then both ways down old Perdido; then steadied itself for the long night ahead. When God alone knew what peanutless monster, what penniless stray, might come there seeking rest.

A moon-faced blonde with her hair in a bun sauntered in, her face dead-white and her brows pitch-black. Dove gave a start, then relaxed: no, this one never could be Hallie.

"Reba, these boys got marcel waves to give away," Mama told her.

"You got *in*surance?" Reba demanded.

"We got insurance to keep your hair from getting nappy," Luke stepped right in. Reba held out her baby hand and he clapped a certificate right in it.

"That'll be a quarter, miss."

"You said it was free."

"The quarter is just by way of a courtesy," Luke told her.

"Keep it. I aint courteous," and gave him back his gift.

"She's from Chicago," Mama explained.

But a girl with a face made up to look like a death mask of Joan Crawford, a real plastic mask of a face, began to plead for one.

"Mama sweet, give the man a quarter for one for me."

"For God's sake, she don't even know what the guy is sellin' 'n she's buyin'," Chicago shook her head in disbelief at the ways of Southern hustlers.

"Meet Frenchy," Mama introduced the mask, "and this is my grandson, Warren Gameliel. Pledge allegiance, Warren G."

The little black boy wasn't pledging a thing. He wasn't even saying hello. "I do it *back*," he warned everyone. No one knew what he meant by that.

"—and this is our Fort Worth girl," Mama introduced a blonde twice the size of the first, with breasts that could better have hung on a cow. No, this never could be Hallie.

Mama handed Luke a quarter for Frenchy, the girl received her paper, gave it one bored glance and handed it to Fort Worth—"You use it, honey, I never go downtown."

She had bought like a child, for the sake of the transaction, and like a child had made a gift of it to the nearest friend. Dove saw that there was nothing easier than selling to hustling women. Reba was the only one who wouldn't buy just for the sake of buying.

Warren Gameliel seemed less a child than the women. Clutching a penny of his own, he watched each transfer of ownership so intently that Mama declared, "I swear I believe that child can add and subtract." And added, perhaps to put the salesmen into a mood that would get the girls their quarters back, "We get lots of married men down here. I've been married four times myself. Shod the horse all around as it were. Once to a businessman and three times to thieves, and the businessman was the only one I was unhappy with."

"Is Looney up yet?" someone asked.

"Which looney?" Fort Worth wanted to know.

"There's no one in this house name of 'Looney' that I know of," Mama defended the missing chick. "If you're referring to Floralee, she's putting on her clothes. I forbade her ever to come down again without them. You know what she told me? 'I don't see the use of all this onnin'-'n-offin','—that's just what the poor thing told me."

"What's so looney about that?" Fort Worth wanted to know.

"After last night I don't see how that broad can get downstairs with or without clothes," Frenchy marveled from behind Joan Crawford's eyebrows, "I don't even see how she can rise."

"She'll rise and she'll get down here and eat grits and ham enough for six, too, you'll see if she don't," Fort Worth promised. "She don't even know she got a stomach, that one."

"Any broad that'll make love *back* to her tricks," Reba reflected sadly, "—no wonder she got a appetite."

"Don't begrudge the child her food," Mama reproved them all, "she got her ways and you got yours."

"If that pimp of hers had a saltspoon of sense in his head," Frenchy decided, "he'd wise her up. What's a pimp for?"

"You tell me," Fort Worth put Frenchy down fast, "you work for one."

The door was swung wide and a legless giant, buckled onto a sort of street-going raft built over roller skates, wheeled in like one who came here every day, making a hollow thunder across the planking as he came. Dove watched him unbuckle his straps and leap, in a single bound, onto a low divan.

The little black boy came up to this enormous torso without fear, to study him comparatively. The great cripple gave him a coin, but the boy remained unsmiling before him. Suddenly he asked, "What they done to *you?*"

"Such a *serious* child," Mama marveled. "Will you boys stay to party?"

"We got a little work to finish," Luke decided to save them both money, "We'll be back later."

As they left, the man no higher than five feet in cowboy boots opened the door for them.

"*Come back by yourself*," Dove was almost sure he heard the little man whisper; yet it had been said so low that they were a full block away before the whisper began to draw him back.

"Sure would of admired to tarry there," he sighed heavily, "a little ying-yang never hurt a man."

"Terrible waste of hard-earned money, son," Luke counseled him like a father.

"Just speaking for yourself, I deem," Dove corrected him like a friend.

"Too much of that thing and they'll be carrying you away, boy."

"Nothin' wrong with that," Dove reflected, "inasmuch as it was that thing that brought me here. I'll tell you just what, Luke," he stopped right where he stood: "I'm just *urnin'* for ying-yang."

"See you back home, boy," Luke dismissed him. "Just don't bring anything home with you."

Dove hurried back up the street, afraid the little man might have left. It didn't seem to him that he could regain entrance without being authorized by a friend.

"My name is Finnerty," he told Dove, "follow me."

And led Dove downhill toward the docks. Halfway downhill he turned into a tiled doorway that still held rusted hinges of a time when the place had had swinging doors. A one-story building built on its incline toward the river.

Although Prohibition was good as done, habits it had

formed in those who had had their living off it for years could not be changed overnight. Every self-respecting speak-easy devised its own secret knock, peep-hole and password. Buyers wanted more than to walk through an open door, they wished to be admitted to a mystery. More, they wished to belong to a mystery.

After Finnerty had given the buzzer three quick shots, he waited a moment and added a fourth; then both stood in silence before a silent door.

"Maybe aint nobody home," Dove ventured.

"He's squirrel-eyeing us this minute from behind the curtain," Finnerty confided without glancing at the window, "to see if we're the type that demands service. If we buzz him again, we don't get in. Doc just won't be bossed."

At last the door opened enough to let a white bug of a nose materialize before them. "Password?" the nose demanded.

"Respect is the key," Finnerty replied, and got past the old man. So Dove said it too and both were inside.

Where along the back bar's thousand bottles, Old Doc Dockery's hundred dolls remembered the twisted twenties.

Dark-eyed, dressy little town dolls and dutch-bobbed blondies from windmilled countrysides, redhaired colleens and gypsy dolls, a cowgirl cutie in a fringed buckskin and a Broadway baby in a fur boa, a geisha whose eyes were quarter-moons and another who had bobbed her hair and gone all out in Babylon; for her eyes were dollar-signs.

A penny-eyed doll and a button-eyed doll whose buttons said "Vote for Cox"; a cross-eyed doll no longer comical, and a doll wearing a bird of paradise. And one little down-and-out bum of a Raggedy Ann with patches on her skirt and wrinkles in her neck; right in the middle where the bar lights could make a small halo about her.

Yet birds of paradise or Raggedy Anns, though one pretended to be Dutch, one Irish and one Japanese, all had seen the headlines on St. Valentine's Day and had dated Harry

Greb. Some had had good luck and some had had bad, but
all had been born to the twenties and had died when the twenties were done.

Some of broken hearts when Wallace Reid had died. Some
had gone on the nod waiting for Dempsey to fight Harry
Wills. Others had grown weary after Starr Faithful had
passed. One by one they had nodded off, taking their good
luck and taking their bad.

(Raggedy Ann's, of course, had been worse than the
others, that was plain enough by her patches. And perhaps
was the reason she had the place of honor right in the middle.)

"There's no price on them," Dockery warned everyone,
"They're not for sale and neither am I. Respect gets you in
here and disrespect gets you out. Respect, respect is the key."
No one was allowed to dicker for his dolls, no hand but his
own could touch them.

Respect for the dead of a dead decade—that was the key.

The old man preferred the kind of drinker who asked that
his glass be washed after every drink. As some men wish to
be always drunken, as some women wish to be always in love,
Doc Dockery wished to be always clean. To be clean and
cleaning.

People, of course, could not be made clean. What kind of
filth the old man had waded in neck-deep, of which he still
fought to free himself in his lonely white-haired age, or what
deep disease was concealed by this passion for hygiene was
not clear. Yet it was plain that it had at last turned all his
women to dolls.

Respect, that was the key. Respect for his women, and
for his music too. His music that was *Stardust, Stormy
Weather, Bye Bye Blackbird, A Good Man Is Hard To Find,
My Bill, Paper Doll, Red Sails in the Sunset* and *Tie Me To
Your Apron Strings Again.*

To this lopsided shambles owned by this unlicensed ghost,

this speakeasy spook who had been alive once but had died
in the crash and was now only haunting the thirties, came
trudging, some uphill and some down, all those who could
not admit that the money was spent, the dream was over; the
magic done. They still wore the clothes they wore before
1929 and no one knew when they might buy clothes again.

By and large they were theater people who had lost their
theater: ingénues, leading men, stagehands, ticket brokers,
managers of road shows, starlets and prima donnas. Albeit
that, just for the time being of course, they were "hostesses,"
con artists, sneak thieves, con men, procurers, cardsharps,
pennymatchers; and a few honest just plain bums.

The first thing Dove saw when he entered the cave was
the lion-headed amputee they had left at the brothel. By
what alley-route he had beat them here only someone who
lived on ball-bearings could know.

Finnerty drank with his back to the half-man, indicating
to Dove that was the wisest way. So Dove felt somehow relieved when he heard the skated platform wheel down the
floor, out the door and onto the open street.

Then, ready to let the murmuring hours spin, he put a
nickel in the juke to help them begin.

I'm forever blowing bubbles
the machine began
Pretty bubbles in the air

"Now I'll come to the point," Finnerty informed Dove
when the bubbles all were blown, "I need the help of a
healthy boy. I take it your health is as good as it appears."

"A might better, mister," Dove made a conservative guess,
"and I'm always ready to make an honest dollar."

"You can call me Oliver, for that's my name."

"You can call me Tex. For that's where I'm from."

"My line of work, as you may have guessed, Tex, is
women. Do you know anything about them?"

"I know that if God made anything better I aint come across it yet, but that's as far as my knowledge goes."

"In that case it don't go far," Oliver decided, "but the question is whether you're interested in going to bed with a young woman who has never been to bed with a man before."

"Mister, I'm a Southern boy and wouldn't disadvantage no young girl that way."

"Southern don't enter into this, Tex," Finnerty assured him, "The young woman is bound and determined to hustle. It's all settled but the bother and inconvenience of breaking her in."

"Your field being women," Dove pointed out, "I reckon that's your job, mister."

"Why, that's precisely the reason I *can't*, don't you see?" Finnerty tried patience. "If I did it she could come back a year from now and law me on the white slave act, for I've a record in that line I don't mind admitting. I've already been busted on that charge once, and I don't cherish being busted again. But someone like yourself that she'll never see again— Oh, don't be afraid of having to use force, for you shant. You won't even have to undress this child."

"That don't sound like no virgin girl to me," Dove told the pander.

"That's her claim, so I take her at her word," Finnerty told Dove. "The point is that, if you did me this one small favor, she couldn't make that claim in the future. Do you follow me?"

"I follow you to a certain point," Dove decided, "after that it's a mite unclear."

"Maybe this will clear things up."

Dove put his hands stiffly behind his back. "Mister, I can't read my own name if it was writ on the side of a barn, but I know a hundred dollar bill when I see one. And I think you'd best put that one away."

Finnerty tucked it into Dove's breast pocket.

"Mister, I can't take that," Dove told him firmly without making a move to give it back.

"Don't worry," Finnerty promised, "You're *not* taking it, country boy. You're carrying it for me, that's all. You're carrying it across the street and up the stairs to a room where this young lady is waiting for you. When you come in the room you'll hand it to her without a word—if I know her greedy little heart she'll put it in her slipper and you take it from there."

"What's her name?"

"She'll tell you that herself, country boy."

They were at the back entrance of the house which they'd entered by the front before Dove hesitated.

"Just one thing I'd like to ask, mister."

"What's that?" Finnerty was too close behind him.

"I'd rather you call me Tex 'stead of country boy."

"Right-o, Tex," Finnerty agreed, and shook Dove's hand to seal the deal.

Dove shook, and stepped through the door Oliver held wide.

A girl with the pallor of one who lives indoors, one low of flesh but high of bone, in red shorts and red halter. Dove heard the door lock behind him.

"What's your name?" he asked her.

"Floralee," she told him, "and I sing like a damned bird. But how did I fly here?"

"I'm sure I don't know, country girl," Dove told her, "but I'm to give you this."

He took his last ten dollar bill and handed it to her. Just as Finnerty had said, she had a greedy little heart, for she stuffed it down her slipper right away without even bothering to glance at it and snapped the button that held up her shorts.

If Dove, in the minutes that followed, heard murmured

laughter from behind a wall, he didn't let that divert him from the sums he had now to do in his head.

"It costes me ten dollars to make a hundred," he figured, "at that rate I don't see how I can lose."

On a morning so damp the salt wouldn't dust Dove wakened feeling like something chewed up and spat out. His seersucker, hung on a nail on the wall, looked like something fished out of the river. Everything his eyes fell upon looked fished-out or spat-out. He had a big bad head and held it hard, mourning "Oh, it drinked dandy but Lord the afterwards. The way the world is going I don't think it'll last."

But the Financial Counsellor was whistling cheerfully as he buttoned himself into a freshly pressed financial-looking suit.

"Happened on a *most* curious certificate," he announced as soon as he saw Dove get one sick eye wide, and drew it forth like a document. "What do you reckon happen when one of them girls trots all the way downtown for a free marcel?"

"Reckon she gets herself fixed up right pretty," Dove took a hazy guess.

"Reckon she do if she got three-fifty. Which you know very well she don't. Did you *read* this thing you're selling?"

For once Dove was glad he couldn't.

Fort touched a prong of his sunglasses to the fatal figures. "I warned you to stay clear of that Georgia hand," he reminded Dove, "now my advice is that you stay indoors. There must be a chance of husbands on the lookout for a country-lookin' gin-head by now."

"I was only tryin' to make an honest dollar in a crooked sort of way," Dove explained.

For reply Fort fastened his face one moment to the mirror and must have been pleased by what he saw. For he left with a confident, executive stride, a man who'd be rich in six weeks if not in five.

Dove went to the window. Street to sky, New Orleans looked shrouded. He saw its fearful loneliness. He felt its dreadful heat. "It's a misling day," he thought, "I reckon I don't deserve to rise, doin' that innocent country girl the way I done. What's to become of her now?"

Fort was back in the doorway. "Was two blocks down afore I missed 'em," he explained, picking up his blue sunglasses.

"Sun aint bright," Dove observed, "fact is it look like we might have a little weather."

Fort snapped his glasses on and left.

"Weak eyes," Dove concluded as the first drums of the rain began. Began, and paused, and began again to a slow and funerary beat.

Soon one mornin', death come creepin' in the room
Well, soon, one mornin', death come creepin' in the room

"I would most likely be married and well-fixed by now, keepin' my clothes in a sweetwood chest and taking the paper in the baseball season if I could but make words out of letters," Dove dressed himself in his daydream now wearing terribly thin, "with a girl who could read 'n write too. 'N little kids—I'd learn them how to do it my own self." Anything could happen to a man who could make words from letters.

The smells of coffee-and-banana dock, warehouse and orange-wharfed shore were borne into the room on the wash of a rain that had no shore at all. Beneath it banana boats were moving out to sea. Trailer and truck were bringing peanuts and grapefruit to town below it. Endless freights moved east, moved west, by plane, by boat, by passenger train. By highways dry and highways wet everyone but himself was getting to be a captain of something or other.

Everyone but one forgotten Linkhorn bogged down in a room where the blues came on and the old rain rapped this

door then, like somebody's grandmother seeking forever her
long lost first born.

And it seemed to Dove that the sun had gone down the
same morning that Terasina's arms had last locked in love
behind his neck, that her good thighs in love had last drawn
him down and her good mouth had last loved his.

"You were my onliest," he admitted at last, "but we only
got to B. These days when I don't get to see you are plumb
squandered like the rest of all them letters. My whole en-
duren life you were the only human to try to see could I live
up to the alphabet. Then I would of had a chance to rise like
others."

Luke came in on a skip and a grin and stood in the middle
of the room drenched, drunk, hatless, the laces out of his
shoes, the shirt out of his pants, the pants half-buttoned; the
picture of a contented man.

"Take off your jacket, Luke," Dove invited him, for the
jacket was clinging to the skin.

Luke slapped his thigh and did his little joy-jig. "It's all
in people's *minds*, boy—business is better than ever if you
only let yourself *think* it is." And shook himself like a duck.

"You're soaking," Dove pointed out.

Luke turned stern. "What the hell *is* the matter with you,
son? Opportunity is knocking the door down and you're
beefing about a little rain."

"You looked kind of damp is all I meant."

"Son, you been alone too much, brooding here by yourself. Smile, damn you, smile. Let a smile be your umbrella,
boy."

"Reckon I am a mite fevery at that," Dove conceded.
"Havin' no breakfastes 'n thinkin' of bygones give me the
morning-wearies."

Luke brought the flat of his palm down on the table so hard
he almost lost his balance. "Why didn't you *say* so, son?" He
began turning dirty plates over looking for something.

"Where's my check? I have a small check somewhere around here."

"Must be so small it's not to be seen with the naked eye. Fact is, the landlady came up but she didn't bring no check. She come up for to tell she wants three-thirty a week for the set of us."

Luke stared at Dove unseeing while his brain, like a pinball machine, toted an unexpected score. His face lit triumphantly. "Chargin' us for a place where the roof leaks so bad a man gets his bedclothes soaked in his sleep!" He leaped on Fort's bed, stabbed the ceiling with a jackknife and down he jumped again. Dove rushed the dishpan to the bed in time to catch the first rain drop.

The second drop preened its muscles a moment in preparation for the death-defying dive, then dropped dead center with a tiny *pingg*.

"Man would be a fool to pay rent for a room where he's like to catch his death by dew and damp," Luke sounded ready to sue. "Borrow me a half buck till Monday, Red?"

"Ef'n I had money I'd buy flour 'n shortenin' for us to have a pan of poor-do gravy," Dove told him.

"You like poor-do gravy, son?"

"Mister, I like *any* kind gravy: red-eye gravy, pink-eye gravy, black-eye gravy, speckledly gravy and streakedy gravy, piedy gravy, calico gravy, brindle gravy, spotted gravy, white gravy 'n grease gravy, 'n skewball gravy. I can eat lavin's 'n lashin's of gravy. Ef'n we had us flour 'n shortenin' now I'd pour a little coffee in the pan too. Yes sir, I *do* like gravy."

Luke slapped him cheerfully on the back. "Pack up your troubles in your old kit bag, son. *Smile*, darn you, *smile*. Laugh and the world laughs with you, Boy. *Look at this*—in six weeks we'll both be rich!"

He was dangling some sort of purple-feathered rubber in front of Dove's eyes. "Whatever *is* it, boy?"

"Look like a little kid's balloon but for the feather," Dove guessed and inspected the device more closely, "only it can't be no balloon because it's hollow and couldn't hold no air. I'm sure I never saw nothin' to compare, Luke."

Luke waved it like a purple flag. "It's a *contraceptive*, son! Combines protection with pleasure," he flicked the foolish-looking feather on its obscene tip, gave it a joyous swing and twist and flung away the certificates in his other hand. "No more knockin' ourselves out rappin' doors for two bits. A buck apiece boy! *One buck apiece!*"

Dove shook his head mournfully. "I wouldn't have the common brass to knock on no lady's door and show her one of them unnatural-lookin' things, Luke." Dove told him, "I'd go plumb through the floor if she knew what it was—and if she didn't know how could I sell it?"

Luke grew serious. "Distribution is *my* department, Red. But there's room for a good man in plain condom mechanics. Later you advance to fancy work."

"How much do plain condom mechanics make?" Dove asked with only mild interest.

"Twenty cents a dozen—that would be about four dollars a day if you just take your own time, Red. And Gross buys your meals besides."

"Who's Gross?"

"Gross"—Luke would have taken off his hat in reverence had he owned a hat—"Gross is the father of the O-Daddy."

"Never heard tell of that either," Dove admitted, "but four dollar a day is mighty good pay."

Luke scribbled an address on a slip of paper, then recalled something and tore it up. "Ask a policeman," he suggested—"but never mention 'Gross' to anything in uniform. Get it, boy?"

"I get it, Luke. And I'm mightily grateful."

"Let a smile be your umbrella, Son. We're finally around

that corner. Business was never better. Weep and you weep alone."

And left Dove to weep or laugh as he chose. "Always downhill and always merry," Dove thought as the little gin-head's demented skip-and-hop step was lost in the brainless titter of the rain. And felt as if he'd not be hearing that foolish step in any weather again.

He never learned how the little man had come upon the address he handed Dove that day.

The room began to fill with a gray-green river light, the very color of sleep. Raindrips pinged faster into the pan. Dove slept with his head in his hands.

To dream of a room where buckets stood about to catch raindrops and men and women encircled a bed to watch a woman and a man. Above the girl's head the gloom was smeared by light like a yellowing streak of shame and Dove saw she had one toenail painted green. And heard Fort's voice toll and toll from some chapel below sleep—"Hasteth! Hasteth!"

In a robe once red and now faded to rose Terasina came toward him wearing dark glasses and extending her arms to find her blind way.

Then one raindrop pinged into a bucket, another and another. It saddened Dove to hear them fall because each time one dropped he lost a friend and he could not leave till the last of all fell. "Boy! Wheah 's mah pot?" A big hand began shaking him.

Under the light the real Fort stood looking down.

"Who poked the holes in my ceiling, Son?"

Dove looked at the dishpan. Its bottom was barely covered.

"Luke thought if the rain leaked in we wouldn't be held for the rent."

"A mighty weak thought," Fort decided.

"I got a little inkle, Fort."

"You got a little *what?*"

"I got a little inkle Luke is fixin' to move on."

"I couldn't be more unconcerned, son. Made *my* rent this afternoon. Picked up six dollar in the rain 'n could of made eight with a mite of help."

"What line of work *you* followin' now, Fort?"

Fort stood up and extended his right arm. Dove reached to shake it but Fort wouldn't shake. "Can't you see my sad condition?" he asked softly.

Dove studied him carefully. "Your eyes look shut sort of," he decided.

"Why, then *lead* me, goodbuddy," Fort asked without opening a lid. "*Lead* me."

Dove rose dutifully and led the big man once about the room.

"Now that's all there is to it," Fort took off his glasses and opened his eyes. "Now wasn't that *easy?*"

"We had a blind Indian home name of Chicken-Eye Riley," Dove recalled, "Wore a tuckin'-comb. But he never went around with his eyes shut. Didn't have to. He'd been gouged."

"Indians don't have to fake it," Fort revealed resentfully, "all you got to be to get sent to a reservation these days is be some damned kind of Indian. The government'll be given out pensions for bein' Hebrew next. A white man don't stand a chance no more if he's poor." Fort suddenly left off complaining and used his executive-type voice—"You understand this is merely a temporary expedient until we get up a stake to get us into the oil business, goodbuddy?"

"I don't follow you, Fort."

"In Cameron County between Harlingen and Rio Hondo. Half a day's hike from your own hometown. All we need to get it is to give the Sinclair man twenty dollar for a tankful of gas. He'll furnish us cots and blankets out of his own attic. One of us takes care of the pump and the other buys up produce from the Mex farmers round about and wholesales it in

the valley stores. The Sinclair man don't have to know about
the produce. So long as one of us is at the pumps when he
calls is all that matters. You dig as good as you sell coffee to
Negras, Red?"

Dove rolled up his eyes like a doll's. "I can dig real good
for I'm bedcord strong—what do I have to dig?"

"Gas tanks, son—one on each side of the station! You dig
one and I dig the other!"

"To be part owner of a gas station," Dove offered dreamily, "I'd start to work before good day. I'll dig 'em *both*
sides."

"There's a deal, goodbuddy."

"When do we start, Fort?"

"Soon as you lead me around a couple days. Then I'll lead
you."

"What do I do when the policeman comes up 'n sees I'm
not really blind?"

"Never said you was," Fort explained, "all your sign says
is 'Help Me.' "

"Don't hardly seem fair after we whupped them so bad,"
it struck Dove.

"Whupped policemen?"

"No. Indians."

"Stop worrying about Indians. What you got to realize
is the blind eye don't reflect the light but yours do. *That's*
why you got to keep them shut. If you're really blind you
can go around with them open, people take one look and
slip you a buck or two. Over and above that you get a state
pension."

"I do?"

"Not you. *Really* blind people."

"So do Indians. That's why I figure to be a blind Indian
must be the best deal a person could have. Still, this fellow
back home didn't have it none too good. In fact he spent all
his weekends in jail."

"They're strong for that firewater, or so I've heard," Fort agreed impatiently.

"Weren't firewater. It was a sow Riley was so strong for. He'd find his way to her guided solely by the sense of smell and his wife would come home and find him missing. She'd go down to the sty and put the flashlight on and there they'd be. That woman got so jealous of that beast she had Riley locked up every Friday night."

"I allow there was hell to pay in the pigsty when Riley got loose Monday morning," Fort conceded.

"He never bothered her weekdays," Dove reported, "just when his wife weren't well. He spent day after day in the domino parlor and seldom lost. He could tell every piece by running his fingers over it once."

Fort sighed.

"Either that or he couldn't find her during the week. As I say, he was guided entirely by a sense of smell."

Fort got him back on the main highway, "Don't you go *gawking*. Just look straight ahead and keep saying 'Who is it? Who is it? Who's there? Who is it?' "

"Who's there? Who is it?"

"That's right. You're learning."

"Who's there? Who is it?"

"You can open them now. I'm going to let you lead me until you get the hang of the thing," Fort promised. "Sunday morning in front of a Catholic church is worth from ten to fifteen dollars."

"That leak'll be wide by morning if this rain keeps up," Dove judged. And blinked up to where the next drop clung, lost its grip and plunged, to become one with the eternal waters.

"How would you like to eat at the best restaurant in town tonight, Tex? Set down at a white tablecloth right amongst the people who got this thing whipped and tell a waiter what to bring you?"

"Thank you kindly all the same, but I lack the means to return the favor."

"Tell you what, Tex," Fort persisted, "you go on the blink with me and I give you my word of honor here and now, the day we get a stake we throw away the glasses. Think it over, son."

Dove thought it over as long as it took for two more drops to ping into the dishpan.

"My stated *in*tent is to rise in the world," he decided at last, "but playing blind man on Canal Street just don't seem the proper way. In fact I'd rather see my box a-comin' than to be led by another as though I were helpless, when all the while I can just about see through that wall."

"Opportunity has knocked," Fort announced like an undertaker. "Opportunity is now going through that door. Opportunity aint coming back."

And left like a man who would search all day, and half the night if need be, for the right flavor of chocolate ice.

To leave Dove alone to tote up the chances a single day had offered.

"I could of took a position as a leader of the blind but I turned it down. That's one. I could be a plain condom mechanic with a chance to do fancy work should I qualify. That's two and I aint yet turned down the second. The way things are coming my way today it must be hard times are over."

He went to the window to see the city. There were lights in the haze but no sun was out. He was about to turn away from the window when he caught a brief glimpse of a sun he had never seen before. It was hiding behind the corner of an eave like a chicken thief at dusk. Dove stood quietly to see what its next move would be, thinking itself unseen. Sure enough, it edged softly off, showed a bit more of itself—a sneak thief sun, a sun with a hooded look. A sun of the alley stalls ready to do anything for a fiver.

Dove didn't want to see what a sun like that was up to. He

opened his Bull Durham sack and sure enough, folded neatly quartered so as to let him read the "100" without unfolding it, Finnerty's c-note still waited to be spent.

"As long as I done it, it was just as well I got paid," he philosophized his guilt away.

Out in the lake-palmed suburbs, far from the dong and the glare, in a house that had once been human, Dove climbed a soundless stair.

The stilly stair to O-Daddyland in a pale hygienic glow. Feeling some sign he could not read must say ZONE OF QUIET. For the weather in the streets, and the seasons there, are no more permitted in O-Daddyland than in a surgeon's washroom. Rainwinds washing children's voices have nothing to do with O-Daddies. Step up in an airless quarantine, go down a passionless hall. Stand before a door without knocker or bell.

Till an anesthetic odor, as of gas or seeping ether, trails from below; as though abortions might be performed here.

Stranger on a strange-lit stair, you have come to a strange frontier.

The frontier of a principality whose only law is Rhino Gross and Gross's many moods. A totalitarian state whose single industry is a curious craft in Goodrich rubber, worked out in forms sufficiently fanciful. Rhino Gross is his state's sole industrial designer and Gross is a fanciful man. Indeed, abortions are aborted here.

(At night in the deep and dead time, old Gross hears again the soft *scraaap* of his curette against the uterus wall in a room that holds no other sound. *Scraaap scraaap scraaap.*)

Now the daylight man, ex-physician, ex-abortionist, ex-quack, ex-con, ex-man, ex-everything, enfolded and armored by layer across layer of swart encrusted fat, clasping his distended gut to keep it from slipping down over his rusted truss, is an aging animal come to the jungle's rim whose hearing is excellent but whose sight is waterish, ready to turn at a tiny twig's crack and lumber back to his forest's protecting gloom. Yet stands one moment snout upturned and quivering, to sniff the dangerous air: now he is wondering whether it would be perfectly safe to try a little mock-charge on whoever that was across the room.

Dove caught a good strong whiff of the sniffer at the jungle's rim without knowing that what he whiffed was actually burning rubber. When you work with guano you live with guano till you smell of guano. Gross's hide was impregnated with it clear down to his money that stank of it.

(Who else but a disbarred gynecologist could have devised that technicolor fantasy so long before technicolor, of liverish yellow dipped at its obscene head in firehouse red and tipped by a delicate rainbow silken as baby's first down? An improvement in style, function and line worthy of its proud name *O-Daddy, The Condom of Tomorrow.*)

"First you learn your craft," Gross told Dove. "How else do I tell what you're worth?" Then deciding to show Whoever-It-Was that he really was a furious charger at heart, lowered his snout and trumpeted terribly—"*Welma! Welma!*"

A swift light step and there materialized a woman whose life had been consumed. She may have been thirty-five or sixty but wasn't quite through burning yet. She was wearing a rubber apron over a gum-colored dress and pigtails bound by a big pink bow that bounced as if the very hair were rubberized. Apparently her sight wasn't much better than Gross's, for she stood dangling one glove, specs in hand, looking about for some way to clean them of particles of reddish dust. At length she stooped, brought up a corner of her slip far enough to serve as a lens-cleaner.

"Look the bow ribbon!" Gross squeaked with mocking glee—"Welma the wulcanized *woo*min! Aint a wife! Aint a mother!"—his voice turned stern with shame for her—"What are you? You think a bow ribbon makes a *woo*min?"

The woman snapped her specs on and beamed upon Dove through them as benignly as if Rhino's derision had been praise. "He'll mouse on me and he'll mouse on you," she explained without heat. "He's a forty-faced pigeon straight from Rat Row, quack from head to toe. Rather steal from his mother than ride a passenger train and I give him eighty percent the best of it at that. Now if you want to see how we get these things out come back here and I'll show you how."

The kitchen, so commodious it might once have served as a slave quarter, was now largely given over to half a dozen small molds of individualized design. About the molds stood cans of liquid rubber, open paint-tins and brushes soaking in solutions. Above a wide white oven a line of O-Daddies hung like sausages to dry.

This was also the place where *Cupid's Arrows* came warm off the forge and *Ticklish Tessies* lounged about. The craze in *Laughing Maggies* had almost died but *Ding-Dong Darlings* had a promising future. *Happy Hannahs* roomed here; *Barney Googles* were having their noses pinched by clothes-pins on a wire line. Here Gross moved *Love's Fancies* by the gross; and a reddish dust lay over everything. For the O-Daddy was not the only creation of the hand and heart and brain of this dishonored genius. It was only his masterpiece.

Yet through the air made thick by gum, by paint, by turpentine, Dove smelled something better than any of these— something was doing inside that oven for sure. When Velma peered in he caught a glimpse of a chicken roasting on a bed of yams.

"Don't mind Gross," she reassured him, "all it means when he hollers is he's scared. I'm sure I don't know what he's scared of because there's nobody here but me. The creature is ill of bad conscience and don't have long to go."

"I didn't pay him particular heed," Dove told her, "but your ribbon bow strikes me as mighty purty, m'am."

"Thank you, son." She seemed genuinely flattered. "Now let me show you how to turn out a condom you can trust."

Painting a skin with a film of liquid gum, she nodded her head to indicate that Gross was listening at the kitchen door and deliberately spoke loudly enough for the old man to overhear. "He'll give it out that his only trouble is that Broomface wants a word with him, but that aint his real worry. He's a man with a double-W on his forehead and Broomface is the least of it. Those other parties who would like a word with him won't bother to give warning."

Gross's big head came through the door: "Old-time shoplifter stealing all her life!" he announced like a station caller. "Wanted by everyone but the church! One hand over her heart and the other in your pocket!" He slammed the door before she could insult him in turn.

Velma the Vulcanized Woman, Dove saw, retained a faint copperish tint to her ash-blond hair and her face bore traces of Saxon beauty. She was humanized as well as vulcanized, he perceived.

"Every bare window in this town reminds me of Arkansas," she admitted to Dove. "I might as well be in jails as the way I am."

Sitting at the window she looked out upon a world of rogues with innocence and wonder, and both her cheekbones smashed. Her ash-blond bangs, streaked broadly now with gray, belied the fact that there wasn't much on the books Velma hadn't tried and a few deals she'd thought up by herself.

Goin' to town Mama, what'll I bring you back?
she invited herself, and answered—

Just a great big bag of candy and a J. C. Stetson hat
She came of a long line of country thieves that had grown shrewd in the mountains. Velma had grown yet shrewder in town. And at last, too shrewd to trust on the common high-

way, had become the shrewdest inmate at the Women's Reformatory at Aldington. Not yet twenty when she'd been first sent up, she had immediately distinguished herself by saying to a colored matron—"Hold this for me"—and had shoved a tableknife with a friction-taped handle into the woman's abdomen.

"Will you spread a clean cloth for dinner?" she asked Dove, "You'll find one in that bureau."

Velma spread the clean cloth with Southern variety—okra, clobber, cornbread, yams, rice, chicken, onion gravy and sweet potato pie.

But Dove had never seen anyone eat like Gross. Velma didn't even bother to lay a knife, fork and spoon for him. He went at everything with forefinger and thumb, being particularly careful, every time he dropped a fried egg, to get every bit of it on his pants.

"Mighty fine chicken, m'am," Dove congratulated her. The chicken was fine, the yams were dandy, the gravy was great and the clobber was super. Unluckily the small reddish dust had gotten into the food as into everything, so it all came to a single dish: rubber. Gross liked the taste of rubber. When you work with rubber you not only eat rubber, but your very dreams arrive in rubberized folds. Within twenty-four hours Dove looked and smelled like Velma the Vulcanized Woman herself. Those weren't dead ants between his toes but only particles fallen from the Flap-Happy mold that had worked their way down his socks.

They poured the rubber and heated the glue, forged the forms and painted the skins, glued the feathers and hung the O-Daddies and sorted the seconds and burned the culls and filled the orders; and never went dancing down below.

Velma taught Dove never to put a Cupid's Arrow on a King Tut rack nor to let an O-Daddy wander among the Happy Hannahs. When the sun beat steadily they risked hanging a line to dry against an outside wall; when it rained or was overcast the big room was full of skins hanging in rainbowed rows above the dark gas range's flame.

In the evening the three outcasts sat in the dark of their old strange house, hearing human voices rise and fall. There was an amusement park at the end of the wide-palmed street, letting laughter come to them from a place where human life was lived out on roller-coasters; while they endured the rubberish dark of O-Daddyland like three ghosts yet to be born.

"Son," Gross always began his nightly lecture with the same phrase, "Son, not all the O-Daddies are hanging on a line. There's one sitting right here in this rocker. Would you mind either turning the lamp down a bit or else not look directly at me? I have a little aversion to being examined. Thank you." Dove turned a bit to one side.

"Son, you look to me like a man of two great weaknesses, either one of which may ruin you. Women and whiskey, in that order. Take my advice, if you don't want to wind up being one more Barney Google like me. First thing you ought to do is throw away that shirt. Never wear light colors. They catch the sun. Blue is best—mailman blue. The whole secret of not ending up an O-Daddy on a line is to look as much like a mailman as possible—who knows what the mailman *looks* like? Who'd recognize him if he changed suits? Get a cap with a peak that shadows the eyes. Wear glasses that throw back the light. Grow a mustache but don't go into bars. If you must drink, lock the door and drink by yourself. Conviviality leads to fist-fighting, fist-fighting leads to rage. Look out for rage, son. People never forget a man they've seen in a rage.

"My own appearance was always such that I didn't have to lose my temper to catch attention. I always fitted into the bystander's memory, so that five minutes after a rumble, my description, complete to hat-size, would be at headquarters.

"Watch out for the inclination to trust, particularly toward

women. It leads to *giving*. Look out for that one, it's the
worst of a bad lot.

"Watch out for flowers, watch out for trust, watch out for
women, watch out for giving. In short, don't give flowers to
a woman you trust."

"He'll come to the point in time. Just have patience,"
Velma assured Dove.

"No woman since the world began," the old man kept trying to say what he meant, "ever accepted a flower as no more
than a token of affection. Does she seem pleased at a gift so
humble? 'What, a *daisy* for *me?*' Why shouldn't she be
pleased? it's a down payment on your hand, your heart and
your brain and she knows that even though you don't. If you
owe her a daisy you owe a box of candy, and how long do
you think you're going to get by just on candy and flowers?
Where's the perfume? Progress, that's what women want in a
man. What is more natural than the step from perfume to
wristwatch—*now* let's see how long you can keep from men-
tioning engagement rings. Your very silence betrays that
you're considering marriage and are only trying to get up the
courage to ask. Son, you're good as done. You're in hock to
a house, a car, children, maid—you give up your freedom and
there still hasn't been a word said about what does *she* owe
you?

"Why, that goes without saying—she's giving you her vir-
ginal white body, isn't she? Don't throw it up to her that
you're giving her your little pink body, that's cad's work—
no, son, you'll never get your daisy back. But you'll find that
appeasing that little white body is a job like any job except
that you don't get three weeks off with pay. If you try, your
friends will fill in for you. Why do you think they pay me
two dollars for a contraceptive that tickles if it isn't because
they're afraid that the cat is starting to slip?

" 'Look for the woman' they tell us—but I take it one step
farther than that. 'Look at them sperms' is what *I* advise. Son,

did you know that under a microscope every sperm looks exactly like his old man when the old man has a jag on? There he is, the old man all over again, with no particular place to go or if he has, he's forgotten it. Just staggering from pole to pole, up one street and down the next, can hardly tell one door from the next, just hoping somebody he knows will let him in. Really not doing anybody any harm. All of a sudden a lady sperm—looks exactly like the old lady opens a door off the alley 'n whispers—'*in here, Jack.*' Pulls him in and latches it. Now you know where all our troubles start?

"Look out for love, look out for trust, look out for *giving*. Look out for wine, look out for daisies and people who laugh readily. Be especially wary of friendship, Son, it can only lead to trouble. And it isn't your enemies who'll get you deepest into the soup, it's your friends.

"You might keep that in mind if you're ever called upon to point the finger of accusation and say 'that's the very man.' Remember that you have to be *absolutely certain*, son. If you have the *leastest leastest* doubt it's your *highest highest* duty to say you're not *absolutely absolutely* sure. Do you realize that if you sent a man to prison on a wrong identification you're a criminal yourself, little better than a hardened murderer?"

"He's cutting in a little closer now," Velma observed.

"Why," for once Gross spoke directly to her, "doesn't an old man have the right to die in his own bed?"

The vulcanized woman made no reply. Her chair was vacant. She had tiptoed out just to make the old man sweat in anxiety—"Where'd she go? How long she been gone? Why didn't you speak up?"

"I think she's in the bedroom, mister," Dove told him, and waited dutifully for the rest of the speech while Gross went to listen at the bedroom door. Satisfied that she hadn't yet crossed the frontier, he returned to his rocking chair; but had no more to say that evening.

(In the deep dark and dead time the old man hears the soft scr*aaap* scr*aaap* and feels the sudden sinking through the uterus wall and the blood running over his hand again. The uterus wall that, once pierced, bleeds till no blood remains. O, Old Gross remembers a thing or two in the deep dark and dead time.)

Gross lived in an unendurable twilight land, a land of in between, with a woman whom he had married in order to make her his prisoner. Now the prisoner was the jailer, he the captive. Velma not only had enough on him to send him to the pen for keeps, but also those inside-the-walls connections that Gross feared more than the uniformed law. He knew that she could have him disposed of without the bother of having him carried through federal gates. In any one day she had only to pick up a telephone and he wouldn't see his rocking chair that night.

Dove's function, he soon saw, was simply to perform errands that Velma would otherwise have had to do. The only ease the old man knew was when she was at work right under his nose. Whatever he had coming, it seemed, he wanted to see it come.

Yet Gross went on little errands of his own that didn't bother Velma at all. Every morning she wrapped a small package in gift paper, tied it with colored string, put it under the old man's arm and sent him off with it. He would be back in less than an hour without the package. It was some days before Dove saw that all the paper contained was garbage.

"He leaves it on a street car or a newsstand for someone to find, thinking they've found something of value and hurry home to undo it, and there it is. What else can an old man do for fun?"

It seemed to Dove there must be *something* else even for an old man.

How she had found him out, here in the lake-palmed suburb where the rise and dying fall of a roller coaster and bonfires on the beach of Lake Pontchartrain made summer sweet, Gross didn't want to know. He had married her in a last despairing hope of winning her loyalty legally.

The woman had wanted a home of her own all her life. She knew a good thing when she found it. Marriage had turned out to be no more than a down payment from Gross. Now she had a legal grip on everything he owned and didn't have to bother arguing with him except to indulge him.

It was his table manners she found most difficult to indulge.

"I swear I never before did see a man dip oyster crackers in coffee," she commented across the table to Dove.

Yet Gross went on dipping placidly. The whole front of his shirt was greased with droppings from his fingers.

"It could be they never seen a oyster cracker in Arkansas," he goaded her a bit by tipping the coffee into the saucer so that most of it spilled onto the cloth. "What was it you said you got run out of Arkansas for? I always forget."

"The point isn't who got run out," Velma corrected him, "the point is who they wouldn't let in. I swear I never before did see a man dip oyster crackers in coffee."

"Talk to my ass," Gross told her, "my head is hard."

She went back to the sink to finish washing the dishes that Dove was drying, and Dove saw her dab furtively at her eyes. "I've taken all the insults I'm going to off that cliff-ape," she warned Gross aloud, "it's more than natural flesh can bear."

Dove patted her gently. "He don't mean harm, ma'am. It's his way of showing affection is all."

Velma would have none of such affection. "That man would be rode out of town on a rail where I come from."

"Look!" the old man commanded her triumphantly from across the kitchen, "Look! I'm *sopping up!*"

Velma was a kind of cross between a gadfly and a ferret,
but like many people streaked by violence, usually maintained
a deep serenity. In which she sang not unpleasantly,

It all seems wrong somehow
That you're nobody's baby now

and went serenely on molding skins and painting them, clamp-
ing, drying, sorting, glueing, counting, counting days till the
old man died. For Dove sensed she preferred that he die in
his bed rather than by violence.

She would not give the old man the peace that such knowledge would have afforded him. Perhaps she feared that, once
allowed to relax, he might just live on and on. After all, she
had had a hard enough time and didn't have too far to go herself. She could no longer afford pity.

So all night long the old man was up and down in his
flannel nightshirt, hiding his money in one place or another.
He would unscrew the top of a bedpost, drop a couple twenties down the hollow of it, then forget to screw the top-piece
down. He had as many stashes as a squirrel in October and
one of his favorites was the water box above the old-fashioned
plumbing. He would bind a bankroll into a condom, fasten
it tightly and tie it to the waterworks. But when he heard it
flushing, and Velma would issue forth, he would race in there
to stand on the seat to see if she had found him out. Thus giving himself completely away.

Actually she had found him out in everything so thor-
oughly she had no need of following him around. When she
needed money she picked his pocket, that was all there was
to it. If the pocket was bare she went to his bookshelf and
leafed through a few volumes until a bill or two floated out.
The old man had no way of banking without betraying his
whereabouts.

Season of heat when skins dry fast below the copper blaze
of noon or flashflood spring when pipes back up and colored

clothespins clamp the skins in rainbowed rows above the dark
gas-range's flames, they pour the rubber and heat the glue,
clean the molds and forge the forms and never go dancing
down below.

"When you start hitting toward sixty," Gross complained,
"you feel some days like you want to take a cab to the graveyard and wait for your maker beside your stone. Yet when
you've not had an hour's true contentment out of all those
sixty years, you don't want to lay down till you've had your
hour. You want something for all your pain."

"Maybe if you'd give more to others, like our Lord said
to do," Velma reminded him, "you'd of got more. Maybe if
you'd change your ways you'd still have your hour."

"If that advice came from anyone else I might heed it,"
Gross admitted. "Coming from you it makes no sense. How
do I change old bones for new? It wasn't give to me to live
so I could give to others. With me it was a matter of take
or die."

"You didn't have to try to take it *all* to keep from dying,"
Velma pointed out.

"I took all I could, that's true," Gross admitted, "now you
take all from me. Here." He crooked his little finger toward
her. "Pull."

One night Dove woke to hear the old man shouting, "Old-
time shoplifter! Stealing all her life!" He was at the bathroom
door in his nightshirt and pounding the wood with both fists.
"Give me a hand, boy! We got her trapped in the act!" Between his shouts the plumbing kept flushing—the moment
the waters had rushed once and risen, down they rushed like
a thundering falls again. A light shown from under the door.
It sounded like Velma might be drowning in the waterworks.

But when they yanked the door open, the place was empty.
How she had contrived to start the fixture flushing automatically Dove never discovered. Yet there she lay, feigning sleep

in her own virgin-white bed all the while, her country-grocer
shoes at the foot of it and her cotton stockings hung neatly
over a chair.

Dove got the plumbing quieted first, then quieted the old
man. When he heard him fall back into a restless sleep he rose
softly and dressed. He had had enough of rubber.

He stood at the old man's bedside until he was sure it was
safe, then carefully unscrewed one of the bedposts. He had
the top of it in his hand when he heard Velma's voice so close
behind him he stiffened right where he stood.

"That one is empty, son," he heard her say, "look under
the hallway rug."

From under the hall rug he pulled out a flattened parcel
of bills and a minute later was losing himself in the shadows
of that wide-palmed street.

And when he thought, later, of that strange-lit stair and
the rubberish nights and days he had spent there he remembered it like a dream dreamt by somebody else.

Once he went back, out of curiosity, but could no longer
find it. And began to wonder whether there ever really had
been a place where O-Daddies hung on a wire line above a
low-burning flame.

And a reddish dust hung over everything.

That was no town for the aged or the aging. There was
love behind the curtains and love behind the doors. Love in
the squares and circles and love along the curbs.

Particularly along those curbs west of the Southern Railway Station. Where every window framed some love bird
lamed in flight. Where every screen door was a cage. What
had been Storyville was now an aviary.

"Come on in, daddy, we don't bite," they invited the stroll-
ing *voyeur*, or pretended to vie with one another as he passed
on. "I'll take *him*."

From wheatland and tenement, hotel and harbor, girls and

women of a hundred feathers had come to nest both sides of
South Basin. Girls downy as chicks who have just lost their
mammas and chorus-line dolls who had long lost their down.
Girls who came scolding like winter jays, ruffing their tail
feathers and ready for battle. But some like little wrens of
summer, seeking hollows to hide in forever.

At evening they watched the stricken street from their
windows like sea-birds seeing a sunless sea darken and recede.

"Daddy, if you don't come 'n get me I'll just throw myself
away!"

"Daddy, come in, we'll have great fun"—but it wasn't great
fun for a woman accustomed to Northern comforts to wake
up on Perdido Street with the kerosene lamp burned out in
the night, feeling drained and doomed in a stall whose floor
looked as if customers might start coming up through the
planks. The bedbugs that clung in grape-like clusters to the
springs, the cracked enamel basin, the old-fashioned bureau,
the greasy portiere that served as a door; the drawling in the
hallway and the mosquitoes wanting out, all agreed—"Baby,
you've been had. Baby, you've been had."

Droning all night long.

You've been had, you've been paid for, you've been rented
by the minute. Now anything goes no matter how wild so
long as it keeps off the Storyville Blues. It was cocaine, it
was whiskey—who wouldn't get the blues? It was brawling
in the alleys, it was falling on the floor. It was everything to
give and not a thing to lose. It was men, it was gin, it was
all night long. It was have a ball and spend it all—"Daddy,
buy me one more drink and do just what you want with me."
That was what they called fun on old Perdido Street.

Who wouldn't get the blues?

Big-town girls found the anything-goes life of the cribs
tougher going than the girls from orchards and barns. Farm
girls could come on rough as cobs. But the coaltown and
cotton-mill kids took to it easiest of all. Hard times didn't

mean a thing to them—they had never known another kind.
They weren't afraid of law, jail or even, seemingly, of infec-
tion. The anthractite had entered their hearts.

Every time an operator padlocked a mine or a mill in West
Virginia, Alabama, Kentucky, Pennsylvania or Southern Illinois, a fresh flock of chicks would hit town and start turning
tricks for the price of a poor-boy sandwich and a bottle of
Dr. Pepper's.

They were thin, big-boned girls, and when they fought
they didn't go for the air or eyes. They went for belly or jaw,
with fists. They fought like men. Out-fought, out-drank and
out-hollered the farm and city chicks. To name only a few
things they did with the greater will.

"Give us your money—you're drunk," with last night's gin
still crippling their tongues they taunted the teetotaling boys
in tortoise shell specs from Loyola and Tulane. Boys working
on sociological theses who'd been told there was fun down
on Perdido Street.

"Professor! Let me talk to you! Did you come down for
what I think you come? You just came to *look?* Girls! Specs
came just to *look!* Okay Professor—*look* at what brought you
here! Same thing that'll take you away!"—the women's
shrieks would deride the looking-man down the street and
into the winding avenues of all his *voyeur's* dreams: curious
streets where he walked as the last of earth's bachelors, hearing window-women snicker as he passed. In those dreams it
was always the women's turn to stare.

Hard lines, hard times, when soft girls grew hard and hard
girls grew soft. Wise hands at the trade would invite with a
whisper, "Daddy, you name it, I'm on my last legs." For men
sometimes came down there looking for someone to push over
the brink or someone to save—it was all the same. Play Christ
or play devil but pay your damned dollar. For two you could
play both. For the lion that roars loudest at the bleat of the

sheep there was lots of fun on Perdido Street. The sibilant hiss from the narrow dark was for a specialized clientele.

Not Yet Twenties bold or humble. Lost or captured, luck-less or loose. The dark and the fair from everywhere who would have been safely married in Minneapolis or Seattle, Kennebunkport or San Francisco had Old Guard economics not demanded more Coca Cola love and less housekeeping.

Minnesota girls with hair heaped like ripe wheat: a north-ern sun shone yet in hair like that. In the eyes of the girls from San Francisco big slow soundless ocean fogs rolled to their final shore.

Behind the eyes of the Oregon girls it was raining again in Portland. Somehow it was always raining behind the eyes of Oregon girls.

Girls with western turnings in their talk and girls with the midland twanging. Who wore their hair long like Anna Q. Nillson or braided like Ann Harding's. Bobbed or banged or flowing to the shoulders, rose-red girls or sallow, they wore their hair in all the styles, they softened their mouths in all the wiles that good girls did.

Sick or silly, maimed or strayed, fresh-fallen leaf or sear, the Storyville hustler chattered as cheerfully about husbands and wives, washday and landlords, lost chances and chances left as the good girls did. And kept souvenirs of their luckier hours, lockets and albums, letters and rings, exactly as good girls did. If she had married a ponce now doing a stretch, the girls who had married legitimate men felt a twist of envy toward her—but isn't that what good girls often did?

She borrowed from one boy friend to give to another, be-trayed those who had helped her in order to do a stranger a gratuitous favor, let some pander debauch her as though she were something that ran on all fours and all the while had some mark completely convinced that she wouldn't go to bed with a man to whom she wasn't legally wed though he hung

jellybeans on pineapple trees. Now wasn't that just how good
girls occasionally did?

Good girls and bad carried on so much alike, in the cheery
old summer of 1931, a Yankee might well have been deceived.

The Southern boy was a bit harder to fool. The moment he
saw a girl behind a door screen naked to her navel and lifting
her breasts, he sensed something was up. When she did a slow
spread-legged grind and threw in a blinding bump for good
measure, he suspected it wasn't free. When she opened the door
and said, "Step in, I don't bite," he went in, of course, out of
simple courtesy. But he wasn't fooled: she was after his
money, that was all. No, it wasn't easy to fool a Southern boy
any summer.

When the white rain ran with the red-lit rain and Perdido
Street doors stood wide. Where here and there, between dance
hall and dive, some nightingale stood with the weight of her
shame so fresh upon her that she couldn't as yet invite someone even though she hadn't that day bitten food.

(Nobody knew where these silent girls came from. Nor
whether their eyes, searching inward, saw a disheveled and
bloodstained bed or a new cash register. Whether they were
eaten alive by regret as they stood or merely counted in indifference to everything: one dollar, two dollars, three and four,
when I get eight I'll get me a dress of tropical pink. When I
get twenty-two I'll get pink slippers too.)

Birds of a hundred varied feathers, hooters, hissers, howlers,
quackers—it was a new kind of zoo wherein the captured
foraged for themselves.

Some were feebs and some were loonies, some were tattoed
girls. There were peep shows and side shows, fat girls and
gawks and a dwarf who called herself the Princess.

There weren't enough keepers to handle the stock. Panders
who had never had more than two women tapping, found
themselves without enough windows to go around. Five or six

all yammering at once for her turn at door or pane, vying
with one another to be top broad for daddy.

It was a daddy's market, but daddy had to take care all the
same.

Oliver Finnerty, ex-exercise boy and currently proprietor
of six peepholes on the second floor of Spider-Boy Court,
once having incurred a debt of ninety days to the parish jail,
had turned over a girl to a friend in the trade for safekeeping.
Oliver had expended a great deal of time and thought on this
child, for he'd seen her promise early. He had told her, "Baby
you go with this man, and when he says, 'Walk pretty,' you
walk pretty all the way." And to the friend: "Don't whip her
where it'll leave her marked, or she'll use it as an excuse for
laying off work. Now good luck and God bless the both of
you."

Ninety days later, his debt paid in full, Finnerty had returned to reclaim his property only to find her wearing a long
black dress and a pince-nez, and his colleague out digging
ditches. Something had gone wrong. Finnerty had had to
spend that whole day talking the girl back into her lounging
pajamas. By the time the friend returned from work, a black
lunch bucket under his arm, Finnerty's patience had been
exhausted.

"Just look what you *done* to his girl," he berated the Benedict Arnold of Panderdom. "You took a nice sweet kid and
twisted her all up. You undone all my good work." Then he
raised the girl's hair off her neck and began cracking her
patiently, without hatred or heat, but mechanically, with contentment in a job he was the right man for. And like a good
little whore she stood and took it, for she knew very well she
had it coming. And that, once done, she had a chance for full
pardon.

But Benedict Arnold would never be pardoned: when this
sort of thing happened it wasn't the girl's fault. Now he could
only sit mute and miserable, knowing he'd never be allowed

to drink among honest pimps again. But would instead drink
in crumb-dump taverns where working men play dominoes
for nickels and envy those who get to work on Saturday too.
Oh, if only Oliver would give him one more chance!

Oliver wouldn't violate his principles. When the whipping
was done, the pince-nez crushed and the long black dress in
the garbage can, he turned to his ex-colleague and finished
him crisply. "*You*. Pick up your lunch bucket and get back in
your ditch."

Dishonored, disbarred, a disgrace to right-thinking pro-
curors, the Man-Who-Would-Be-A-Pander shuffled wearily,
without a word of goodbye, out onto a street that other lunch
buckets had laid long ago.

And was never seen in respectable circles again.

Finnerty, who looked like one of those little Australian
foxes with ears half the length of its body, claimed to be five
foot but had to be wearing his cowboy boots to make good
the boast.

"Aching Chopper's giving me trouble again," he would
complain of the girl who had been with him longest, the moon-
faced Chicago blonde. "I know she been faithful as a broad
can be but her teeth give me trouble. It's a new plate now
near every month. I'm supporting half the dentists in town."

"If you'd stop busting her in the mouth you wouldn't have
to support that many," the mulatto woman once called Lucille
suggested.

Oliver owned five women, a single-motored plane and a
captive mouse. He claimed to be the first pander in the entire
South to transport women by plane. A claim making every
single one of the five proud of their five-foot daddy.

He'd crowd all five into the single motor, deposit one on
the outskirts of Baton Rouge, two near Hammond (where a
fast track was operating at the time) and take the other two
to Gulfport. To the women he pretended that his motive was

to save time, but to his brothel brothers he readily admitted that the idea was really to save listening to all that yakking— "I can't bear to be with one broad a whole half day, not to mention five."

He had the identical weakness, as a pilot, that he had had as an apprentice jockey. He'd get so high on Panama pot that he couldn't make up his mind. On a horse he had never known whether to go for the whip or tighten rein so that sometimes he had done both at once. In a plane, with five silly women high as himself and every one giving him orders, he wouldn't be able to decide whether to land on roadway or grass. The road burned up the plane's tires so badly it would mean a new set—but the risk of flipping over on the grass, inviting loss of his working principal, was even greater.

The second the women saw that Daddy was in the switches, they fought to be first to help. One would decide for the roadway and grab for the stick simply to have her own way. But one of more economical habits, wishing to say later she had saved him a whole set of tires, would scream right in his ear, "Idiot! On the *grass!* The *grass!*" At the very last possible second he would holler, "I can't please everybody," fling out both fists and make earth in a shrieking, careening lurch like a chute-the-chutes hitting water. Road or grass, the women loved it. It was a kind of thrill not another pimp living could provide. Small wonder that to say "Finnerty swings her" afforded a girl real distinction among the women of Perdido Street.

The mouse was one that had barely gotten away from Hallie's lame brindle cat. The cat, that belonged to one woman who would have nothing to do with Finnerty, had been going on three legs so long that it no longer killed, it crippled. After she had crippled it, the mouse had dragged itself into a corner behind the juke. Finnerty had fished it out and given it a home in a little box with a cellophane window that had once held face powder. When he had to induct a new girl, or

to straighten up an old one growing recalcitrant, he took her
to watch the mouse. His own face would be expressionless as
he and the girl saw it trying for freedom in spite of all pain.
He said nothing while it hauled its wrecked hindquarters
around and around. Just as it seemed the animal had made
good its escape at last, he would plop it back in its box and
say to the girl, "When you get as much sense as this mouse
we'll get along better, little baby," and close the box. It was
a warning that she ought to try to do better by her little
daddy, lest he had to put his mittens on.

"Daddy dear," his Chicago blonde once complained, "take
me to the hospital, I got to get a little something or other took
out." And leaned her head on her hands.

"I can't afford to be carting you in and out of operating
rooms twice a month," her pander told her, "every time you
go you're out of action for days. One more visit and by God
you get *everything* took out. Make up your mind to *that*,
Aching Choppers—I said *everything*. This piddling around
with part of a gut at a time disgusts me."

"But Little Daddy, why get *disgusted?*" the girl wanted to
know," if you went to a doctor about a little prostate trouble,
say, you wouldn't want the man to cut off your balls, would
you? A woman got things she don't want to lose neither,
Little Daddy."

"Don't give me that," her little daddy closed the discussion,
"you can get along without all that crazy stuff."

"That's no way to talk to a girl, not even a pimp ought to
be that hard," Mama scolded the pander in front of everyone.
"The good book tells us 'A woman is as a precious fruits in a
garden shut up.' "

"Shut up is correct," Finnerty commanded, "and anyone
who says I ever hit any woman with anything bigger than a
small housebrick is a coon-assed liar."

He was as heavy in the shoulders and arms as a well-grown
six-footer and the right arm bore a strange tattoo: A narrow

cigarette whose smoke formed a burning boast: KING WEED-
HEAD.

How much good this would do him in event of a pinch he
never explained, and modestly disowned the implication of
the tattoo. "It don't really mean I'm the king *of* the weed-
heads, or course," he pointed out, "it just means that *as* a
weedhead I'm a king." His distinctions were sometimes too
fine to follow, and actually weren't worth the bother of following anyhow. He'd been known to trade off a woman no
older than thirty-five for a twenty dollar bill and a spring-
blade knife, but explained he had reason to think she had been
unfaithful to him. Faithful or not, if you threw in half a can
of greenish tea with the twenty, he was ready to let loose of
almost any one of his women. Except, of course, Reba, for to
her Finnerty had been true: hadn't he once been offered a
cartload of green bananas plus a full can of potoguaya for her
and turned the whole deal down?

But before letting that offer go he had taken a look at the
tea, that had been of a light greenish cast. "If it had been the
real *boge*," he admitted later, "I couldn't have answered for
my actions."

Meaning, by *boge*, the deep-purple plant that only grows
on Mount Popocatepetl.

He went in for broad stripes and coats almost to his knees,
sometimes draped out and sometimes semi-clad—a man a full
ten years ahead of his time with eyes as pale as the whiskey
in his glass.

"Oh, how I wish I could get off this *killing* kick," he'd
complain. "Why do I *do* it?"

"You might throw away that thirty-eight," Lucille advised
him again.

"Why, then I'd be without help," Finnerty told her in mild
surprise. She was his housekeeper and was half-fond of him.

Yet when asked by a stranger, half-amused at the outra-
geous little sport in cowboy boots and smelling of cologne,

"How tall *are* you, Shorty?" Finnerty had replied, "About ass-high to a tall Indian. You figure you're higher?"

The stranger answered softly, "I figure we're about the same height, mister."

"That aint good enough."

"Could be you're a little higher."

Yet if he really liked you he'd warm right up. "I've decided not to bury you," he'd congratulate you then, "I've made up my mind I'm on your side against everybody. I'm not even going to drop you. It's time I got off this killing kick and I'm going to start with you."

Once Oliver was on your side he'd stay right at your side. He knew you needed him. And who could deny so close a friend certain small favors, such as buying him drinks all afternoon? What would be left of a friendship that couldn't stand up under a few whiskies?

Of women he asked no favor. They had no more side for a man to be on than so many fishes in a stream. Indeed, they were so many fishes. And the bait with which he hooked them hardly varied. It was the immemorial chicken farm story procurers have used since procuring began:

"We don't spend our money foolish like other couples, little baby," the story went. "They won't catch us wasting it on strong drink and folly. After all, you and I both know you're no more a whore at heart than I'm a pimp. We're just a lover and his little sweetheart up against it for the moment. You listen to me, little baby, and everything will be perfect. So much in the bank every week come rain or come shine. I didn't want to tell you this, sweetheart, I wanted to save it as a surprise, but I've had my eye on a little chicken farm upstate for you and me for some time now. We get that for ourselves, just you and me, little baby, and in five years we're on Easy Street. The day we move in we stop by the justice of the peace, little sweetheart. Because if you take care of me in the little things I'm going to take care of you in the big ones."

What kind of a little sweetheart would it be who wouldn't take care of Lover in little things till he got on his feet again?

But the weeks stretched into three and the three into a month. The months to six and a year passed by, and she took care of Lover in the little things and he took care of her in the big: he kept her out of jail or visited her there when he couldn't. He saw that she always had enough tricks and never let them come on too strong. He saved her from drunks, thieves, pederasts and fiends, and once or twice a year took her fishing with him.

But nothing was said about chicken farming any more. Once, long after it was too late for farming, he might catch her crying and pet her a bit. "What's the matter, little baby? You got a fever? You want to take the night off?" She might murmur something then about candling eggs, but he wouldn't be able to understand what she meant. And after a while she cried on without knowing what she meant either, as a girl cries over a bad dream long after the dream is forgotten.

In time the tears dried. She could no longer cry over anything. All the tears had been shed, all the laughs had been had; all the love long spent. Leaving nothing to do but to sit stupefied, night after night, under lights made soft beside music with a beat, to rise automatically when someone wearing pants pointed a finger and said "that one there."

Then just like an animal trained to sit up at sound of a little bell she found her way to the bed assigned her.

Where lay all she had claim to in the world: a towel, a tube of jelly, an enamel basin, a bar of Lifebuoy and a bottle of coke, half to be spilled in the basin and the other half for a douche.

Her ears heard the pants inquire her name, and her answer to that too was assigned. ("This week you're Pepper, little baby." If you let her pick her own she'd come up with something like Jane or Mary.)

So she fixed her mouth to smile in reply, washed him in

water a little warm, lay down and shut her eyes; felt his hands roll her breasts and a long weight upon her, turned her head to avoid his breath, sensed some little convulsive jerk of his backside and opened her eyes: time was up again, time to begin again. By the time she returned to the light made soft beside the music that had a beat, another finger would be pointing "That one there."

"*Now* you finally got her where you can trust her," was Finnerty's view. "So long as she wants to pick her own name you still aint got good conditions."

Until a girl had relinquished every claim but those to basin, bed and towel, you couldn't trust her. You couldn't trust her until she had forgotten it was money she was working for. It took a man years of dedication to bring a girl to that. Only when he had madams sending him cash—no money orders—from half a dozen parts of the country might it be truly said of a man that he was a good pimp.

Finnerty's talent lay in his limitless contempt for all things female. He treated women as though they were mindless. And in time they began to act mindlessly.

At the moment he actually had two hooked on the chicken farm story working under the same roof, and both well on their way to becoming "that one there."

Frenchy and Reba worked side by side, each satisfied that it was the other whom Oliver would betray when the Judas hour struck. Meanwhile they competed, week in and week out, to show Oliver his faith wasn't misplaced. If one week Reba was top broad, Frenchy was moping all the next, feeling so useless and so untrue that Oliver had to buck her up a bit— "Don't feel so bad, honey, you done your best. That week she had was just lucky breaks. You got the looks all over her, you know that. I'm laying the odds on you this week."

Inspired by the knowledge that her owner was still betting on her, Frenchy went all out, getting tricks to finish their business almost before they had their pants down, hustling

them out the door to make room for the next, clucking at
them like an enraged hen if they didn't hurry and—lo! At the
end of that week she had made half again Reba's take.

"I never been so proud of anyone in my life," Oliver congratulated her that Saturday in front of everyone. "Don't
bother me, you," he turned on Reba—"buy your own drinks,
bum." But bought Frenchy drinks all night, paraded her
about, asked her what she wanted for her birthday, where she
wanted to go New Year's Night (this was July) and told her
the chicken farm was now actually within reach. "Only two
more weeks like this one, little baby, and we got it made for
life."

But for the next two weeks Reba topped the whole house,
they had to hold her back from pulling tricks in off the street
—and so it went, week in, week out, playing the one against
the other till it was a standing joke at Dockery's Bar to ask
who was Finnerty's top broad now.

A joke which only the two butts failed to understand.

"You must despise women something terrible," Mama
once grew bold enough to challenge him.

"I believe, whatever you are, be a stompdown good one,"
was all Finnerty replied.

And no one could deny that, at his trade, Oliver was anything but a stompdown good one. In fact, he was a perfect
little dilly. For he never came on cheap and loud, such as
"Meet the Stinger from St. Louis, have a piece of skin. Got
six broads in Miami, six in Kansas City," and all of that.

Yet why should any right-minded girl ruin her health just
to keep some unfinished product in sideburns looking sharp?
What right-minded girl could let any forenoon lush bounce
himself off her fine pink hide to wear off his hangover before
going home to his wife, in order that some Finnerty could bet
the daily double? Why wind up, scarred from ankles to
breast, in some panel house in Trinidad?

It was something Mama pretended not to understand, but

understood better, than she let on. The fact was that an un-
protected girl got into all manner of mischief, such as getting
drunk on the job and ripping off her joint togs and trying to
catch a Greyhound for home. It took a good pimp to keep a
girl honest, Mama knew.

Mama Lucille abhorred violence; yet hardly a week passed
but she was forced to say, "Honey, don't make me get Finnerty here with his mittens."

Yet when he put his mittens on, Finnerty always said,
"Baby, this is going to be a wonderful lesson to you. Some
day you'll thank me for it."

More than one innocent, deciding she'd rather keep her
earnings than give them away, would shake some half-breed
ponce in Omaha and go into business for herself in New Orleans.

But sooner or later, wherever she rented, rooming house or
hotel, desk clerk or landlady would make certain arrange-
ments with or without her consent. The line the landlady
used might be, "Honey, I'd like you to meet a nephew of
mine in the sporting goods line. He's a sweet boy, good-
looking and lots of fun, just in New Orleans for a weekend.
Would you let him show you a good time?"

Desk clerks didn't bother with that. There was a knock
and there he was, checkered vest and one hand in his belt.

"I'm not hard to get along with," he'd assure her after he
told her the score. "Whether you want to come along easy or
come along hard, that's just up to you, baby. I've got us a
nice little flat above a bar in the class part of town. There's a
smart girl."

Mama boarded only one girl who had never been pandered
and never would be. Hallie Breedlove had found her way to
Perdido Street when small-town gossip had gone around that
a certain schoolteacher wasn't really white. Hallie had suc-
ceeded in passing as white half her life, and had married a

white man who would not have married her had he had the faintest doubt of it. When the gossip had forced them to move to New Orleans, she had kept him believing it was no more than gossip. Then their baby was born and the secret was out. She had not seen him since.

She held herself higher, and took greater care of her health and earned more money, than any of the other women. If any of them actually wound up with a chicken farm, it would be Hallie.

Yet when Finnerty propositioned her, he made no allowances for the fact that he wasn't, for once, talking to a demented child. He went at her exactly as though she were as mindless as the others.

"Why, that sounds almost too good to be true, Little Daddy," Hallie tried not to appear too excited at his offer. "Only I'm *mad*—" she stood half a head higher than him, but she baby-pouted.

"*Mad* at your Little Daddy?" Finnerty couldn't believe it. "*Why?*"

"Because you promised Reba *she'd* never have to pull feathers and you promised Frenchy all *she'd* have to do was candle—but me you got stepping over droppings, carrying feed and slapping new coops together. Little Daddy, it just don't seem *fair*."

"*Them* two fools," Finnerty scoffed merrily, "you don't think I'd let a couple city clowns like them on *my* chicken farm, do you? You and I know what hard work is, we know what chicken farming is. Now wouldn't I look good trying to tell a smart country girl like yourself that all she had to do is candle? That's why with you I'm *sincere*. A country girl and a country boy. We know you don't get nowheres without hard work. Don't we, little baby?"

"What country exactly is that, Little Daddy?"

Not until then did Finnerty see he'd been had.

"Go on turning tricks till you're sixty," he gave up on

Hallie. "Just don't come running to me for help, that's all."

"I didn't say I *wouldn't*." Hallie kept a baitless string bobbing.

Yet when Frenchy would shake her head and say sadly, "Reba, poor thing. I really don't dislike her, I just feel so *sorry* for her, the fool Oliver is making of her," Hallie would be noncommittal.

For Reba was equally concerned about poor Frenchy, and worried what would happen to the girl when she and Oliver left for the farm.

Hallie pitied both, and Floralee as well, and nearly everyone.

Everyone, that is, but Oliver Finnerty. There was no place in her heart, inside or out, that did not freeze over at sight of him gnawing his little nail. And while Finnerty could respect her lack of interest in his farm, he could never forgive her indifference to his physical charms. He was hurt.

"The broad carries herself mighty high for one I got reason to think aint even got the right to be working the doors of a white house." He had tried and she had mocked him. There was only one answer now: force.

So he caught her alone petting her lame cat, the very one that had crippled his mouse, and came right to the point:

"Baby, you got all that education working for you, let's see you walk to that bureau drawer, take out every penny and come back here and hand it to me. If you hold out so much as a nickel it's as bad as trying to hold out the whole roll and that's plain stealing. Move, you."

Hallie stopped petting the cat long enough to give the pander a gray, grave look. Then bundling the cat comfortably in the crook of her arm so as not to jog it, went to the bureau and put her back solidly up against it. In the bathrobe once red now faded to rose, her hand dropped casually to her pocket.

Finnerty closed the door behind him and dropped the key

into his pocket. "You know I'm not without help, little baby," he warned her.

"I don't plan to cut you," Hallie told him quietly. "I got cut once myself. I won't scratch you because I don't like to see a man walking around with scratches on his face. I won't throw acid in your eyes because it makes me sorry to see a blind person. All I'll do is kill you where you stand. If you get through the door I'll kill you on the stair. If you make the stair I'll kill you in the parlor. If you make the street I'll kill you on the curb. I'll kill you in the alley. I'll kill you in God's House. I'll kill you anywhere."

Finnerty stood with his head slightly bent, his brow lined by doubt.

"Did you lose something, Oliver?"

"My key," he told her, "I lost my key."

"*My* key I take it you mean."

"*Your* key."

"It's laying in your cuff. You got a hole in your pocket. Bring your pants up later and I'll make you a new pocket."

Had he actually appeared with the pants she would have sewed both pockets to the seat, but he gave her no such chance.

It was Mama upon whom he conferred that opportunity, Hallie was later mildly surprised to discover. There she was, the bespectacled mulatto housekeeper-informer with gray in her poll, a rosary around her throat and Finnerty's boy-size trousers across her knees, plying needle and thread as though she were his mother. "I'm putting in a new pocket for Oliver," she explained, chattering on as the needle plied. "Oh, I know people say a pimp is the most pitiful shame, but little they know what such a man has to go through for his hustler's sake. What if she's sick or in jail? Who else has the poor thing to stand by her side?

"Oliver didn't invent his trade no more than we invented ours. I never heard of a pimp being elected mayor nor even of one who bothered to vote, so why blame *them* for the way things are? They weren't the ones who made the laws that let the trade go on. If nobody wanted there to be pimps, honey, there wouldn't be no pimps. Isn't it strange that it's the very ones who say we're a public disgrace who pay us best? You know yourself that it's the ones from the Department who come down early on Saturdays to holler, 'Bring us two women and a bottle!' "

"What's wrong about two women and a bottle?" Hallie asked, just to find out.

"Honey, there's nothing wrong with two women and a bottle, or three or four women and a whole case, so long as you don't sneak it and preach against it the next day." Mama wetted the thread and pointed it through the needle. "If there was another craft open to Oliver he'd try it, and make quite a success."

Sometimes Hallie wondered a bit about Mama.

For how disapproving Mama looked later, in the kitchen, while Reba and Finnerty were having a bite together.

"Are you having coffee, baby?" she heard Finnerty invite Reba.

"Yes, daddy."

"Then make enough for two and bring mine here."

"Alright, daddy," Old Faithful agreed, "but butter me a little piece bread. After all, I work for you."

Reba had been brought up in a Chicago orphanage although both her parents were living. They had taken turns visiting her on alternate Sundays—but one Sunday neither had come. "See," one of the other girls had told her then, "your father's no good," —and had shoved Reba's head against a flathead nail. The accident had caused a permanent squint in the girl's right eye.

Now she had found a sort of father, one who was surely no good at all, but at least he came to visit her every day and sometimes twice. It was "my Oliver this, my Oliver that" and "My Oliver is just so *tickled* with them raw silk lounging pajamas I bought him he been lounging two whole days so I'm going to get him cowboy boots to go with them. Won't that be *cute?*"

"Not the way I heard it it aint cute," the big girl from Fort Worth needled her. "How I heard it, you've been hiding them pants to keep him from loading up a sheeny wagon of green bananas and making hisself a nice profit by the time he got to Chicago."

"If my Oliver ever worked a sheeny wagon I'll kiss your ass before God!" Reba came swiftly to the defense of her household honor. "His whole life he aint worked one single mothering day! Never rolled up his sleeves except to exercise horses a little. Even then he was just *settin'* up there, takin' his own good time. Why, he won't even take off his own shoes to climb in bed!"

That nothing could lower human dignity faster than manual labor was understood. "Go get yourself a lunch bucket and get back in your ditch" was the ultimate insult on Perdido Street.

"Any pimp whose broad don't take off his shoes for him," Finnerty backed up Reba, "I defy him to claim he got good conditions."

"Oh, who cares what conditions you and your old lady got?" the Fort Worth blonde dismissed them both. "Why, *I* got a daddy friend don't take a dime off me. He buys *me* things. He's going to buy me a Cadillac so long I'll have to back up to turn a corner. Whatever Fort Worth's real name was, no one ever called her anything but Five, to honor a navel formed to that figure. When asked to show her wonderful navel she would show it, sweetly and simply, just like that. Men pinched her bottom, yet she did not hold herself proudly just because of that.

No chicken farm story was likely to catch Five. She had

been brought up on one, and had had enough of *that*. Yet she was wide open to the Cadillac story, which was nothing more than the chicken farm story on wheels.

Oh, that long easy rider with the real careful driver. When promises would buy Cadillacs, Five would own a whole fleet.

Until that time Five would go on her feet.

The courts were against them, the police were against them, businessmen, wives, churches, press, politicians and their own panders were against these cork-heeled puppets. Now the missions were sending out sandwich men to advertise that Christ Himself was against them.

"If it weren't for Mama who'd take *our* side," Frenchy demanded to know, and stick up for them Mama did. She took their side against Oliver, ordered him out of her house, and told him not to come back till he could show respect to ladies and forced him to apologize to one or the other at least once a week.

A cruel game, tricking children. For one word from Finnerty would be enough to send the woman back to the alley stalls from which she'd risen. Colored women were not legally permitted to manage houses employing white prostitutes. But every house was required to keep a maid on the premises during working hours. To the police therefore Mama was a maid. This was Finnerty's arrangement, and he didn't let her forget it for a day.

Leaving Mama troubled by the part she played. At times she tried to justify herself by remembering that she had been deceived by many white men; therefore it was only fair that she should now deceive their daughters. Yet disappointment wide as the world would surprise her out of her sleep: "When had she ceased to belong to herself?" Some mornings she would have to go for the cognac before she could go downstairs and say, "How is my chick today?" to each and every one.

Between forenoon and evening her chicks descended the stairwell like separate blessings, one by one.

Hallie came down first, with a cup of tea steaming in her hand and the brindle cat limping at her side. It was a cat that took offense at nothing simply to have some sort of life. It walked beside her down the stone, but when it felt dew beneath its paws it drew back. Then Hallie would point her foot, the cat would leap, hobble and claw its way clear to her shoulder. Then they went together to say good morning to the jonquils growing between the cobbles. Though between the cobbles of Hallie's heart no jonquil would grow again.

A heart like a lonesome gravestone, winter weeds covered it now. Below the weeds the child lay buried who had been but three when he'd died. One who had surprised his mother that sad and sudden fall by asking "Mother, are my mittens ready for winter? Are my earlaps ready? Will my coat be warm?"

His last Christmas he had put a hand behind a glowing ornament, passing it about his face, dreamily taking up the heat until she had made him stop.

Now nine shuttered Christmases later she walked powdered, Maybellined and gowned in the mascaraed evening light and something swollen in a mushroom's shape, boredom like a living growth, bore down on her heart and brain.

Morning was not the hardest time, for the lame cat needed her, and the other women were not yet about to smile a little to themselves when they talked to her: "How you doin', philosopher?" they would ask, though she could not recall who, nor why, anyone had first called her that. But she had once been a country schoolteacher, so it must have something to do with that.

"I got no philosophy but I topped you last night," Frenchy especially liked to tease her.

So she and the cat went visiting jonquils, and had a bit of

fur-to-ear chatter in the ancestral understanding of woman
and cat. Sometimes she read, in the quiet forenoon, out of
books she still loved. But when the morning was past and the
cat lay stretched on the window ledge through the sweltering
afternoon, then she was left alone in this strange house, and
ennui came down like a foe on her mind and she shaded her
eyes with her hand.

To hope she might spend her yet unspent hours bedside to
bed in some common ward, under some final quarantine, some
ward where go all those whose lives are untouchable, from
streets for whom nobody prays. Where it is one where evening falls and one the sad return of day.

Till the violet evening had mercy at last. Then she stood
in the portiere and chose what guests she would.

The other women regarded her with a strange mixture of
admiration and pity. They felt she held herself apart because
she had once taught school—yet at other times they perceived
she was somehow defenseless against all of them. Then it was
that, hearing the low grinding of metal on stone, they looked
the other way to spare her, while Finnerty held the big doors
wide.

They did not look, yet sensed as if the lights had gone up
a bit, that at the sound of little wheels, life was beginning
again in Hallie.

Her lover was the legless man.

"I'm a philosopher, too," Reba challenged Hallie—"because
I got my *own* goddamn philosophy. For instance. You take a
woman married to a good man and she cheats on him. Their
baby is born dead. Well she had it coming to her, didn't she?
Everyone gets what's coming to them, that's my philosophy.
I picked it up working for loryers. They said they never
heard anything like it."

"I can believe that," Hallie was inclined to agree with
loryers.

"I had to run down two flights and up one across the street to get a coke," Reba recalled, "because across the street is a whorehouse with a coke machine. Why wear myself out running stairways? A job is a job. One with cokes is better. That's my philosophy too."

"Say you don't go for cokes, you're on hard liquor. Okay, be a B-broad and get drunk every night. Say you're a heavy eater, a regular fat glutton, get a job as a waitress 'n stuff yourself. Say you're rapping doors with a box of silk stockings under your arm and you start freezing. So what? Get a job as a dance-hostess and work up a sweat.

"I got half my choppers out and no ovalries. So what? I can still be a practical nurse, can't I? My people come from that part of Europe where they say 'fis' for 'fish.' I don't know where it's at exactly but when my mother sent me to the store she'd always say 'Honey, bring back a nice piece fis.' Hey! How'd you like all the cigarettes you could smoke? Just go down to American Tobacco and give my name, they'll give you all you can haul in one trip."

"Baby, I don't know what you're on," Five marveled, "but I never heard nothing like it neither."

Reba read all the papers, and always shook her head when she'd finished one. Someone in South Carolina had received two boxes of poisoned candy by mail, signed merely "B'rer Rabbit, R.F.D." Now what did anyone hope to get out of poisoning somebody else by mail? "If you got a grudge like that hire somebody to bust his damn legs, don't go sneaking around signing yourself a damn rabbit."

Postal delivery poisoners were among the few who fell out of the range of her sympathy. It troubled her to read that a tenant farmer had drowned his three daughters in a well because "Jesus says we got to go." "If Jesus said *that* why don't he jump in the well hisself and let Jesus decide for the babies?" Nor was she satisfied with the explanation of the brakeman who killed his wife with a hammer. "Grace aint fitten to raise a dog. This is the only way I know to make a lady of her."

"I don't know what people are coming to, they act like a bunch of damned pistols," was Reba's reaction. When she read of a widow woman who fell and broke her leg on a downtown street and someone stole forty-eight dollars out of her purse while she lay helpless, Reba was helpless too. "That's too much" was all she had to say for that day, and threw the paper away.

One evening an actor stumbled in. "I've had too much to drink," he told the women as though otherwise they'd never catch on.

"Sweetie, I seen your picture in the paper but why don't you just go home?" Reba asked. The next morning the actor had his picture in the paper again, having been picked up for drunk and disorderly down the street. "I had too much to drink" he had repeated his explanation to reporters once more. Reba's patience gave out.

" 'I had too much to drink.' 'I had too much to drink.' What did I tell him when he was here? 'Sweetie, you've had too much to drink' is *just* what I told him. Honest to *God*, when a man *knows* he's had too much and goes on drinking more all the same, that's just too much. I refuse to adjust to peasants of a environment like this, that's all."

The excuse of the dunce who drowned his infant daughter because his wife had run off with another man didn't get him off the hook with Reba. "Something snapped in my head" he had told the police, "I didn't know what I was doing."

" 'I had too much to drink,' " she mocked all erring mankind. " 'Something snapped in my head,' 'I didn't know what I was doing'—of all the bum excuses. Give me animals, at least *they* know what they're doing."

Especially elephants. Elephants *always* knew what they were doing.

"Do you know about elephants, how *they* come on?" she asked anxiously of some sport adjusting a black wool tie in a cracked mirror while she was preoccupied with the ritual of the douche, shaking the bottle madly to make it foam.

"If you'd stop sizzling maybe I could hear what you're saying," the wool-tie sport suggested.

"Well," the girl explained, "I read about how the old man elephant whips up a big pit in the ground with his trunk 'n then whips the old lady into it. Otherwise they could never make it and there wouldn't be no elephants."

"So what?"

"Well, it just goes to show you, animals *do* know what *they're* doing."

"I'm in theatrical work," the girl called Frenchy explained to a date. "See—" she stretched her pale hands before his eyes— "I'm double-jointed too. Double-jointed hips, but I lost my partner."

"Can't you find another?" the date asked.

"You don't understand. I probably couldn't find another partner in the entire country. Not everyone's double-jointed you know." She was a high-cheekboned girl with consumptive coloring. "We'd swing down the coast and come back west— Philly, Cleveland, Cincinatti, Chattanooga—that's where my folks are, they spent thousands on my education."

Out on the walk, up and down in the rain, the man with a cap that shaded his eyes carried a sign that said BEWARE THE WRATH TO COME.

If the pale lost blonde wasn't down the stairs by the time that street lamps came on, somebody went up and fetched her down. Should lamps be lit or no lamp burn, all was one to the pale lost blonde.

Nobody had counted, for nobody cared, how many lamps had come up and gone down since the night she had stood where Loew's marquee lights flickered in an uncertain rain, when a cabbie had held a door wide for her and she'd told him, as though she were awake and not in deep dream, "Lake Pontchartrain."

Nobody was home at Lake Pontchartrain. She had spoken a name overheard, nothing more, and offered him a pressed flower out of her purse for her fare. He preferred coming into the back seat with her to collect instead. Then had turned her over to Finnerty to satisfy the meter.

"I'd rather not be whupped," she'd told Oliver—"*if* I got my rathers."

"I'd rather not whup you," Finnerty reasoned with her, "all I'm asking is that you let me take care of you in the big things so that you can take care of me in the little ones. Or am I asking too much?"

"Little ones, big ones," the girl repeated, offering him a smile itself a pressed flower.

"Do you remember your name, little baby?" he asked her.

"Floralee"—and that was all she remembered.

First he had made her his pleasure, then he had made her his trade. But the ease with which he'd accomplished this troubled him. He had Mama spy on her. Mama reported back.

"Haven't you any pride at *all?*" he asked Floralee in his injured tone, "coming on with a trick like it was love, love, love? Do you realize you spent the better part of an hour with that bum for a lousy four dollars?"

"Daddy, I lost track of the time," the demented girl replied.

"*I'm* here to take care of your needs," he reminded her. "Try to remember that."

But a few days later he heard a great thump and crash overhead while she was entertaining.

"What was that?" he asked her half an hour after.

"Why, daddy, we fell off the bed and kept right on going, that was all," she told him so innocently he hardly had the heart to give her the beating she now so richly deserved. But it had to be done to protect the fool from herself. He hung his coat over the back of a chair.

"If you'd just as soon," she had seen what was coming, "I'd as soon not be whupped—if I got my sooners."

"I'd sooner not," Oliver told her, but put on his mittens, lifted her pony-tail off the back of her head to get at the nape where bruises don't show: A few rabbit-punches, enough to make her head spin, and that satisfied him.

"But next time when you chippy with a date daddy won't put his mittens on," he promised her.

She never committed the sin of chippying again.

Although Oliver's other two faithfuls, Reba and Frenchy, were at needle's points day and night, somehow neither was jealous of the wandering blonde. "Nobody home at Lake Pontchartrain is right," was all Frenchy had to remark. For Floralee's life was too remote for envy. She lived enwrapped in some private cloud through which the light of the outer world filtered sometimes dimly and sometimes bright; but never like the light of the world in which the other women lived and bargained.

The girl had days when she seemed so sensible no one could have guessed there was anything amiss. But before night she would be ecstatic, singing upstairs or down—

> *The beasts of the wild*
> *Will be led by a child*
> *And I'll be changed from the thing I am*

And the next morning would be utterly cast down. Once Oliver went to fetch her and found her lying naked on her side, eyes shut tight, knees drawn to her chin and the sheet over her head. There was no sound in the hot little room save the incessant hum of an electric fan.

"There are little people a-prayin' and a-singin' in there," she told him and he understood she was hearing the voices of her people at their old spirituals in the hypnotic hum of the fan. He shut it off, returned with a small radio and tuned in a Sunday morning choir—

> *The son of God goes forth to war,*
> *A kingly crown to gain*
> *His blood-red banner streams afar,*
> *Who follows in His train?*

Floralee opened her eyes to see her little daddy standing on a chair, pretending to lead a congregation—
Who best can drink his cup of woe triumphant over pain?
"—it takes your little daddy to get them real good programs," he told her, and jumped down. She listened closer, growing proud of the way her little daddy made them real good programs come in. By noon she was downstairs singing with faith restored—

> *His blood-red banner streams afar—*

"That just won't get it, honey," Mama finally had to put a stop to it—"I'm a church-going woman bound to die blessed, but there's a time and a place for everything and that song just isn't right for a place like this. If you just *have* to sing when men are around, try something like 'Mademoiselle from Armentieres'—something to put them *in* the mood, not take them out of it."

"I won't sing brashy tunes with vulgary words," Floralee suddenly grew stubborn. "I sung one once 'n that same night God said He couldn't bear me."

"God wouldn't say a thing like that, sweetheart," Mama promised.

"He said it all the same. He was standing right outside my door, I heard him plain as day. He said, 'I've took all I can off that girl. I can't bear the sight of her.' "

"What makes you think God would talk like *that*, sweetheart?"

Floralee's face clouded as she struggled to remember, then

her eyes cleared. "Because, whoever He was talking to, He kept saying 'No. By *no* means. No.No.No.' That *must* have been God. If it had been the devil he would have been saying 'Yes, oh, yes, by all means, by all means and don't think I don't appreciate it." And in her anxiety that God bear her, applied to Him right there and then despite Mama's instruction—

> *What must I do to win a diadem?*
> *When I reach that shining strand?*

The only solution was to play the juke with the volume turned up.

"To hear that looney holler," Reba shuddered after things had quieted down a bit, "you'd think all they did in them hills was bury their dead."

"Let us not begrudge the child," Mama reproved Reba, "she got the innocence God protects."

While God protected her innocence, Finnerty figured her finances. He supplied her clothes, her meals, her amusements and what in all seriousness he called her education. The grift on joint-togs, such as parade panties, ran to a hundred percent and higher.

Small wonder He had forgotten entirely about the escapee from O-Daddyland.

The escapee came down Perdido Street with a sample case in his hand. He wasn't offering coffee pots nor finger waves any more. Now He was the Watkins Man.

Of course being a Watkins Man in 1931 wasn't what it had been before the wilderness had been pushed back. Then it had been something more than a matter of taking orders for lotions and salves. The Watkins Man had once been the bringer of news of the world outside to the Louisiana backbrush; and he'd been more than a news bearer. He could tell the farmer what ailed his horse and could cure the brute as

well. More than a horse doctor, he had cured people too. He
could preach the Word, act as midwife, and recite *Evangeline*.

In Dove Linkhorn, unhappily, these arts had declined.
Indeed, they had vanished altogether. And by his clothes one
had to wonder whether this particular Watkins Man might
not even have the notion that his true trade was lovemaking
rather than salesmanship.

Dove had spent every last cent of his O-Daddy gold on a
suit of O-Daddy clothes. It was tropical white, over a shirt
with narrow pink stripes. His hat had a yellow feather that
matched his shoes of yellow suede. He had come a long way,
that was plain to be seen, from the boy who had come to town
barefoot in blue jeans.

As he came down the street for whom nobody prays, in the
evening hour.

It was that slander-colored evening hour before the true
traffic begins, when once again sheets have been changed,
again Lifebuoy and permanganate have been rationed; and
once again for blocks about, pouting or powdering or dusting
their navels, each girl wonders idly what manner of man—
mutt, mouse, or moose—the oncoming night will bring her.

Perdido Street, in the steaming heat, felt like a basement
valet shop with both irons working. The girls in the crib doors
plucked at their blouses to peel them off their breasts. In the
round of their arm pits sweat crept in the down. Sweat molded
their pajamas to their thighs. The whole street felt molded, pit
to thigh. It was even too hot to solicit. For normal men don't
so much as glance at the girls in heat like that lest the watery
navels stick.

Yet the very heat that enervates men infects women with
restlessness and the city was full of lonesome monsters. Side-
street solitaries who couldn't get drunk, seeking to lose their
loneliness without sacrificing their solitude. Dull boys whose
whole joy expired in one piggish grunt. Anything could happen

to a woman available to anyone. Boredom of their beds and terror of their street divided each.

They had died of uselessness one by one, yet lived on behind veritable prairie fires of wishes, hoping for something to happen that had never happened before: the siren screaming toward the crossing smashup, the gasp of the man with the knife in his side, the suicide leap for no reason at all. Yet behind such fires sat working cross words while prying saltwater taffy from between their teeth: passion and boredom divided each.

In Spider-Boy Court the blinds, drawn low, left the room in a dappled gloom where dimly fell the shadows, darker yet, of bars. For little windows lined the side that paralleled Perdido Street. And a ceiling fan, cutting the restless light, caused shadows to tremble along wall and floor.

In this moted dusk a juke played on and so long as it played the women sat content. But the moment the music stopped, a creaking, regular and slow, began right overhead and they began shifting uneasily from divan to doorway and back to the divans, opening another coke or lighting a fresh cigarette at each new post—they never finished anything.

Dissatisfaction was a disease with them. Reba was sure the fan was giving her a chill, Floralee needed something to warm her up, Frenchy wanted someone to tell her *why* she couldn't spike a coke with gin and Kitty said she was simply suffocating.

Wherever they powdered, wherever they paced, envy and ennui divided each.

"A light drizzle would be good for trade," Mama took a guess, "but a heavy fall would ruin it." At that moment a cab honked from the curb.

Though someone was always watching the street, no one had seen it drive up. A cab that appeared out of nowhere, like a cab in a misting dream. Mama simply scuttled to the curb and the girls crowded forward in their watery gloom, shading their eyes against the street.

And saw step forth in the greenish light a naval lieutenant in full regalia, a sea-going executive in rimless glasses, a hero of sea fights yet unfought. Bearing like a rainbow across his sky-blue breast all the ribboned honors a peacetime navy could pin. From the gold-braided cap to the gold-braid sleeves, there were not many such sights above deck in 1931. Mama had never captured a sight so glorious just to behold.

Yet the sight seemed reluctant of capture. He held Mama in some earnest discussion speaking low to keep his driver from hearing.

"Mammy-freak," Mama *thought* she heard him say, "stick out so fah behind she hahdly got time make a child behave."

Mama stepped closer. "I don't quite catch what you're saying, officer." He leaned toward her cupping his lips— "Made a lemon pie. *Me* a little pie. What do you know? A little lemon pie *all my own.*"

Mama took one step back. "Lemon? All your own?"

"The very day after I broke the churn."

"Then I have *just* the girl for you," Mama decided. For whatever the rascal had in mind she couldn't afford to lose any prospect so prosperous. "Every man likes a little change now and then. I know exactly how you feel."

He drew himself up. "*Nobody* knows how a mammy-freak feels," he informed her point blank. "How could anyone but another mammy-freak know how a mammy-freak feels?"

If it was an organization he was the president. Mama simply turned to go but he held her back with a wheedling touch. "You know yourself," he cajoled her, "how they stick out in back."

"*Who* stick out in back?"

"Why, all of them, when they get in a hurry. Now admit it."

Mama shook off his hand. "*Who* stick out? *Who* get in a

hurry? Admit *what?*" Mama was getting angry but she didn't know at what.

"Why, old black mammies of course," he told her as though everyone knew old black mammies were the coming thing.

"Maybe you ought to come inside before it rains," Mama invited him, feeling they'd both be safer in the parlor.

"It isn't going to rain," Navy sounded certain as God, and began unfolding a little apron from under his coat. He bowed to tie it about her waist. It was striped green and white like peppermint and as he tied it Mama wondered how she had become the prospect. Her fingers plucked without strength at the apron's price tag. He picked the tag off himself and the cab dusted off in disgust.

"A good many black mammy-freaks visit you I presume?" he presumed confidently.

"It's been several days since one called," Mama played it straight, "and he didn't leave his name. Would you care to offer yours?"

"My men call me Commander," he informed her stiffly.

"That," Mama thought, "isn't what my chicks will call you." And led him inside like leading him home.

Just as the first drops began.

Inside the parlor the five-year-old boy with the mind of a forty-year-old pimp, the one his grandmother called Warren Gameliel and the women called the King of the Indoor Thieves, stood on a divan ready for anything.

In a shirt that never reached past his navel and a tight little hide not exactly high yellow, Warren Gameliel was actually closer to being high-brown. He was even closer to dark-brown. As a matter of fact he was black as a kettle in hell. He was so black you'd have had to put a milk bottle on his head to find him in the dark. He looked a cross between a black angus calf and something fished out of the Mississippi on a moonless night. One tint darker and he would have disappeared altogether.

Turning his head proudly upon his iron-colored throat, he fluttered his beautiful lashes modestly at the women's flattery.

"Meet my grandson," Mama always introduced her menfolks first—"Aint he fine?"

"Five year old 'n weighs sixty-nine pound 'n she asks is he fine," the woman called Hallie Dear mocked Mama fondly as the big overdressed man saluted the small naked one.

"Pledge allegiance, boy baby," Mama encouraged Warren G. to his single legitimate accomplishment. But Warren G. just planted his black toes the wider, as if to say he'd have to know more about this gold-braid deal before he'd pledge so much as a teething ring.

Reba honked with hollow glee: the boy was growing up so fast.

"Aint you *shamed?*" Mama reproved him in a voice that simply *donged* with pride.

Warren Gameliel felt no shame. That belonged, Hallie Dear saw in a single shocked glance, to the hero beside her. For the ghost of a smile that strayed down his lips belonged to a beggar-ghost, a penniless pleader hunting a handout— then it was gone. Leaving him cowering within himself in some cave of no knowing save his own.

Hallie hooked her arm in his to let him know he really wasn't as alone as all that, and he peered out slowly, warily. Feeling her support, he began coming out of it.

Slowly, warily.

"In Shicawgo I worked in a office for loryers," Reba hurried to keep the man from confusing her with certain common whores trying to crowd him—"I specialized in tort 'n see-zure—" but Floralee elbowed her aside. Floralee was fond of gold braid too.

"I can sing just *ever* so purty, mister," she offered in a voice

strung on little silver bells "—only modesty songs of course,
for I don't know vulgary words—" and did him as pretty a
little curtsy as ever he'd seen.

Warren G. tried to regain the spotlight, but Mama yanked
the cap, that he had taken off the officer's head, far down
over the boy's eyes, as if shutting off his vision might improve
his manners. Somebody got the juke going just then and
someone else called for gin. Someone said, "Make mine a
double" just as the juke began—

> *All of me*
> *Why not take all of me*

"I can sing purtier far than *that*," Floralee insisted amid
pleas, claims, threats and tiny squeals, for now all vied for
Navy's attention.

"Why do people down here all talk so *Southern?*" Chicago
Kitty complained. "Why do they have to talk like the niggers? Why can't they talk like their selves?"

"We do talk like ourselves, honey," Hallie assured her,
"the Negras learned to talk that way from us."

"May I recite now?" Floralee begged.

"As soon as the juke is through, sweetheart," Mama promised, and turning to the guest, "This girl is a regular angel."

"She's a whore like everyone else," Kitty put in—"*anyone*
can be a whore. I feel rotten about everyone but myself."

"Is that true?" Navy asked Mama curiously. "Can any
woman become a whore? Any woman at all?"

"Anyone at all," Mama was optimistic. "Aren't we all
created free and equal?"

"Tell me one thing, sailor boy," Chicago Kitty demanded.
"Where do you keep your submarines?"

"Why ask me a thing like that?" The lieutenant looked em-
barrassed.

"I have to know. I'm a spy on the side."

"I don't want anyone calling our guest sailor boy," Mama

scolded Kitty and everyone. "Look up to this man! He's honoring us! Hear this! Commander! Report all insults directly to me! Warren Gameliel you little black fool, get that fool hat off your head and pledge allegiance in-stan-*tane-ously!*"

"Mama!" Hallie scolded in turn, "stop giving orders as though we were in battle formation! This man didn't come here to have *you* pin a medal on him. Can't you see you're spoiling his fun?" And brushing everyone aside, she framed his face in her palms to make him return the look she gave. "Navy, don't mind Mama," she told him, "she's just impressed by your uniform."

"Don't *dare* call our Guest of Honor Navy like that!"—Mama was getting worse by the minute—"This man represents the entire Atlantic fleet!"

"I represented two loryers," Reba remembered wistfully.

"I represent a tube of K-Y jelly 'n a leaky douche bag," Kitty commented bitterly.

"I can sing like a damned bird," Floralee marveled aloud, "only how did I fly here?"

Outside the drunks were coming out of the country's last speak-easies and the street lamps began to move like the breasts of a young girl under the hands of a man who has bought too many. Warren Gameliel reached out blindly and secured a black stranglehold on the officer's neck.

"If you don't behave I'll send you to the nigger school," Mama threatened him.

And in an odd little silence a girl's voice said, "I was drunk, the juke box was playing, I began to cry." And all the air felt troubled by cologne.

"I think our guest wants to see me," Hallie guessed, and pulled Navy's head right against her breast. He nodded strengthless assent.

She helped him to rise, and he rose more like a sick man than one drunk.

"Send two double gins to my room," Hallie ordered Mama, "the rest of you drink whatever you want."

The door shut behind them and a lamp lit a room that might have served a whore of old Babylon: a narrow bed in hope of bread, a basin in hope of purity. A beaded portiere to keep mosquitoes out and let a little music in. A scent of punk from an incense stick to burn off odors of whiskey or tobacco, a calendar from the year before and an image above it of something or other in hope of forgiveness for this or that. A whole world to millions since the first girl sold and a world to millions yet.

The lamp's brown glow on her amber gown made of Hallie a golden woman. For her eyes were gray, her skin was olive and about her throat she wore a yellow band.

Her gown, unfastened at one shoulder, was kept from falling only by the rise of her unbound breast. Still she said, "No matter how often I trick, as soon as I'm with a man I get shaky."

"You don't have to bother to get shaky with me," the seagoing executive assured her, "don't even bother taking off your clothes."

So he had found some fault in her. "What's the matter, don't you like dark girls?"

"It's not you, it's me," he reassured her, "I'm of no use, that's all. But I'll gladly pay you for your time."

"I don't need charity." Hallie was hurt nonetheless.

"It isn't charity. You've already helped me in a way that can't be bought."

"Then I'll take the money all the same," Hallie recovered herself and sat beside him on her dishonored bed, letting the gown drape loosely over her breast in event he should prove not so useless as he thought.

"I'm from Virginia, of course," he announced as though that were more important than a woman's flesh.

"I'm from Louisiana myself," Hallie went along. "Of course."

"What I *mean* is"—he felt it time to be kind—"I'm a gentleman."

"I'm certain you are," Hallie told him he really was. "When you're a lady yourself that's something you can tell about a man right off."

"What I'm trying to say," he tried afresh, "I'm a *Virginia* gentleman."

"I don't mean to be sarcastic, mister," Hallie promised him, "but so what?"

"Why," he had never thought that being a Virginia gentleman might not be self-sufficing, "well, it means I can teach at Washington and Lee!"

"It's nice to have two jobs," Hallie was sure, "and in times like these amounts to a real curiosity."

"I'll tell you what is a yet mightier curiosity," he got down to business at last, "and that's the way old black mammies stick out in back—" his voice took on a secret excitement—*"the way she come by with a broom 'n most knocks you down—'Boy!—stay outa mah way when ah'm cleanin', Boy'—'n here she comes by again with bucket 'n mop—'Boy, when you gonna learn to behave? Didn't ah tell you stay outa mah way? Boy!'—'n you just about turn around 'n here comes Mammy back again—'Boy! You got nawthin' to do all day but stand in mah path? You fixin' to get y'se'f soaked?' "* He composed himself only with an effort.

"Mister," Hallie asked gently, "how long you been in this condition?"

"Since the day I broke the churn of course. Black Mammy's been dead nineteen years—otherwise why would I feel this way? Hand and foot she waited on us and when that day come when all she could do was just to set in her old cane chair, there wasn't a soul but myself to fetch her a glass of water.

" 'Mammy,' I told her, "you waited on me, I'm goin' to wait on you. *I'm* takin' care of my old black mammy."

"I slept by her chair, for she couldn't lie down. When I woke at night I could reach out and touch the back of her skinny black hand and know if she was asleep or awake just by the touch. Mostly she'd be awake. You know what I'd ask her then?"

Hallie felt his hand on her own. "What you ask her then?"

"I'd ask her, 'You want anything, Black Mammy?' That's just what I'd ask her."

"She must have been grateful for your care."

He looked at Hallie so evenly. "More than I knew. For the very day she died she raised her weary old arm and give me a back-handed slap."

"You broke *another* churn on her?"

"It was her way of letting me know that she had understood all along what her first back-handed slap, when I was ten years old, had done."

"She forgive you at last for breakin' the churn?" Hallie kept trying.

"We were too grateful to one another for forgiving," he explained—"Don't you think I know it was Black Mammy's hand made a mammy-freak out of me? That I might have had a wife and family now if it hadn't been for her hand? Yet I'm grateful to her still. Who else ever thought I was worth human care? I'm *glad* the porch was slippery."

Hallie was lost.

"Mister," she shook her head sadly, "I just don't take your meaning."

"The water from the churn made the porch all wet. When its handle snapped she saw what I'd done and aimed her hand. I slipped and fell so she paddled me face down. I lay hollering, pretending she was half killing me. Black Mammy had a good strong hand. That was the first time I was made to behave."

Hallie saw light faintly.

"What happened *exactly?*"

"Why, what happens when a man is having a girl, *that's* what happened. And I've never been able to make it happen any other way since." He laughed in the watery light yet his face looked stricken.

"I'm terribly tired, I don't know why," he said and put his face in his hands.

It came to Hallie then that this wasn't at all some monster of the nastier sort, but only some sort of lonely suckling boy playing Commander with his nose still running.

"Mister," she told him quietly, "you don't need a girl. You need a doctor."

"There aren't any doctors for black-mammy freaks," he explained dryly, as though he'd tried looking one up in the city directory.

"Then just try to rest," Hallie told him.

Fast as she could pin, Hallie was preparing Mama for the great impersonation.

"You don't think he stole his ship's money, do you?" Mama had to know. "He isn't going to get us all in trouble, is he?"

"You never made an easier dollar your whole enduring life," Hallie reassured her, "he's just a green boy been kept on black titty too long. All you got to remember is this rapscallion keeps getting in your way. Just don't hit him too hard—just hard enough to make it look good."

"You wont catch *me* hitting no member of our armed forces," and Mama stuck right there.

"Getting whupped by his old black mammy is what he come here for—turn around so I can pin you." She began stuffing a small pillow into Mama's bosom. "The more you stick out in front the more you stick out behind. I'll have you sticking out so far you'll look like Madame Queen."

"Girl, I was born in this country."

It was plain Mama hadn't caught the play even yet.

"*Mama,*" Hallie pleaded, "*forget* the man's uniform. I'm trying to tell you he isn't *like* other men."

Mama stiffened like a retriever. "Honey, he aint one of them O-verts?"—She was ready to rip off her handkerchief-head masquerade and run the whole O-vert navy out of town "I wont cater to *them*. Not for *no* amount."

"If he were he'd be better off," Hallie reassured her. "Now turn around," and pinned skirt over skirt till Mama, weighted down, sank heavily into a chair.

"Honey, I'm starting to sweat," she complained.

"Sweat till you shine," Hallie encouraged her, "but don't show your face till I give you the sign." And stepped through the portiere.

Beneath the ruin of the gold-braid hat the King of the Indoor Thieves had collapsed at last, his undershirt tangled about his throat as if someone had tried to improve his manners by finishing him off altogether. He snored till his toes were spread, he stretched till he creaked in dreams of some final assault for an earth about to be his for keeps.

"All of you stop talking out of the corners of your mouth like you were Edgar G. Robinson and everybody was in the can," Hallie quieted the woman—"You've got a guest tonight that means gold from way back, so try to show manners."

For down the stair with an admiral's tread came the hero of sea fights as good as won, looking like the dogs had had him under the house; with a gin glass latched to his hand.

Hallie crooked one finger toward the portiere.

Mama came forth with forehead shining, bandanna and broom, all sweat and Aunt Jemima, in the peppermint apron that hung like candy.

The second he saw her Navy dropped his glass. "I didn't *mean* to do that," he apologized immediately, and began trying to clean the floor with his sleeve, glass, splinters, and all, making a worse mess than before.

(*Long-ago Mammy who made me behave the day the
big churn broke, who backhanded me to pretend she
didn't know something had broken forever. Who knew
how it was going to be with me, and made me a little pie
all my own. Who's left to make me behave?*)

Mama seated herself across from him, in all her preposterous
gear. Hallie put a warning finger to her lips. The girls ex-
changed looks part fear and part wonder.

"I'm a Protestant by birth but a Catholic by descent,"
Mama felt it was time to explain the curious no-man's land
of her faith, "I've shod the horse all around." Meaning she
had had four husbands. "So I'm not acceptable to the Church.
But if I can't die sanctified I hope to die blessed."

His elbow touched Floralee's glass. It tottered, he reached
as if to keep it from tipping and knocked it over, of course,
instead. The girl pushed back her chair and he began mopping
it up with a silk handkerchief, although all he was doing actually was swishing the handkerchief around in it. "Go on with
your story," he told Mama, "I'm sorry to be so clumsy."

Mama had lost the thread. All she could remember was that
she had four husbands.

"Three of them were thieves and one was a legit man—I'd
never marry another legit man. Did you know that a prize
fighter is more gentle than other men, outside the ring? That's
because he knows what a man's fists can do. Do you know
that you're safer living with a man who kills for hire than
with a man who has never killed? That's because one knows
what killing is. The other don't."

"Why," Navy remarked, "in that case ill-fame women
ought to make better wives than legitimate girls."

Again that odd little silence fell. Nobody knew what to
say to that.

"Navy, I think that's the nicest thing I've heard anyone

say since I've been in the trade," Hallie said—and his elbow
tipped Mama's glass into her lap.

"Now don't tell me that 'just happen,' " Mama scolded in
real earnest now—"Don't tell me *any* man is that *clumsy*.
Mister, my frank opinion is you done that a-purpose."

"Honest, I didn't, Mammy," he lied patiently.

"Don't whup him, Mama," Floralee pleaded for him.

"I'm *sure* he wont do it again," Hallie defended him too.

"Give me *one* more chance, Mama," he whimpered.

"Only out of respect for your uniform," Mama issued final
warning, "and one more is *all* you gets." She turned to shake
out her skirts, somebody tittered and somebody honked and
she whirled just in time to catch him with two fingers to his
nose. Now Mama scarcely knew what to feel.

"Why, that isn't the least *bit* nice, a man of your back-
ground to have such manners—"

"He didn't *mean* anything, Mama," Hallie was sure.

"*Don't* whup him," Floralee *begged*.

"*Cross my heart* I didn't mean anything," Navy swore in
that same unbearable small-boy whine that in itself entitled
him to a thrashing.

"O he *meant* it all right," Kitty informed, "I saw him with
my naked eye—and I have a *very* naked eye."

"I *will* try to do better, please mum," he promised so hum-
bly, "I *will* try to behave and be a *good* boy—" and standing
to cross his promise, yanked tablecloth, bottle, glasses, trays,
cokes, decanters and four bottles of beer crashing to the floor.

"O you *fool's fool*," now Mama roared right at him, black
with rage as he turned white with fright, neither pretending
in the least—right under the table the two-hundred pound
hero ducked. And cowering there all could hear him plea—
"*Don't* whup me, mama, *please* don't whup me."

Unable to reach him with her fist, Mama seized his black
silk ankles and hauled him forth floundering on his back, his

eyes closed and covered by his arm to ward off anticipated blows.

"I don't like the looks of this," Mama told Hallie, "he aint got no right to be so loose without being drunk or sick, neither."

"He's sick enough for twenty," Hallie informed her. "Somebody get some water."

"Wouldn't beer do as well?" Floralee inquired, and emptied a full pitcher right in his face. Then, looking into her pitcher, grew sad. "Why, it's empty, fun's all done." She looked ready to cry.

"Use cokes," Hallie ordered.

Now who but Hallie could have thought of *that?* Floralee leaped for the half-finished bottles standing like small sentries on ledge and divan, and in no time at all had her pitcher full again. This time she poured it down the front of his shirt.

"That *was* fun," she told Hallie then.

"The fun is done," Hallie told her.

"Fun done," the girl accepted matters.

But on the floor the fun had only begun. There he lay licking his big ox-tongue, a coke-licking Lazarus too languid to rise.

"I've been everywhere God got land," Mama announced, "but this is the most disgusting sight yet seen."

"You can drop his legs now," Hallie pointed out, and Mama released the ankles, that dropped like a dead man's legs.

Both women stood looking down. Hallie herself didn't know what to do with the fellow.

As Navy finally opened his eyes.

His eyes so blue, so commanding.

"That was the nicest party I've had in twelve years," he congratulated everyone.

Mama lowered herself in all her finery, onto a divan and sighed, just sighed.

"Bring me the evening paper," she asked after a while, "I want to see what the white folks are up to."

The figure, the face and the gleaming braid of the madman who had spent a month's pay in a night dimmed swiftly. His money long spent, nobody cared what had become of the Lieutenant-in-Command.

"I wonder," Mama grew suspicious later, "whether that officer told us the entire truth."

"So far as he knew it," Hallie took a guess.

"You figure he left out a little something or other?"

"Black Mammy wasn't as simple as he likes to think. I think she had lapped the field."

"I don't follow your meaning."

"Why, I think from the day she paddled that little boy, she knew what kind of material she was working with. I think whether that little boy became a man or stayed a little boy was entirely up to her. She had a choice between herself and the boy, and she chose against the boy. That was the only way she had of not one day losing him to a white girl."

"I'd purely hate to believe that a common field darky could be that evil," Mama turned Hallie's theory down cold.

"She wasn't a field darky. She was a house darky with scores to settle in that same house. Everything she had the white folks had taken. She saw her chance to get something back. I'll take my oath she was getting even on somebody."

"No," Mama still declined to believe, "everybody got to love somebody and that woman wasn't give nobody but a little white boy to love, and he wasn't give nobody but an old black mammy. When things are like that color and age even don't matter. In love, not even price matter. Yes, Black Mammy genuinely love that child."

"It's what I've been trying to tell you all along," Hallie agreed. "In love price don't matter nor which lover pays.

It's why he can't hate her even to this day though he knows now what she did to him."

Though the languid lieutenant was far to sea—gone without trace never to return, his visits began a slow sea change. He had spent so freely Finnerty had been encouraged to believe there must be other such fools about, in uniform or out. Finnerty was right.

"It's the age of specialization is what it is," he began preaching a new faith, "Do you go to a eye doc to get a tooth yanked? Do you go to the ice cream parlor for stamps? New fields is opening and one is the bug field. Hundreds of bugs loaded with gold, the depression aint even touched them, willing to pay somebody to make them happy. It don't make a bug happy to come into a joint, point out a girl and go to bed. Nowadays he wants the bit spiced up. He wants the girl to tell him, 'Do what you want with me.'"

Perhaps too it was Finnerty's new girl, a spare and bitter child just out of a Houston jail who had encouraged him, for she seemed not to care in the least what became of her. "My name is Kitty Twist," she had told him, "and I do everything."

Her breastless, sexless personality was no matter, Finnerty knew. For this was the kind of girl upon whom a man might recover something of which a wife or mistress had robbed him. The city was full of hatless Harrys seeking not so much love but vengeance for wrongs, real or fancied, forever imposed by women: wife, nurse, sister, daughter, mistress or aunt. Woman, *there* was the cause of it all.

A traffic founded on self-pity that paid off better than the old-fashioned traffic in love. Love's dividends came in single bills; but hatred's comes by twenties.

"It's the new way of doing things," Finnerty approved.

And the men who came buzzing in the lieutenant's wake had the twenties. Apparently they didn't read the papers, for they gave no sign of knowing that the country was in the very depths of an economic disaster. They were men who had been sheltered all their lives and were sheltered yet. Their world was the world of their own needs alone, and if they looked out of a window at the street below, nothing they saw, or nobody down there, had any relationship to their own safe halls.

Brokers and buyers, efficiency experts with private means, personnel managers from banking families, men who had been born to ownership of ships or banks or mines or wells—the whole contented clan of white-collar foxes whose hearts were in their collars and their love locked in their files, who yet wanted to know of life—"What's the answer?" Without pausing once to wonder what was the question.

"These are *class* people," Finnerty tried to impress his girls. "If one tells you to swing from the chandelier, baby, you swing."

"Why not just sell the beds and buy trapezes for the money?" the new child wanted to know right off.

"You're always in there with the wise answer, aint you?" Oliver warned her.

"Because you're always there with the right question, Little Daddy," Kitty tried quickly to soften her new daddy.

Against the collar clan the lunch bucket brigadiers—boilermakers, janitors, construction workers, merchant mariners, grease-monkeys, slaughter house bullies, plasterers and brick layers didn't stand a chance. The collars had fancied love up until the best looking and youngest of the women were out of range of the bucket boys. Why tie up a piece of merchandise for half an hour with a date smelling of fish or tar, when one smelling of nothing but after-shave lotion would pay five times as much and perhaps not even soil a towel?

"Mama," Oliver gave out the news, "we're going to forget these workin'-ass bums who don't even know a girl has a soul. I know one pimp willing to stand on the corner waiting for a broad to turn a three-dollar trick so he can get a haircut,

but I don't call that a pimp. I got every one of my broads in-
sured and I got a plane to keep up too. What the workin'-ass
man wants he can get elsewhere. From here on out we cater
strictly to the bug who wants something he's afraid to ask his
wife for—or what he'd rather not have her give. Or what she
can't give."

"I'm not sure I'm following, Oliver."

"You're following all right," Finnerty assured her.

"Well, I don't care for where I think you're leading. What
can any girl of ours give a man that his wife can't?"

"*Virginity*, woman," the pander almost spat the word—
virginity. Else how is it that when I say to some clown—
'Would you like to see the girls, mister?' he just dogeyes me
and keeps on walking. But when I say, 'Mister, are you interested in a girl who's never been had?' it's just too much for
him. He slows down, thinking it over, turns the corner, comes
back on the other side of the street and all I have to do is
wait. He comes to me then. 'What did you mean by that?'
he wants to know and by the way he says it I know whether
he's the law or a bug. 'I meant are you interested in witnessing
a girl giving in for the first time?' Mama, you'd be astonished
how almost every one will come up with a ten-spot just on
a promise like that. Honest to God, some days I feel rotten
about everyone but myself."

"Some days I feel rotten about you too, Oliver," Mama
admitted.

The little man sat clasping his stomach as though in pain.
"What kind of a sport wouldn't hop to a chance like we're
offering? Why, it's like having a girl's very soul. Love he
can get at home—but the *soul*, the *soul*—Did his mother neglect
him? Did his auntie seduce him? Did his mother-in-law rob
him? Did his wife desert him? Did his mistress betray him
—Here's a chance to get even with them all."

"Calm yourself, Oliver," Mama urged him, "because no
man is coming for no such purpose to any house of mine,"

Mama found her voice at last, "I've been an underworld woman all my days. I have faith my Lord will forgive me for that. For I've been straight with Him and straight with my-self—"

"—and straight with your girls too, of course," Finnerty stopped her. His very tone stopped her. "Sit down, old woman. There's something I've been meaning to have out with you and this is as good a time as any."

Mama sat down.

"It's a little matter of a bill that went into your hand a C note and came back to me as a ten spot. If it had been any broad but the Looney I'd think maybe it was her and not you. But it's true that the girl never actually looked at that bill— I've watched her take money time and again and she never looks at it, just puts it away until she sees me, then hands over the lot. So I know she gave it to you as she got it—old woman, it was you pulled the gypsy switch on your best, your only friend. Do you call that being straight for the Christian-killing Moses's sake, old woman?"

"Oliver, if I know what you're talking about I'll kiss your behind before God."

Finnerty cocked his head a bit at that. "You know what you just said is as strong a statement I've heard a Louisiana nigger make to a white man for some time?"

"Oliver, it's the truth. I *don't* know what you're talking about."

"Look," he began losing patience. "I whupped the broad and she said 'No.' I whupped her harder and she still said 'No.' Finally I took my mittens off, ready to give her the real thing. She still said 'No.' Mama, I don't want to whup *you*. But I *know* it wasn't the broad. I *know* it was you."

Mama could scarcely bear the injustice of this. "For God's sake, boy. What makes you so sure it wasn't the mark who switched on you?"

Finnerty smiled thinly. "I was wondering how long it was

going to take you to come up with that. It don't go, old
woman. I never took eye off that bill from the moment I put
it in the mark's pocket."

"Were you *in* the room when he gave it to the girl?"

"As good as. I had my eye to the hole."

"How could you see the number on the bill through a key-
hole?"

The shadow of a doubt passed across the pander's mind—
but he recalled the sheer simplicity of Dove's face and the
shadow passed. It just couldn't be. For that redheaded country boy hadn't been just an ordinary mark. He had been a
mark's mark, the kind a man might wait a lifetime to meet,
so simple it was pathetic.

"Any one but *him,* Mama," he told her—then suddenly
realizing how very near she had come to throwing him off the
track he made up his mind twice as firmly as before—"Mama,
I'm going to hear from your own lips that it was you who
switched on me and nobody but you."

Mama knew that tone and could only sit shaking her head
miserably, "No. No. Let me die the worst death there is if
I took it."

Finnerty rose.

"Oliver, I know what you're going to do. But I just can't
fix my mouth to say what you want me to."

Finnerty pulled on a single mitten. He drew the cloth down
tight over each separate finger. When every wrinkle had been
smoothed he turned his wrist slowly to test its hinge. Then he
drew on the other glove.

"Yes," Mama told him. "Yes. Yes. Yes."

"I knew you done it all the time," Finnerty said, "and I'm
not billing you for it. But never let me hear you say again
that you play it straight. Not to *me* you don't say it. Here."

He poured her a cognac and offered it full to the brim
without a spilling a drop. But Mama's hand shook so when she
took it he had to help her to bring it to her lips. When it

was empty she held it out for more. He filled it again. This time she drank more steadily. And still she wanted more.

"If I can save one sparrow a single misstep," she began.

"That'll do for now, old woman," Finnerty told her, "I've got work to do and so have you."

And left to study his mouse.

What passed for the Wrath To Come on the walk and what passed for the Wrath inside the parlor were hells an earth apart. Though that amateur savior warned the women of the middle-pits of Hell, the women themselves felt sure that the pits were reserved exclusively for finks. Certainly no reasonable God would hold a grudge against a girl for earning her bread by the sweat of the sex with which He had blessed her. But to save one's own skin by crying off on a sister—no God worth the name would overlook as lousy a trick as that.

Beside, God must be on their side because He was on Mama's. And wasn't Mama forever bringing home moulting canaries or bargain goldfish because she felt sorry for them? Didn't she say almost every day, "If I can save one sparrow a single misstep it makes my own missteps worthwhile?"

Long after midnight old lonely trains called up to Mama like lovers forever arriving too late for love. Up from the long grieving river they called, past track and tower and dock, to windows long darkened and doorways long locked; old beaux that had walked Perdido Street long ago, returning to mourn the names of girls they had loved. They had plenty to spend and all night for loving. But the windows were darkened, the doors were locked, and the only girls whose names they knew had no name now but dust.

Mama would rise from her bed so wide, the Woman The Pope Didn't Want, so fierce to defend the weak and the motherless, so watchful of the sparrow's fall until a dollar was involved. And saw some too-late lover come to stand below a lamp that made the whole night look hired.

Down on the corner she heard some woman jangling around for a straight four dollar trick. Then her husband, down the block, signaling with a set of keys of his own—"I got a trick here, Baby, so come on home." And the empty night came down again.

From somewhere upstairs or somewhere down, a mountain girl's voice began telling the dark—

Oh blow away the morning dew—

And knew, Mama knew that soon or late the hour would come when the hurry-up wagon would haul girls with pride and girls with none, those who had saved and those without Penny One, to that cellar below the cells where one door leads to freedom and another door leads to jail. One back to the street and one to a tier. That some would buy out then and some would bail out and some would cry off on their sisters.

Oh blow away the morning dew
How sweet the winds do blow

"If I can't die sanctified," Mama crossed herself where she stood, "at least let me die blessed."

Because the air was so close, the whiskey so bad, the prices so high and the place so hard to climb up to, every one came to Dockery's Dollhouse night after night while other bars stayed empty.

Every one came, that is, but the law. To this lopsided shambles, where the floor slanted slightly, no police ever came. When the big hush fell that meant trouble was starting, the old man drew the shutters until the trouble was done.

The old man had himself never fought another man in his life—yet he took a senile pleasure in watching others go at it. He pretended that it was the manly thing, to "let them fight it out"—but the titillating joy he took when the first blood flowed was a womanish delight.

And though there were frequent brawls, he took care that none attracted the attention of strangers on the street outside. Only the steady thud of the fans overhead and a desperate scuffle of shoes and breath would be heard when two panders fought up and down the floor.

Suddenly as it began it would be done. Doc would be letting in the light, victor and vanquished would be having a shot on the house, the babble of voices would rise once more, the juke would start *Dream Train* or *It's Only a Paper Moon* —and everyone would feel something real had been accomplished at last.

"Let's see what them damn mackers are up to," hustlers would suggest to each other on afternoons off—"I'd rather see a fight tonight than ride the New York Central—"

If a man were hurt so seriously that he could not rise to drink, old Doc poured a shot down his throat personally, and friends hoisted him and deposited him behind some less lucky dive.

Yet all the fights were strangely unnecessary, and not one of them ever solved anything. The mackers never fought over anything real, like money or love. Had High Daddy really told Easy Rider's woman that she didn't dress her man with class? Had Easy Rider actually said that Spanish Max would stool on his own mother? They fought for their honor, that must have been it.

Not because they had too much whiskey in them, but because they hadn't enough. Their lives went dry as their glasses; lack of love parched their throats. They wished to be drunken, forever drunken.

"Too much salt on the potato chips," someone was always complaining to Dockery.

"Them chips is what gives people a thirst," Doc explained,

"it's why the mustard bowls is always full and plenty of good old salty pretzels too."

To be drunken, forever drunken.

Yet Dove came there at noon, long before the drinkers' hour, only to put his sample case below the table and his book above it, to order a poor boy sandwich and a bottle of beer.

Then the book before him, the beer forgotten, at last he saw for himself how different an A was from a B.

He was studying M and N one noon when a shadow fell across the page and Finnerty's finger shut the book like shutting it forever.

"What kind of con is this—*Fairy Tales*—you connin' little kids or something now, country boy?"

Dove took his book and pocketed it. "Hello, Oliver," he said.

Finnerty shook his head incredulously. "To think I took you for the simplest fool in town. To think that I thought that W on your forehead stood for Watkins."

"I'm in the field for Watkins, Mister," Dove reminded the pander with understandable pride.

"Man, you *are* great. Simply great. And the sample case tops it. Just tops it. Lugging that thing with your country look, who could ever have guessed what your real line of goods was?"

He pulled a chair beside Dove's, and sat so near and talked so low, his mouth right at Dove's ear and his little finger hooked to Dove's, that Dove felt trapped between him and the wall.

"Buddy, *as* your buddy," Oliver whispered wetly, "it's now my duty to tell you that my new child got one terrible hard edge out for you. It's all I can do to keep her from coming in on you. No, I don't mean that real hard swindle where she took the rap and you went south with the bundle. I doubt Texas will extradite you for that. But how's your conscience resting, buddy? Did you know the broad done a hundred

days without commissary? You and I both know what it is
to be busted without a pack, Jack. Of course if that's how
you expect your broads to do time that's your business. But
I wouldn't treat a yellow dog like that."

"Mister," Dove tried to get his little finger unhooked, "Mister, that old gal quoted you a mistruth."

"I hope you aren't thinking I'd take a hustler's word against
that of my own sample case buddy? The very buddy who
broke in my top-earning broad for me?" Oliver was hurt
that Dove should even suspect him of forgetting a favor like
that—"*Naturally* she lied. Who ever heard of a hustling
woman who wouldn't rather lie than ride a passenger train?
Buddy, what I'm telling you is I'm going to get you *out* of
this. Man, I *been* to Hurtsville, I *know* what it is. They made
me regret the day I was born there but they aint going to
make my sample case buddy regret the day *he* was born.
What if she *does* claim she was underage when you transported her across a state line in a moving vehicle? That don't
cut ice with Oliver Finnerty."

"Mister," Dove got in a word at last—"I never transported
nobody. We just rode a old freight train a ways together,
that was all. You'd scarcely call that 'a moving vehicle' I don't
reckon."

Finnerty unlocked his little finger as though that had been
Dove's idea—"What would *you* call it, Mr. Bigass? A possum
up a telegraph pole?"

"Well, it weren't no *passinger* train."

"Brother," Finnerty put a hand on Dove's shoulder,
"Brother, it don't matter was that a box car or on roller
skates, that broad can swear out a hold order for you in any
district station in town—"

"I pulled her out from under the wheels!" Dove remembered in a shout—"I treated her *good!*"

Finnerty shook his head solemnly. "You can *always* treat

one too good," he reminded Dove, "but you can never treat
one too bad."

"I saved her dirty fool life," Dove added, yet felt his courage sliding down all drains.

"I'm sure you did," Finnerty agreed sympathetically, "but
still it don't cut ice."

"She were *willin'*," Dove recalled desperately. "Fact is, she
were more willin' than me. She got more willin' all the time.
Fact is I took to sleepin' on my stomach, she were that
willin'."

"Willin' don't matter. Under age is statutory rape though
she put a gun at your head."

"She didn't have no gun," Dove conceded, "but I sure
didn't sexutory-rape nobody, mister—" yet strangely flushed
with guilt.

"We've all done crazy things from time to time," Oliver
lowered his voice for he read that flush aright—"What I always say is if you're not champeenship material, you might
as well let the women get you now. Buddy, a broad is only
a broad but a pal is a pal, so put your mind at rest. I'm not letting Texas get no holder on you because some broad wants
to cry off. It'd be as good as her life and I've told her as much.
'Baby,' I told her, 'when you held out on me that was one
thing, but crying off on my pal is another.' Now do you
want me to see you through this sorry situation you got yourself into or don't you?"

Dove was beginning to feel scared in a way he had never
been scared before.

"I'd be mighty grateful for your help, mister."

"One good turn deserves another. But I'll expect your complete cooperation from here on out. I'm the general. You're
the private—when I give an order I expect to see it carried
out. For I'm not without help," he added softly.

"You're my captain," Dove agreed, "I'm your hand. But
there just one little favor I'd like to ask."

"What's that, old buddy?"

"Don't call me Mr. Bigass."

"Shake—Tex." Finnerty extended his hand.

Dove shook it with gratitude.

"I've kept my part of the bargain, mister," Dove told Finnerty in Mama's parlor half an hour after.

"That you did, and I'm that proud of you I'll brag you up all over town," he promised—"Come and get it."

He held out a five dollar bill.

Dove turned it over as though the number on the other side might be different, then passed it to Frenchy.

"Tell 'em where you got it and how easy it was," he told her, and walked indolently toward the door.

A huge disbelief dawned in Finnerty's brain. He caught up with Dove at Dockery's door. He was a little out of breath and waited till they were inside to offer Dove a drink.

"Give this man what he wants to drink," he told Dockery breathlessly, "*any time he wants it.*"

"Any time this man wants a drink," Dove assured Dockery, "he'll pay for it hisself," and laid a C note on the bar before the pander's eyes.

Finnerty started to reach for it. Dove put his hand gently down.

"I understand the price is ten bucks per peeper, Oliver," he told Finnerty. "You had a full house. I'll take my thirty now."

Finnerty went for his wallet. Slowly. Yet he went.

"I'd never of believed it," he admitted, laying three tens on top of the C note, "I wouldn't of give you the credit for the having the cold nerve."

"You provide the virgins, mister," Dove promised, "I'll provide the nerve."

"I guess you know I had to give a poor broad a ninety dollar whupping account of you?" Finnerty reproved Dove as he watched a hundred and thirty dollars disappear in Dove's wallet.

"It's what I always say," Dove told him cheerfully, "you can always treat one too good. But you never can treat one too bad."

Airless days when panties of purple and braes of black, silver g strings and dappled halters hung on the clothes lines in a kind of joint-tog jungle still as all Brazil. A jungle whose foliage was such garments of bright shame as were washable, whose cries were those of the pepper pot man—

> *All hot! All hot!*
> *Makee back strong!*
> *Makee live long!*
> *Come buy my pepper pot!—*

Odors, and cries, a chemise stained by mascara, the spill of water into a basin before the long day's first-risen lover locked with the last girl left awake. They went at it like foes, navel to navel, still his two dollars of passion was spent. Then just as he stood with one sock drawn on and the other foot bare, he was touched by a perfumed disgust.

Disgust like a perfume pervading a forenoon that felt perpetual; till noon mixed with evening and evening with night.

Then a reddish scent as of soap or blood and the voices of women and an air of haste began somewhere upstairs or somewhere down. Then cigar-smoke mixed with eau-de-cologne and incense with whiskey and whiskey with gin. Then sometimes upstairs and sometimes down Dove Linkhorn could always be found.

Sometimes in a red shirt, sometimes in a yellow, wearing cowboy boots and a black silk bandanna, one foot on Dockery's bar-rail or leaning on Dockery's juke, he wasted no time in letting strangers know who he was.

"Shake hands with Big Stingaree! Just up from the Rio

Grande! See these boots? They cost forty dollars. See this
hat? Cost thirty-five. I do most of the drinking here 'n all the
buying. Anything you want, just point. I take care of my
friends. You want to say hello to a girl, just say which one.
They're most of 'em mine but I'm not the jealous kind, I pass
'em around 'cause I know they'll come back. They always
come back to their Daddy-O. It's what they call me, their
Daddy-O, but you can call me Tex. Any time you drop by
and I aint here just tell that old man behind the bar you're
waitin' for Tex. Tell him what you want to drink—he works
for me—and sooner or later I'll be by with one on one arm
and one on the other and most like a new shirt one of 'em's
just bought me. See this belt? A girl give me that."

The whiskey brown, the rum so black, the beer so dark,
the gin so pale.

"Couldn't read my name were it wrote a foot high on the
side of a barn but I make more in a single day than some
educated fools earn in a month. Drink up."

Whiskey, corn liquor, gin or rye, Big Stingaree drank it
down. Big Stingaree drank whatever was poured, till drops
dribbled down his shirt red or yellow and beer stood in his
boots. Once he stood up in a puddle of urine or wine, and his
face looked lopsided with its load of rum. He waved his arms
till somebody shut off the juke. Big Stingaree had something to tell all panderdom.

"Burn down your cities!" he demanded; and wove a moment to remember what else had to be done. "Burn down
your cities 'n save our farms," he concluded lamely.

"Well, go on, go *on*."

But whatever it was he was trying to recall, that was all
Dove could remember.

For sometimes once a day, sometimes twice, Finnerty's
gentlemen stood with eyes fixed to a wall to achieve vicari-
ously that ancestral lust: the deflowering of a virgin.

Finnerty was right: it was a fantasy that had pursued them,

every one, all their lives; they had not pursued it. They had
only made of it a secret mystery that never could come true.

A mystery as false as it was secret. Yet Finnerty made it
whirl with fiery colors, like a pinwheel in the dark; that be-
comes, when it is not spun, no more than a piece of painted
wood. He instructed the girls not to yield their chastity easily,
but only with tears, after a bit of a struggle.

At this game Floralee was no hand at all, for she couldn't
understand that the old game now had a new twist. Nor did
she wish to understand. As soon as Dove entered and hung
up his stetson she threw off every stitch and in a voice like
little bells on a silver string began play-partying—

Cat had a kitten, kitten had a pup

she invited Dove to clap hands with her—

Say old man is your rhubarb up?

Nobody could make her understand that that wasn't at
all how lovely reluctant virgins carried on.

*There's plenty of rhubarb all around the farm
And another little drink won't do us any harm.*

Reba, on the other hand, played her part too well. Racing
from one corner to another, she would shrink like a wild
trapped thing, burying her face in her hands and crying
"*Never!*" to the walls, "Never! Never! Never!"

Beating Dove's chest with both her fists, again her plate
slipped as she pled for her honor. Yet that in no wise dismayed her. Good trouper that she was, she kept right on
beating her gums in time to her fists, "Never! Never! Never!"

Considering the abortions she had survived, she was sur-
prisingly fleet. Feinting Dove out of position, she would leave
him breathless there in nothing but red garters and boots. At
length he was forced to complain to Finnerty.

"I admire talent in a woman," he protested, "and I don't
expect one to make things easy for me—but chasing *that* one

up and down and around is simply wearing me out. She's a fine little broad and all of that, but she's just too zeelious."

Sometimes the virgin was Frenchy. Kitty clamored to get into the act but the amateurish tattooing on her arms and legs, that she had inflicted upon herself as a child, disbarred her.

"Who ever heard of a tattooed virgin?" Finnerty dismissed her.

"I'll keep my clothes on," she offered.

"They'd want their money back," Finnerty told her, "get down to the door where you're supposed to be and don't let me catch you off your post again."

She did not perceive that had she only acted reluctant about performing, he would have appointed her to be deflowered upstairs instead of merely to stand guard below, hour upon dull hour.

It was never Hallie. It never could be Hallie. Yet what Finnerty would have given to get *that* one in there! There was no way of debauching her. She had been in a thousand corners with a thousand men and had come away with herself untouched.

It gnawed at him, just as it gnawed him that every time one of these Never! Never! innocents was deprived of her maidenhood he had to divide sixty dollars with Dove—admittedly a generous wage for that type of work.

"There are those who'd be happy to give me a hand for nothing," he told Dove.

"Fly-by-nighties," Dove reminded him, "here today and gone tomorrow."

It was true, and Finnerty knew it, that Dove could not be replaced. Every time Finnerty put an eye to the wood to check on him, he was giving an honest day's work for an honest wage. Reliable to the bone. And, nothing, it seemed, impeded his tidelike powers.

Like the sea, he came and went.

Indeed, Finnerty could not contain his secret enthusiasm for Dove's prowess. "You never seen nothing like it," he invited Legless Schmidt to see, "God has put his arms around that ungodly clown."

"Why would God put his arms around something like *that?* You can leave God out of it, for I won't pay a nickel."

"I wouldn't think of asking *you* to pay," Finnerty employed his injured air. "I just thought you'd get a laugh out of the thing."

"It's nothing to laugh about," the big half told the pander.

"How can you tell till you've seen it?" Finnerty insisted— "How this mad stud comes on! Man, it's *educational.*"

"Thank you, I'll stay ignorant," the cripple decided firmly.

"Think it over, friend," Finnerty suggested, "the offer is good any time."

Why he wanted to involve Schmidt, Finnerty himself wasn't clear in his own mind. He resented the crippled man's air of independence as unbecoming when able-bodied men were out begging, but that wasn't all of it. It was Hallie's dismissal of his own charms, made so lightly, that was at the bottom of it. How could a woman prefer a man without legs to a little beauty like himself?

If you couldn't get at somebody yourself, Finnerty knew, your next best bet is to get at somebody who has already gotten to her.

And whether for laughs or whether for lust, his mathematics of the soul began to add up nicely. Some white collar bug would wander in pretending to look for a friend; then another friend-seeker and another, till there were five or six. One by one Finnerty would take them out for a little private talk, and then his voice could be heard, confident, promising, reassuring from behind a half-open door. Till the bargain was sealed and a ten dollar bill changed hands.

When the buyer put his eye to the peep-hole for which he had paid, he saw only a pale, demented girl, blonde braids bound tightly about her head, wearing a simple cotton frock and her pale hands folded in her lap.

Then in strode some kind of redheaded hayseed in a sheriff's hat with a flashy cord and boots that were all but spurred—the hiders could almost smell the whiskey on him. When the hayseed took off his hat the pale girl loosened her frock. What a dunce the fellow looked after that! The only sound in the room was his heavy breathing and the whirr-whirr-whirr of the ceiling fan slicing the obscene heat. What a clown! He was going about his job in there as though it were hero's work, a thing no one else could possibly do.

Some felt contempt of the shameless dunce, but not all. Each watcher was affected differently.

One paled slowly as he looked and, after a minute, left for good thinking how sad such things were so.

Another laughed smugly deep as his liver, to see proven at last what he had long suspected: a man was a two-legged animal and a woman a four-legged one, nothing more. And left thinking how lucky it was, such things being so, that he had been there to see.

Yet a third looked thoughtful, as at a demonstration in carpet weaving: see, there was still money to be made in small enterprise.

Another felt stale lusts grow swift and bit his lip for lack of cash: had he every dollar in town tonight, all would be spent by morning.

But the great cripple neither laughed nor paled. Only the lines of his heavy head hardened and he swung his torso on its tiny wheels and wheeled off down the hall, making a rolling thunder to hide his indignation.

No, Schmidt didn't believe in this sort of thing at all.

The other peepers would be sitting in the parlor once more when Dove returned downstairs—that was when the fun really began. The sight of the fellow combing his hair or playing the juke, seemingly innocent that he had performed publicly, sent such glances of cold glee back and forth that soon every one had their money's worth. That the joke, after all, was on themselves, was a bit of knowledge Finnerty took pains not to divulge. Had they understood that the dunce in the stetson was not only aware that he was watched, but was secretly proud to display his powers, they might have mobbed both Dove and Finnerty.

Schmidt, of course, knew the story, and didn't share the amusement others felt. From a corner where the light hardly fell he studied Dove. Big Stingaree's shirt was open at the throat and his throat was flushed to the chin, for he had thirty dollars to spend once again. And was spending it the way he'd found it went fastest, by buying drinks for everyone.

"He don't know the show is over," Schmidt realized, just as the juke began to sing—

> *They needed a songbird in Heaven*
> *So God took Caruso away—*

Dove began mugging silently with the singer, pretending it was his own voice mourning Caruso. "I wish I could sing truly," he would lament when Caruso was done, "but I lost my voice hollerin' for gravy."

This legless man was an old carnie hand who had lived among human skeletons, 500-pound women, dog-faced boys, spider men, living heads, geeks, half-men-half-women and dwarfs in the maimed world of sideshow exhibitions; but it seemed to him he had never seen anyone who filled him with such disgust as this grinning pimpified country braggart pretending he was Enrico Caruso.

When the song was done Dove spotted Hallie. He came up beside her, raised her glass, drained it and called—"Bartender! This lady needs a drink!"

Hallie covered her glass with her hand.

"What you settin' at the bar for if you don't want to drink?" Dove demanded.

"I'd rather buy my own."

"What's the matter, Hallie?" his bravado began to crumble, "I done nothing against you."

"I just don't like to drink on someone who don't know what he's doing, that's all."

For reply he took a whole tumbler of gin and gulped it down in a single breath, then set it back on the bar with a sigh.

"What did it prove *that* time?" she asked him.

"It prove I can drink gin," Dove informed her.

"That you've already proved. I haven't seen you sober in a week."

"Whose money is it, mine or yours?"

"Yours," she assured him, and turning away, left him weaving.

Schmidt was waiting for her at the door.

"What were you two whispering about?" the cripple barred her way.

"I told him I think he's killing himself."

"Then let him. The sooner the better."

Yet once it was morning when she came down to the parlor carrying her lamed cat. After the long night of riot the spiders, that at midnight had twisted and swung on their metal wires, now hung motionless. The night was done and the early light lay scattered about like broken glass, as if people had picnicked in a mausoleum here. And as in mausoleum the air felt exhausted. So close, so very still, that a sun mote in its silent play seemed like a sick-ward child told be quiet while its nurse sleeps on.

Hallie saw the pale mote searching a floor where the dead lay against the dead: a whole platoon of cokes had been wiped out at the foot of the juke, and the juke itself looked like it might never play again.

A single gin-fifth, the last of its line, lay face down where it had fallen, surrounded by dead butts and snipes that had burned themselves out on the floor. Bobbie pins, kleenex wads, beer caps, wine corks, a deck ripped savagely in two and tossed across the carpet in despair, made the whole place look like a field on which no quarter had been given.

Yet from somewhere heard a murmurous breathing, regular and slow. She followed the mote that searched, like herself, for the sole survivor too.

Hunched in a corner so deeply bent she thought he was sleeping, sat the boy with the face too young yet too old.

"Wake up," she told him. He rose and stood trying to pull the various parts of the Big Stingaree together while hiding something behind his back.

"Now what are you up to?"

"I'm sober," was his curious reply.

"But you'll be drunk by noon."

"It's my money."

"You told me that yesterday."

"I made sixty dollars yesterday. How much did you make?" He had Big Stingaree's parts almost together.

"If that's how you feel, give me back my book."

He brought it from behind his back. "I don't know how it happen to come my way," he pretended. "Of course it *must* be yours because you got all the knowance of books and I got nary knowance at all. Yet I don't see how that give you the right to mock others for ignorance."

"I never mocked you, Dove. You can have the book."

"It don't do me no good, for I can't read as you well know and you're mocking me in offering it."

"If you can stay sober till noon for a week, I'll teach you to read."

He took her up so quickly she grew suspicious and touched the book to take it back. "If you're sober at noon you can have it back."

He wouldn't let her have it.

"If I'm not sober I'll bring it back myself. That's a promise."

"You'll be too tight to remember any promise."

He was sober at noon. He was still sober at four. At five Finnerty's show went on. At five-thirty he came to her, still sober, and without a word handed her the book.

"Bartender!" he shouted to Dockery, and his knuckles were white on the bar—"Gin! Gin! Gin!"

That night Dove dreamed he was alone in a hotel in Houston. Somewhere in the room a cat was trying to throw up—it had something in its throat it couldn't swallow. He looked under a divan for it and behind a juke and then below a cot bed but everything was swathed in a mist, he could see nothing plain. Then a shadow moved in the mist and Hallie's cat made a dash for it right across the floor and disappeared into somebody's room. She was hiding something there she didn't want anyone else to see; she'd been up to something for some time now. Something was wrong with the animal but nobody dared to say what.

Behind a radiator it had hidden the baretoothed carcass of a kitten dead for weeks, and was suckling it. The kitten's teeth were bared to the bone of the jaw but the brindle put her mouth to the wasted belly and pushed against the death-stretched hide. Dove began beating it to make it quit but it felt no blows; though he beat it a long time. At last it looked around at him.

Along its whiskers fresh milk gleamed, and the dream went out slowly, like a twenty-watt night bulb saying goodnight.

Nobody on Perdido Street considered the legless man a freak. No one told that once, for a few brief weeks, he had once let himself be billed as one. For no one who knew that lion-browed gaze could doubt his profound naturalness. Below the heavy brows his eyes, set wide, burned even as candles in a room with no wind. Schmidt never blinked. He sat his platform like a saint of the amputees and gave you gaze for gaze. When at last you turned your eyes away he touched his little brown beard as much as to say, "I've seen enough of you too, friend."

He sold his wares and made his bets and drank his beer both dark and light and never forgot his dignity; nor permitted others to forget it. Once a girl had told him, "Keep your money, you need it worse than me," and had meant it kindly. But the man waiting like a mutilated statue on the low bed's edge, had paled below his tan.

"You should never have said that, sis," he told her and lowered himself and left.

Yet, the very next afternoon, the same girl had handed him a five dollar bill for a twenty-five cent bottle of perfumed water and he'd pocketed the five without even the pretense of making change.

Some saint. When you gave, he felt, you gave it all. When you took you took it all.

Now, nearing forty, having rebuilt his whole life on the rock of sheer courage, he felt the rock shift and could not believe it. Surely a man who has been once destroyed and fought back to the land of the living would not be picked for destruction twice. God would not permit it.

He was Schmidt who needed nobody, he was Schmidt who could never lose. And yet when he thought of Hallie, surely the rock slipped. How had his life, that he'd held so hard, come to be cupped lightly in a woman's palm, and the woman herself to be held in any nameless stranger's arms?

The thought sent him kneewalking about his small room, pounding his stumps in a blood-colored tantrum; for the neon traffic light beside his window flashed from red to dull gold and back to the hue of blood again. The stumps! The stumps were to blame for everything!

"One at the hip and one at the knee"—he punished both at once with his hands like hammers, sending a wire of white pain zig-zagging through his breast to his brain.

The stumps! The dirty stumps! He gasped like a great seal for air, air. Not again. Not twice.

Then composing himself began to wheel slowly, for wheeling was therapy for his rage. And as he wheeled remembered, and remembering, loved again. Saw her standing in a bead-curtain doorway as though even now she were waiting only for him; and how she would turn her head slowly when he rolled in, and how she would not look at him with pity, and how her mouth would say "darling" just to him.

"I'll get this out of my system tonight once and for all," Schmidt promised himself.

But before he'd go to Mama's he'd have a taste of Dockery's booze, to numb the pain in the stumps before making love. And a bit of talk with other cripples to numb the pain in his breast.

Dockery catered to cripples, and one that was almost sure to be on hand was Kneewalking Johnson; whose handicaps were greater even than Schmidt's own. Johnson was a Negro, and owned no platform. He had padded his stumps with leather and reinforced the pads with tin. To Schmidt there was something so backward about stumping up and down the city's walks on tin plates that he felt it his duty to modernize Johnson.

"Get on this thing," he ordered. Johnson didn't want any part of the platform, yet didn't wish to offend the Big Half.

"I get along alright, Mister 'chilles," he reported without looking at the raft, "I got my own way."

"Can you *back?*" Schmidt demanded. "Can you swivel? Can you move sidewise? Can you make good time?" And to show just what he meant he wheeled straight toward the juke, made an airbrake stop—"back!" he backed, "swivel!" he swiveled, "sidewise!" his hands on the wheels seemed mechanically driven, pimps and cripples and their girls scattered while cool heads got chairs in front of them—it was like being in a swimming pool with a rudderless motorboat.

Dockery stayed in the dark of his bar so that none might see his narrow smile. He loved seeing men and women in panic and flight, did old Doc Dockery, closed in with all their sins. Whatever ran over them only served them right, that smile revealed.

"Now let's see *you* try it," Schmidt paused at last.

Johnson had no choice. Hands lifted him and other hands buckled him fast, then everyone stood back.

"Give the man room," Schmidt commanded, "give the man a chance."

So the old man with kinked hair gone white, and nothing beneath his chest but a pair of short pants that small boys wear, put his hands, that were only half the breadth of Schmidt's and yet a full inch longer, to the wheels. And rolled himself gently back and forth, forth and back. Only a timid roll forward, only a shy roll back. As though he had not a room as big as a dance floor to move in but just a tiny cell.

It was no use. Nobody could get Johnson to be more daring. It grew tiresome watching him roll those few feet up and back till someone put a coin in the juke thinking that music might liven the old man up.

But when the music began all that happened was that the old man sang along with it and rolled no faster than before.

Ninety-nine year so jumpin' long
he made a strange, sorrowing cripple's dance—

> *To be here rollin' an' caint go home*
> *Oughta come on de river in 1910*
> *Dey was drivin' de women des like de men*
> *Well I wonder what's de matter, somepin' must be wrong*
> *I'm still here rollin' but everybody gone—*

"Now you see how much better it is *my* way?" Schmidt told him when he'd performed as best he could and had been allowed to unbuckle himself and kneewalk to the bar for the beer that was his reward. "Once you get used to it," Schmidt

assured him, "you'll be ashamed that you ever went around in
that old-fashioned way. I'll get you the wood, I'll get you the
skates and straps, I'll even put it together for you. Man, you'll
be *proud* to be on skates."

"Mister 'Chilles," the Negro felt obliged to assert himself at
last, "what you don't keep in mind is I caint work main-town
routes like you. I aint allowed on Canal, I aint allowed in white
neighborhoods. They tells me to get my livin' off my own
people 'n the walks is all bust and cracked out there. Lots of
places aint no walks at all, just old rutty wagon roads. I come
to a broke walk or a mud-hole after rain, what I'm gonna do
with a big old board like that? I got to unstrop myself, haul
that old board through the mud or down a drop, then strop
me up again. So you see, Mister 'Chilles, I wouldn't be savin'
time, I'd be losin' it."

But Schmidt had suddenly lost interest. Turned to a total
stranger at the bar and asked, "Jack, what's your frank opinion of a woman who'll go to bed with a man she don't even
know his name?"

He'd torture himself like that, as lovers always have.

For what would begin when he'd wheel into Mama's was
one of those mysteries born only in brothels—a relationship
with a deep river's surpassing strength: that had swept two
unready people into its current and now carried them past
dumb faces on the shore. Faces awe-struck or compassionate
at sight of so strong a woman and so strong a man suddenly
made more weak than those still safe on shore.

Finnerty was holding the big door wide when Schmidt
rolled in.

Like a statue of serenity calmly smiling.

"Hallie! At last your husband's come!" Mama called at once.

He had a greeting and a smile for every girl in the place but
Hallie. Floralee kissed his big hand, Frenchy stroked his hair
dark yet silvered, the one half-out-of-her-mind child and the

other with no mind to be out of, letting the pair of them compete to see which could get his straps unbuckled first. When each stepped back with a captured strap it was as though his stumps had springs—he leaped right into the center of the divan, tottered, regained his balance and glanced all around with triumphant pride.

Yet had not so much as noticed Hallie. Instead he shoved his hands down his pockets and came up with his palms filled with nickels, dimes, even half dollars—"Count it, girls! Count it!"—and slung every cent into the mildly astonished air—"Count it! Count it all!"

Frenchy and Floralee went down on all fours, diving under divans, hopping like rabbits, scurrying like mice. In a moment Kitty Twist followed, crawling, creeping, elbowing the others.

But the sallow woman in the portiere standing so silently never moved, though a coin rolled right to her feet.

"The most generous man I've ever known," Mama decided right there.

"Just buying like everyone else as far as I can see," Kitty Twist perceived.

"I notice when he's 'buying' you're right in there with your elbow in everybody's eye getting your full share," Hallie reminded the new child.

"You get yours," Kitty told Hallie quickly—"You stoop like everyone else."

"Why, I make my living here, honey, if that's what you mean," Hallie replied without heat, "what line of work are *you* in?"

Kitty grew more careful after that, for as much as the women heckled one another about their dates, they spared Hallie's relationship to Schmidt.

"You in the brown dress," he called to her as though he had not noticed her till now, "step out here where we can see what you got."

Hallie was obliged to stand alone in the parlor's center between Schmidt and the juke's unblinking eye. Like a sultan, he gripped the point of his little brown beard as he studied her manner of walking. And like a sultan swung his hand, to indicate he was now ready to view her from behind.

"Is this one healthy?" he asked Mama after a moment. "I hold you responsible."

But Mama was counting her beads, the others were looking out window or door—it was plain they felt their big daddy was overdoing things tonight.

Big Dad didn't feel he was overdoing a thing. He slid down off the divan and kneewalked around his selection.

And turning her head on her olive throat to follow the torso as it stumped, she thought, "What a man he must have been!" For even on stumps Schmidt moved with grace.

"I'll have a go at this one," he decided aloud, and swung himself after her through the portiere, his head just barely higher than her waist, with the satisfied pride of a man who has driven a cunning bargain.

But the moment the door shut behind them both pride and satisfaction fled—he seized her hand, kissed each separate finger, pressed his head hard right under her heart and clasped her as though she were the life he had lost. It was the stumps made him act like he had, he told her. It was all the fault of the stumps.

Hallie stood quite still, pitying the power that could not be contained. And after a while smiled down, stroked his hair and agreed as with a child: yes, it was all the fault of his stumps.

To such tenderness he reacted like an enormous cat. And rolled within his massive arms, pressed to the great cave of his chest, his lion's breath against her breast, she felt his passion relentlessly driving. And then it was as though no man till Legless Schmidt had possessed her.

Many had rented her, none had possessed her. Not for one moment, not even to the man she had married, had Hallie been subjugated as this shattered athlete subjugated her. To be re-

duced to a thing for the use of lust was her trade, and to that
trade she was long resigned. But to feel, below his lust, love
running like a river in flood terrified her; for she abandoned
herself to it, she lost herself in it, she could not help herself
against it. And then was ashamed—not that she had given herself to a cripple, but that she had violated the first rule of her
craft.

There were moments with him when she cried weakly and
begged his flesh, as if it were something apart from him, to let
her be. And at the same moment drawing his flesh so tight and
deep toward her heart, so fierce not to let him escape her, that
the man himself was brought close to tears as he lay back limp
and done.

Schmidt had never felt a woman like that before. With him
it was as if he had never had a woman completely till Hallie.
Only with her, not until her, never at any moment except
those with her was he a man, able, loved, possessing and possessed—his own true man again.

In her he spent a lifetime's wrath. In him she too lived once
more. Nine Christmases she had been buried, and twice that
many for him. And with each time together, each lived a little
while again.

Once, waking from sleep she became aware again of how
the Santa Fe wheels had rolled back his thighs, one at the hip
and one at the knee, into raw volcanic folds. She threw the
sheet across him to conceal, at once, his deformity and her
own disgust.

"I'm afraid you'll catch cold," she pretended.

"Don't worry"—she hadn't fooled him for a moment—"you
don't look no better to me than I do to you."

It always ended like that. And she never tried directly to
answer his insults, as bitter now that he'd had her as before.

"I don't want to go through this any more," she told him
what she had told him often. "I'm clearing out."

"Sister, if you think I'm going to say 'Please don't go,' you're barking up the wrong tree. When I get a bit of the booze in me it don't make no difference what girl I pick. All you tramps look alike to me."

"In that case you won't miss me. So goodbye."

But after he had dressed and she still lay on the bed he stumped to the dresser with a handful of bills. She lay with eyes closed pretending she didn't know what he was up to.

"There's a hundred or so under your comb and brush," he told her—"that's one way to anywhere. See you in jail." And so, having salvaged his pride at the cost of his heart, he left.

"I might just take you up on that one of these days," Hallie promised herself after he'd left.

Then in the damps and glooms of her little room, Hallie slept.

Schmidt's greatest joy was Armless Charlie, a panhandler whose face was a mask of fright and whose arms ended in delicate nibs, more like fingered fins than hands, where another man's elbows would be. What stray wind off what derelict's row had blown him down Perdido Street nobody knew. But there he was with a dime between his teeth, placing it carefully on the bar—"Listen to this,"—Schmidt would command silence. And in the silence the beggar would ask, in a boyish lisp out of some eastern preparatory school:

"Mister Dockawee, might I have a beah pwease?"

"Everyone watch this!" Schmidt ordered as soon as the beer was put down.

Charlie would grip the glass with his teeth and tilt it till the beer ran over his face—he gulped frantically, catching every drop he could. Drenched and choking, yet he never unloosed the glass till it was empty. Then would set it down as carefully as he had picked it up, bow slightly and say,

"Thank *you*, Mister Dockawee."

"My *God*, what a pig!"—Schmidt would race back and forth on his platform, slapping his stumps. "Aint he the *worst*?"

A different brand of innocent was one who didn't come into
Dockery's at all, but always chose Mama's instead. This was
an ancient Negro carrying a curtained cage more ancient than
himself. He would set it down on its wrought-iron base, doff
his little red monkey-cap to each woman individually and at
last would pull a little string that caused the cage's shade to
rise.

Revealing a parrot that took one glassy glance around and
screeched, "Let me out! I'm a married man! Let me out!" Then
hung upside down in a clench-beak rage while biting the bitten
wood.

The old man stood a bit to one side, implying the bird was
now on its own. But kept his cap extended should anyone care
to drop a penny. If someone did, he would pull out a drawer
at the cage's base, where small pieces of colored paper lay folded
promisingly. The parrot would snatch one and permit the pur-
chaser to take it out of its beak. The message on each was the
same:

> *Dummy! Don't try to come back the way you came.*
> *Don't you know a tiger is trailing you? Stay*
> *off footpaths—they have been mined just for*
> *you. Don't peek under that stone, fool, a*
> *pit viper is planted there especially for you.*
> *If you have any sense left at all you'll stay*
> *downwind, six blunt-nose hyenas have a good*
> *whiff of you. Avoid open plains—buzzards*
> *have spotted you. Pay no heed to anyone in*
> *the trees, it is only the apes laughing their*
> *heads off at you. Natives are beating the*
> *brush for you. And you still call it*
> *'Civilization'?*
>
> *Call it what you want. I call it a jungle.*
> *Now you owe me 15¢ for a bowl of gumbo for*
> *being the only one not pursuing you.*

"I don't believe that old man wrote all that, he aint got the sense for it," Finnerty decided.

"Who did then?" Hallie wondered.

"The damned parrot, of course," Finnerty assured her.

And went off to see Kitty Twist. The new child who still had a thing or two to learn from his mouse.

Yet another wonder, neither snatch-mad nor prophesying, taxied in one narrowing twilight, made one brief scene; and no twilight brought him back again.

"In *per*son!" this one announced himself—"Adler! King of the acrobats! Good as ever!" Paunched and pallid, bald and tattooed: a man at least as good as ever. He came to the center of the parlor wearing seersucker so soiled and stained one wondered how many places he'd been thrown out of since the last time he'd changed.

. "Once an acrobat always an acrobat!" he announced—"I invented the double high-wire back somersault."

"You invented it but who *did* it?" Kitty Twist asked, but the king ignored all questions like that. Just stood back beaming until everyone had had a good look then asked so benignly: "How does it feel, now that you've met the king?"

"It feels like hell," Kitty told him.

"These young ladies are waiting for you to say hello, Mr. King," Mama let him know no one cared a doodle in a wood how great he was. If he wanted to stay he'd have to let loose of some loot.

That didn't disturb Adler. He knew how people loved to tease, pretending they hadn't heard of Adler.

"Are you with a circus or something, mister?" Floralee inquired hopefully, and somehow that set him off.

"Clear a space!" He met the challenge as a motion picture director might, or at any rate so we're told—"Women off the set! No crowding! Put out that cigarette!" Then pointing

right at Dove, who wasn't even wearing cowboy boots—"You
there! Tables end to end!"

Dove leaped to action, tumbling girls upon one another until
Mama gathered them up and put them safely behind her. In
rushed Finnerty to discover Dove placing two tables end to
end and the king in command.

"A little lower," the king instructed Dove. "No, a little
higher. There, that's just right."

"What the hell is this? a whorehouse or a circus?" Finnerty
demanded.

"The man has signified, let him qualify, Oliver," Dove urged
him to indulge Adler.

"It better be good, all I got to say," Finnerty compromised.

The king had stripped to the waist and the hair of his chest
gleamed white where it wasn't grizzled; a chest as good as ever.
Yet he dallied—"The king always says a few words first."

"Then *say* a few, king," Floralee pleaded.

"Very few," Kitty suggested.

"By God, this *better* be good," Finnerty resolved.

"Ladies 'n gentlemen," Adler nodded toward Hallie, "I dedicate this amazing demonstration of human agility to the lady
in the brown dress with the green earrings."

"Bust your damned neck instead and dedicate it to me,"
Kitty invited him.

Hallie didn't acknowledge his gift lest he take it to mean her
price tag was off. Ex-clown, ex-cop, ex-acrobat—ex-anything,
all sought to please this indifferent dark woman in every way
but by overpaying her. Money, they seemed to think, could
never please her.

"Do what you're gonna do," Finnerty said.

The king turned his back to the tables, did a knee-bend and
arched his back with surprising suppleness, bounded one short
confident step forward, pitched himself ass over appetite,
beaned himself beautifully on the table's edge and crushed flat,
shoulders shaking in noiseless laughter.

"Why, he didn't qualify after all!" Dove was just simply incredulous.

"Why don't we sell the juke and buy beds for the money?" Kitty asked, "every time I look around someone else is stretched out."

Finnerty kicked the fellow to his feet, booted him through the door, made a bundle of his cap, coat and shirt and pitched it through the door after. Then threw a spittoon just for good measure. It clanged loud as it struck the stone, rang less loud as it bounced, then splashed faintly into the gutter. For a moment after, all was still. Then Adler's foolish phizz popped right back in—"Good as ever!" he defied everyone, and cap in hand and draggle-shirted, scurried off to seek some door where everyone would cry out on sight—"Champagne all around! The king is back!"

Some place where he could back-somersault all night to applause that would never cease.

"Now don't you go faultin' me, Oliver," Mama told Finnerty. "I didn't invite the man. And why every fool who hits New Orleans has to head right for my door is more than I can understand."

The tables were back in place when the legless man rolled in. Immediately everyone but Floralee began trying to tell him at once what a show he'd just missed. For Floralee felt so elated by the whole thing all she wanted to do was sing—

> *"Joy! Joy! Joy!*
> *Since Jesus came to stay!"*

"Honey dear, run upstairs like a good girl," Mama asked her, for she knew how the girl loved to run any errand involving Hallie. "Tell Hallie her husband's come."

Floralee was so very long in coming down that at last Mama waddled up the steps herself. She found Floralee standing in the middle of Hallie's room looking vaguely around as if Hallie were hiding from her.

But the closet was empty, the shoe holder hung shoeless, the dresser was swept of brush, compact and comb.

Everyone was so stunned by the news that no one even thought to ask where Big Stingaree had gone, leaving his cowboy boots under his bed.

Achilles Schmidt had had his sniff of fame—a scent that prevails against all perfumes. Born on the outskirts of Mobile in a carnie show, he had grown into a shrewd wild boy who had learned reading and writing by working the bingo tents. He could still guess a woman's weight to the ounce by running his hands once down her clothes.

He had begun boxing professionally at seventeen and had lasted two rounds of his first bout—he'd never make a boxer. At seventeen he was already too heavily muscled for that.

He had billed himself as ACHILLES THE BIRMINGHAM STRONG BOY and country girls came to stand at the feet of a boy with an IBM brain in the body of a honeyfed bear. To bring the yokels crowding, he could scale a house and threaten the local sheriff, and give the wink to the girls all at once.

Yet it wasn't until he'd gone on the road as a professional wrestler in a coast-to-coast tour, stooging for a claimant to the world's championship, that he had found his own trade.

A trade that soon taught him such physical superiority over other men that he began, like the honeyfed bear, to protect others against his strength. For it wasn't just in the biceps and chest that he was greater than others, he saw without arrogance, but in the mind and the heart as well. That he was incapable of the meannesses he observed in others the boy did not consider a virtue in himself so much as an advantage, like the breadth of his chest, and was grateful. Who had put him together so generously he did not know, and yet wished to honor the wonderful luck of it. Leaning on the ropes in a great red cape, looking across row upon row in the smoky coliseums and tents, he saw how surely the wealth of all earth's tents, the women within them, the fame as well, would come to him.

There was time, and more than time for everything to come to Schmidt.

"When are you going to stop growing, Achilles?" a town girl once had waited outside his tent to ask.

"When I win the undisputed title," he told her jokingly, for his awareness of his powers had come to him so swiftly he had not yet had time to realize fully that there was actually nothing in the way of his winning that disputed title. Yet he could take the hand of a girl like that like any nineteen-year-old brother and say, "I don't want to grow bigger. I don't like to scare people."

"You're big enough now to scare the champion," she told him that night, "but you're not big enough to scare me," and turned her face to his own for the taking.

A face forgotten these twenty years. Yet the hand that had lain so light in his lay there lightly yet.

She had been right. He had been big enough for anything that night. On the road with the Strangler, he had had to hold himself back to keep his job. By the time they had reached the eastern mining towns he knew that no one in the world could beat the shrewd wild boy with the heart of a honeyfed bear.

But the Strangler had only a few years left, he himself had a lifetime. And he liked the Strangler, poor brute.

An old-time promoter, one of Dockery's hangers-on, admired The Birmingham Strong Boy yet—"He could hit you in the ass so hard you'd break your leg. And still I've seen him suffering the agonies of the damned, letting some country athlete haul him from one side of the ring to the other while he scaled the house, though nobody who was unarmed could really hurt him. Once some brave guy pitched him into the folding chairs before he'd finished counting the balcony. Achilles picked up two sets of them chairs, stretched the brave guy cold with one set and his manager with the other and held off the house till the cops arrived. Neither man nor box office could whip him. If you ask me, he could hold off the cops today."

Yet in the time it takes for a second-hand to move from

twelve to six he had been beaten for keeps and his glowing manhood beginning so luckily, so clean, was smashed into something half man and half-platform. Santa Fe freight wheels had proved even shrewder than he.

What had been extricated, after hours of extremest pain in which he had not once permitted himself to faint, was no longer Achilles The Birmingham Strong Boy, but only Legless Schmidt. One-At-The-Hip-And-One-At-The-Knee Schmidt to whom every two-legger might be the one who had rolled him beneath the wheels.

Sure he'd been drunk but what of that? He'd been on the drunk before and gotten a bit of sleep with one leg locked in a box-car's spine between one county fair and the next.

If it had been his own doing, no one's fault but his own, it would be easier to accept even now. Yet, moving behind his memory there lurked forever the suspicion that he had been deliberately shoved over. At moments he could almost feel the hands at his shoulder, the knee in his back.

Two years in a dusty desert hospital where the power that once had moved dead Achille's thighs began to flow with a wilder pride through crippled Schmidt.

All he now recalled of the hospital was the bitter blowing of alkali dust all day against the pane. And the face of some interne's wife who had cut a turtle-neck jersey for him from his red cape.

Where in letters once gilt now long washed to gray all that remained of his brief fame kept fading—

Young Achilles

Lost lost, all lost, swift as the desert dust that taps once and never is blown again.

Blown, blown, the fame and the gathering strength, the girls, the money, the power. Profession and pride gone in one night's passage—and gone so uselessly.

After that he had let himself be billed briefly as *The Living*

Half. He had sat his home-made platform in the freakish sun, looking down at farmers in town to see the freaks. And the honeyfed bear, that once had drawn in his claws, wished as he sat that he could be no more than one great claw.

The sideshow billing had been his greatest humiliation, one upon which he had drawn a shade. He never spoke of it himself and felt his secret was safe enough among the lost and the damned of Perdido Street.

Yet in his heart had never evened up for *The Living Half*—a thing like that.

Once while he chatted with several girls crowding behind a Perdido Street screen, a man with a metal support compensating for one short leg came hurrying down the street. He carried a brief case under one arm and pens and pencils in his coat. Late for some business appointment, that was plain.

Schmidt flared at sight of him, and wheeling after on noiseless bearings, sent the rival cripple spinning so hard that, had he not caught himself against a wall, he would have ended flat on his face. Then swerved with one deft twist of the wheels and faced his man, head lowered in challenge.

But all his man wanted was to be allowed to go his own way. He clubfooted it, hippety-hop, off the curb and around and went free.

Schmidt wheeled in triumph back to his girls. "Well, why give *him* a chance?" he asked. "What chance would he have given me?"

And the mascaraed, Maybellined eye-shadowed girls agreed with a cold vindictive glee—

"Why give *him* a chance? What chance would he have give you?"

Hallie and Dove lived behind a wrought-iron rail a long winding way from old Perdido. The rail enclosed a tiny balcony two stories above Royal Street. Across the way someone long ago had painted a white tin moon against a blue tin sky. A sky of midnight blue. A moon of Christmas snow. Long ago.

Now rust and rain had run the colors, sun had flaked the midnight snow. Nothing remained but a ruined moon in a sky that had fallen through.

Here in the hour of the firefly, while he and Hallie watched the lights of the Old Quarter flicker, the happy time came at last to Dove. The one happy time. From an unseen court or honkytonk, now far, now near, a piano invited them to join the dancers. Each night they heard the same piano and knew the dancing had begun once more.

Behind them a room, no bigger than a beer bottle turned upside down, held little more than a bed where the pupil slept with his fingers spread on his teacher's breast; and as she slept pressed to his side.

Till morning woke them with vendors' cries—

> *Here comes your skin-man!*
> *Bring out your dishpan!*
> *Cracklin's at five cents a pound!*

Once he wakened to see she had been smiling at him. When he asked her why the smile she told him it was because he made her sad "being such as you are and still not seeming to mind."

Along a bureau stood a set of morocco-bound books, all that was left of Miss Hallie Breedlove's schoolroom hours. Sometimes it was his turn for reading from them, sometimes Miss Hallie Breedlove's. For in that first swift rush of their days together he had learned, by the making of wonderful o-shaped mouths, to read unaided—

> *Water now is turned to stone*
> *Nurse and I can walk upon;*
> *Still we find the flowing brooks*
> *In the picture-story books*

We may see how all things are,
Seas and cities, near and far
And the flying fairies' looks
In the picture-story books

How am I to sing your praise
Happy chimney-corner days
Sitting safe in nursery nooks
Reading picture-story books?

And when he had finished the last round sound, would
flatten his lips in a grin so contented she would protest, "You
look like a cat eating hot mush on a frosty morning," and
would snatch back the book. "You haven't done anything a
six-year-old couldn't to look that pleased," she reminded him
to make the fat cat-grin go. *"Here"*—and gave him a passage
wherein he immediately mired himself in such tongue-thud-
ding woe that she took pity and began it from the start—

We shall not sleep, but we shall all be changed
In a moment, in the twinkling of an eye, at the last trump:
For the trumpet shall sound, and the dead shall be raised in-
*   corruptible, and we shall be changed*
For this incorruptible must put on incorruption.
And this mortal must put on immortality—

"Now what do you think of *that?*"
"I don't think purely *nothin'* of that," Dove decided—"it
remind me too near of my poor crazy pappy. Teacher dear,
read me that one where somebody's pappy got entirely
drownded."

Full fathom five Thy father lies
"*That's* the good part," he assured her.

Of his bones are coral made;
Those are pearls that were his eyes:
Nothing of him that doth fade
But doth suffer a sea-change
Into something rich and strange.

"Didn't take much changin' to make Pappy strange," he reflected. "He were a little on the odd side, from the life he led."

"We're all a little on the odd side," Hallie guessed, "from the life we've led. The life we've all led." And taking his hand led him to the bed.

"I don't mean for you to love me," she had to tell him a minute after, "just hold me. *Hold*."

Dove held her, sensing only dimly that in holding her he was saving her.

For around the margins of her mind, as about a slowly tilting floor, a tyrant torso wheeled and reeled.

Hominy-man is on his way!

someone shouted up from the street below—

To sell his good hominy!

The last metallic cries of day rang in the tootle and low moan of the earliest evening ferry. Then in the big blue dusk she told him of battles lost at sea and cities half as old as time. Together they read:

> The ashes in many places were already knee-deep; and the boiling showers which came from the steaming breath of the volcano forced their way into the houses, bearing with them a strong and suffocating vapor. In some places, immense fragments of rock, hurled upon the house roofs, bore down along the streets masses of confused ruin, which yet more and more, with every hour, obstructed the way; and as the day advanced, the motion of the earth was more sensibly felt—the footing seemed to slide and creep—nor could chariot or litter be kept steady, even on the most level ground.
> Sometimes the huger stones, striking against each other as they fell, broke into countless fragments, emit-

ting sparks of fire, which caught whatever was com-
bustible within their reach; and along the plains beyond
the city the darkness was now terribly relieved; for several houses, and even vineyards, had been set on flames;
and at various intervals, the fires rose sullenly and fiercely
against the solid gloom. To add to this partial relief of
the darkness, the citizens had, here and there, in the more
public places, such as the porticos of temples and the
entrances to the forum, endeavored to place rows of
torches; but these rarely continued long; the showers
and the winds extinguished them, and the sudden darkness
into which their fitful light was converted had something
in it doubly terrible and doubly impressive on the im-
potence of human hopes, the lesson of despair.

"Fishee! Fishee!" yet another peddler called—"Mullet! Mullet! Flounder! Blackfish! Shark steaks for dem what likes 'em!
Swordfish for dem what fights 'em! Fishee! Fishee!"

Toward midnight they went, by backstreets, to the ferry.
As the lights of the eastern shore swung toward them he suddenly made up his mind—"Pack of fools! To keep right on
livin' smack at the foot of the mountain 'n that volcano gettin' ready to pop any minute! Didn't they care if they lived
or died?"

"Why did you keep on living in a place where nobody
cared whether you lived or died?"

"I got *out*, didn't I?"

"And you're going *back*, aren't you?"

"Reckon so," he admitted, "some day. It's home."

"Well, the foot of the mountain was home to the people of
Pompeii. Fact of the matter is they'd been there lots longer
than your people been in Arroyo."

They walked through Gretna to Algiers, to a tiny bar
where they could drink red wine or white and a Negro piano-
man played and sang—

Every time the sun comes down
My love comes down for you—

yet by docklight or ferry, by white wine or red, the lessons
went on hand in hand.

"*I* wouldn't of marched on Moscow," he leaned earnestly
toward her, having examined the issue from every angle.

"Listen to the music, Dove."

Every time the rain comes down
My love comes down for you—

"—*I* would of waited till the ice bust up, so's the horses
would of had spring grass."

"Drink your wine, Dove."

"For you see, *I'd* be willing to eat horse-meat a few weeks
to be the king of a whole darn city."

Every time the sun comes up
My love comes up for you.

By boatbell, by bed lamp, by love song or star, the lessons
went on hand in hand, back through the narrow European
streets of home and up two flights till they were safe above
their firefly street again.

"If we had such good good generals and all of that, how
come we got whupped, Hallie?"

"North had more guns. Go to sleep, Dove."

But in the big blue middle of the night she felt a nudge.

"Why, in that case it weren't a question or right makin'
might after all. It was more a matter of might makin' right."

"Might makes might," she murmured sleepily.

"Yes, but how *I* look at it," he made one more ageless de-
cision, "the reason the North got most guns was because they
had the right to start. What I fail to understand is how come
it taken them four years to whup a bunch with such a sorry
cause as ourn."

He knew how to wake her up all right. Hallie was unrecon-
structed with a vengeance. She came awake as though he'd
fired on Sumter.

"To *your* people, hiding out in the Cookson Hills, any cause but that of making corn likker was sorry."

"It was for *your* people to drink."

"*My* people? *My* people. What do you mean by *that?—my* people?"

"You know darn well what I mean alright," for he was touched to the quick himself, "just because you have nappy hair—"

"I'm French and Spanish and one-sixteenth Indian."

He had her going now and wanted to keep her going. "Now about that one-sixteenth—"

"I've had enough." She was out of bed, the light was lit, she was pulling clothes out of closet and drawer.

"Where you goin', Hallie?" Dove was frightened.

For reply she upended a handbag, one she had not carried for weeks, and the contents rolled on the bed—all the tools of her ancient trade.

He scattered them to the floor with a kick and pulled her to him, and found her mouth with the red wine still on it. She yielded wearily, a woman who had had enough of love to last a lifetime of red wine.

Later in sleep she accused someone unseen—"If you had accepted the child he wouldn't have died."

She wore a hat of white straw that day at the zoo when the season of sun met the season of rain. That day when they were happy enough together to make it all one, rain or sun. Dove, in a blue serge suit out of a second-hand store, let her pin a little green feather into his black-and-white checked cap and felt more the sporty-O than ever. And as she pinned it, love lightened his looks a little. Love, and pride that he could read the *Times-Picayune* or the *Item*, either one.

Love, and pride. And the sense of a certain c-note yet unspent.

Merry-go-round music drew them—around and around great stallions raced, some white as snow, some black as night, but all with manes that furled and curled as the music beat, and he wanted to ride, but was ashamed to speak. Beside him Hallie smiled to herself, it wasn't hard to tell what he wanted to do. She drew him away from temptation.

When they came to the monkey house he stopped dead. In one cage a hairy little character was banging his knuckles on his girl friend's skull to make her climb a tree for some special purpose all his own.

"Why! There's Oliver and Reba!" Dove called to Hallie in real glee, and pitched popcorn at Finnerty. Then of a sudden it didn't seem so funny after all, and they moved on.

A single iron-colored owl waited in the shadows of noon like a dream waiting only for nightfall to be dreamt. And a scent of decay blew off him, as though he were rotting under his feathers.

To watch where the elephant, crowned with children, swayed as he walked to excite the children. He looked like a great fool of a child himself. Yet he bore the weak upon his back.

Dove bought two boxes of crackerjack. Hallie's prize was a tiny red and blue clown made of tin; she pinned it on Dove's lapel. His own prize was a toy tin whistle that he blew at the candyland sun.

Crackerjack whistles and children's voices, pony rides and merry-go-rounds, everything Dove heard and saw that day at the zoo lived within a new city innocent and bright.

Belonging just to himself and Hallie.

In the snake house the bended serpent writhed. One attendant held its tail neck and tail, another pried its jaws apart to let a third man bottle-feed it.

When the lion roared Dove backed up a step. "He must be hungry too," he told Hallie.

"More likely homesick," was Hallie Dear's guess.

The great gray wolves of the snowplain wilderness lay stretched waiting for December. But in the cages beside them the small restless foxes raced and raced as though summer never could be done.

Dove marveled at the way the changeful light followed rain across the littered grass: he had never noticed how light fell before. In his mind a hurdy-gurdy played autumnal tunes he had never heard before.

In her hay-smelling dark the quick gazelle tiptoed about in the delicate gloom, practicing a ballet of which she would certainly be the queen.

And like a sidewalk drunk careless of wet weather or dry, the great bear lay with his paws in the air while his brood toddled and wrestled about him. Slowly from out the primeval stone came forth the ancient mother of bears, all brown. A working mother wed to a useless hulk, sole support of himself and a growing family.

Came forth bowlegged, honest paws inward; as she had come toward the earliest man. Dove tossed her a peanut and just this once she decided to settle for that.

In mid-afternoon the rain came again, sprinkling walk and cavern and cage. They ducked, newspapers over their heads, into a latticed pavilion. A place for October lovers. They had just ordered soft drinks and two poor boy sandwiches when an old woman in gray stockings came up to them with a wet newspaper in her hand.

"Forty years a good life," she assured them, "forty years married to a good man. It is damp, so you may have it for only a penny," and offered them her paper.

"It's also yesterday's," Hallie told her; and gave her a nickel. "Keep it."

"I cannot accept charity," the old woman replied with injured pride. And would have left. Dove made her stay.

"I'll *buy* your paper," he offered, "something happened yesterday I want to read about, so you can charge yesterday's price." The woman understood. She handed over the paper. Dove handed her a dollar bill and waited for his change.

"*Must* I give back money?" she pleaded.

There was no change.

As they ate the sun came out though rain still fell. "The devil is beating his daughter," Hallie explained such changeful weather.

"Is that who it was just beat me out of a dollar?" Dove asked a little bitterly.

For some reason Hallie began telling him how she had become a prostitute. For a long time after her baby's death and her husband's desertion she had been unwell, and a friend of her husband had become her only white friend. She would waken and he would be standing at the foot of her bed, watching her sleep. When she grew better he brought her a pair of shoes, just the right size, with French heels. Then he took her to a beach.

He had lain in the sun watching the small waves wash the heels as she walked up and down at the water's edge. Then he had taken her home. That was how easy it had been.

"But I'd still rather have a man sleeping beside me than standing at the foot of my bed without my knowing he's there," she told Dove, "it makes me afraid of what goes on in the mind of a man like that."

Now the devil's daughter was back, begging for her damp newspaper as though she had never seen either Dove or Hallie before. "May I have your newspaper? I've had a good life, forty years of marriage, forty years a good life. Thank you. I don't know *how* to thank you—perhaps I'll come by another day and you'll give me another paper."

It felt like a lucky day for everybody.

Toward evening a small breeze came up and began blowing the minutes away until it was time to go.

As they left they passed once again the prisons where the wolves lay sentenced, though now their fur had been damped by winter's first rain. Where still the summer foxes paced made even more restless by the changeful weather.

And still the obedient elephant went bearing children on its back, swinging its trunk like an orchestra leader conducting an old-fashioned waltz.

Where the white-maned merry-go-round stallions raced, one a nose ahead, then the other, then coasted when the music-box stopped.

The homesick lion roared for home. The iron-feathered owl waited only for night to wing soundlessly into people's dreams and be back in his tree by morning.

Finnerty's girl friend, trapped out on a limb too fragile for him to follow, whimpered between fear of falling and fear of Finnerty.

In the haysmelling dark the quick gazelle tiptoed, rehearsing forever some animal's ballet in which she was sure to be the leading lady.

Deep in the primeval stone the ancient bear had curled, and this time would not be seduced outside for peanuts or people, devil or daughter.

So they turned back at last to those streets whereon the wildest beast of all roamed free.

At the foot of Canal Street they saw a great white excursion steamer that had come down the river from Baton Rouge that day. With a brave invitation at the foot of the gang-plank—

TONIGHT:
OTHELLO

Hallie had not seen a play since her schoolroom days. Dove had never seen one. "It's your day, and that's all there is to it," she decided.

She herself was too heavy with the long day's sun to wish to do more now than sit on the lower deck and watch the big old river bearing broken box lunches to the sea.

Every ten minutes he returned to her with news: the boat would pull out at eight-thirty and the play would begin at

nine! He had been below and was sure the engines were ready
to start. Now they were testing the lights in the ball-room.
He had seen a tall young fellow and a young woman drinking
beer at the bar and had been told they were O-Thello and
Dessie-Mona.

Just then they felt the ship tremble and the big wheel began its first slow sure turn—heading for the open sea! He
turned and lumbered off to see whether the captain needed
his help.

As the lights of the eastern shore swung out, Hallie heard
singing down below out of years she barely remembered—

> *We'll have a bunch of little by-gollies*
> *And we'll put them in the Follies—*

and felt an air of joy and a water-born courting, then a stirring within herself she had felt all day but to which she had
paid no heed.

She saw the fore and aft lights of a freight barge being
towed downriver. And men and beds and odors, the whole
monstrous nightmare of her years since the baby had died
seemed to be towed downriver with the barge. And, in the
place her heart had been, again felt the faint deep stirring.

The boat rocked in the passing barge's wake, she shut her
eyes, for she felt a pleasant nausea. And in her mind saw,
around and around, the white-maned merry-go-round horses
race once again. "One-sixteenth," she thought for no reason
she understood, and wanted to laugh but didn't know at what,
unless it was the redheaded boy coming toward her as though
bearing news.

She listened but hardly heard. It was only when he took
her hand that she understood that a play was about to begin.

In the middle of the first act the boat was caught in a wash
and the whole stage tilted a bit. It was by this time obvious
to the front rows that Othello, with a bad job of makeup,
was tilting slightly on his own. But retained sufficient presence

of mind, when he needed to lean against the air, to bear against
the tilt of the stage rather than with it. By this instinctive
device Othello held the front rows breathless, wondering
which way he'd fall should he guess wrong.

But the boat could have turned on its side and Dove
wouldn't have noticed. He had been captured by the roll and
trump of lines so honored by old time they justified all mankind:

> *I kissed thee are I killed thee: no way but this*
> *Killing myself, to die upon a kiss.*

"One-sixteenth," Hallie's mind insisted as the stage tilted
back and heard herself making a curious prayer all her own:
"Lord, make it a woman or make it a man, make it black as
midnight but let it be *mine*. This time let it be mine." And
her heart closed fast on the very thought that any white man
might share this child. And in her mind began to toss her
French and Spanish forebears like emptied box lunches over
the rail.

She wished, and realized she had wished it for some days
now, to return to the mulatto village in which she had been
born. And there put her hair in pigtails in her people's ancestral way until the baby came. Things would have to be
done quickly before this white man could guess.

But a languid ease arose in her, bringing an irrational contentment that there was plenty of time for everything.

When they left the boat, wearied out with the long day,
Dove heard a tiny tinkling and saw a little ice cart at the curb.
The night was hot, and ice was what he wanted.

"What flavor you want, Hallie?" he asked her.

"Orange."

With the orange in his hand and three cents in debt to the
vendor, he stood trying to decide between raspberry and pineapple, when a voice behind him said "chocolate," and a long
shadow fell across curb and cart.

Dove didn't wait to decide, he would do without ice to-night.

"Someone you know?" Hallie wondered.

"Used to."

"Why you afraid? He after you?"

"I don't know."

At the corner he dared one glance back. Fort was bent so far over, to make sure the vendor didn't slip one over by giving him maple instead of chocolate, that Dove realized how hard it must be to tell colors at night behind dark glasses.

In the days that followed Hallie wearied a bit of hearing "I kissed thee are I killed thee: no way but this, Killing myself, to die upon a kiss."

"If I only thought you knew what you were talking about I'd feel better about it," she told him.

She could never be certain that he didn't know what he was talking about. One evening she heard him read aloud—

As far as to the sepulchre of Christ
Whose soldier now, under whose blessed cross
We are impressed and engaged to fight,
Forthwith a power of English shall we levy,
Whose arms were moulded in their mothers' womb
To chase these pagans in those holy fields
Over whose acres walked those blessed feet
Which fourteen hundred years ago were nailed
For our advantage on the bitter cross—

and when she asked him what he thought it all meant he replied as if he had known all his life, "Oh, somethin' 'bout old-timey kings 'n other folks there too. There's goin' to be a war 'n it looks like our side might get whipped. You want me to go down and bring some srimps?"

Later, when the shrimp question had been settled and the shrimps eaten, she read—

When that I was and a little tiny boy
With hey, ho, the wind and the rain;
A foolish thing was but a toy,
For the rain it raineth every day.

But when I came to man's estate,
With hey, ho, the wind and the rain
'Gainst knaves and thieves men shut their gates,
For the rain it raineth every day—

"Why, that's as good as anything," he assured her. And never suspected how, across behind the words she spoke, a tyrant torso wheeled and reeled.

The Southern nights grew cooler. The rain came every day.

Long after Hallie had gone to bed one night Dove sat alone on their balcony. Every time a breeze from the river passed, another of the lights below went out, till it seemed the breeze was blowing them out. When the windows both sides of the streets were darkened he turned up the lamp in the small room where she slept.

Across her face a shadow lay, leaving her mouth defenseless to the light. She slept on not knowing how the river breeze had just blown out the last of the lights. Nor how the rain-wind was making their room cooler than before.

Nor yet how softly now the night traffic moved two stories down. And how all the anguish he had felt for his ignorance was gone for the first time in his life. And nothing mattered, it seemed in that moment, but that this woman should sleep on, and never know that the wind was blowing out the lights.

Somewhere in the court below someone began playing a piano softly, as though fearing to waken her. Sitting on the side of the bed, hearing the music now near now far, he remembered the first time she had made words out of letters for him—

Water now is turned to stone
Nurse and I can walk upon
Still we find the flowing brooks
In the picture-story books

We may see how all things are,
Seas and cities, near and far
And the flying fairies' looks
In the picture-story books

When he turned down the lamp and lay beside her, she half turned on her side away from him.

How am I to sing your praise
Happy chimney-corner days
Sitting safe in nursery nooks
Reading picture-story books?

He must have fallen asleep almost at once, because it seemed only a few seconds to him when he wakened and saw that the lamp was burning.

He stared into it a moment, dully wondering if he had forgotten to turn it off. The air outside was all mixed up and noises on the street went stamping.

Along the dresser he saw her lipstick, compact and comb. It wasn't till that moment he realized he was alone in the bed.

She was neither in the bathroom nor down the hall. He dressed, feeling sure, for no reason except that he could think of no other, that she had gone back to Mama's.

The last Dove saw of the little room above Royal Street was a broken comb lying in a pool of light.

He left in a ceaseless rain, the saddest that ever fell. He went by streets both steep and narrow and the rain fell all the way.

In that hour when tugboats call and call, like lovers who have lost their way.

THREE

OLIVER FINNERTY, disgust high in his throat, went into Dockery's hoping to drown it. Chicken farm promises, Mama's warnings, Reba's entrails, mouse-in-a-powder box, broads haughty broads humble, broads sober broads drunk, amputees tossing dollars to broads on all fours—fever and fantasy, hot dreams and cold cash lumped like dead meat at the back of his throat too far back to bring up and too high to swallow.

"There's one sick pimp in Storyville tonight," he reported himself in without pity. Then tossed down two shots of Canadian rye so fast they hit together, yet served only to bring the dead meat higher.

The little man leaned his head on his small pale hands and peered straight into the dark of his brain: a low motionless pall, like coalsmoke or smog, hung there over the roofs of a curious street—two short rows of bungalows long unpainted, like company houses down some company street; with one porch light left burning.

Yet it wasn't smoke nor lack of paint nor even how, below the porch, a rain puddle burned like living fire that troubled the dreaming pander so.

For though in their narrow closets the women's clothes still hung and their stoves still faintly gave off heat, the beer buckets stood half empty and the whiskey stood half drunk.

One had steadied a dresser mirror by jabbing her slipper between it and the wood. Outside a dog kept trotting and
sniffing between the deserted cribs. And an air of rage and
terrible haste that could only mean the worse was yet to come
walked the empty rooms.

It came by car splashing mud to the fenders, men and wild
boys leaped out—he heard the first glass smash and saw the
first flame reach.

Bringing the ponce a pleasured sorrow, a kind of release
from everything.

The same sick pleasure at the same dead dream. Though he
could not place the curious name of that place nor its women's
names either dark or fair.

He had never seen those wild boys. Nor how a rain puddle
made fever fire below a last porch light left burning.

Whether as a child he had seen such a raid from the window of a moving train or whether it was all nothing more
than a wish to rid his mind of all women for good and all,
poor pimp Finnerty had no way of knowing.

"Oliver, you're looking poorly."

The pimp raised his face that had lost all life, like that
of an embryo more clever than most but stillborn all the same.
And thought it must be part of his illness that he should now
see his old Texas studbum standing right beside him.

His own good old studbum, the one and only studbum.
Waiting for a live one with his tongue out a yard.

Someone had put a black-and-white-checked cap only a
size too large on his head and someone had stuffed him into a
blue serge suit only one size too small. Someone had given
him a hair cut, someone had polished his boots. Someone had
pinned on his lapel a little tin clown of red and blue—but
it was still the same old studbum. Like dust before the hope of
the world the pander's sickened soul was swept. A sense of
well-being filled him as a cup. He felt grateful for joys both
small and great, he wished it were mealtime so he could say

grace. His own old stew-faced studbum. The same big stink-
ing crawling creeping loud-mouth just as useless as before.

"Big Stingaree!" he greeted Dove, and stepped back shading his eyes as though unable to believe that the biggest wonder on the character side of town had come back for a bit of
a visit. "You know for a second there I actually didn't recognize you in that disguise?"

"You looked like maybe you was mad at me, Oliver."

"*Mad? Me* mad at *you?*" He slipped the knot of Dove's
tightly tied tie with one deft jerk and retied it, with elab-
orate care, into a looser, more fashionable knot. "*Mad?* When
was there ever a prouder sight? *Mad?* Man, I made you what
you are and I'm not ashamed of my work. Now what's *this?*"
He slipped a small book out of Dove's side pocket and his
smile thinned—"On that little-kiddy con again? What *are*
you sellin' them? I know you got a hot angle by the shift of
your clothes and I'm deeply interested in that. When I had a
hot thing I counted you in, so I scarcely doubt you'll count
me in on yours."

"I can read 'n write now, *that's* what, Oliver,"—a touch of
bravado returned to Dove's voice as he returned the book to
his pocket.

"Why! I'll just take your word for that! I'll stand for
drinks on it in fact!" Finnerty seemed somehow relieved. "For
aint I been the one been telling them all—'Don't worry about
Mr. Bigass! A *certain party* is giving him lessons! She's *too-
terin'* him! Tex, they laughed till they howled—they thought
I'd said '*tattooin'* him'! 'The bum'll show all of you a trick or
two yet' is what I been sayin' "—and dropped his voice to
imply the moment had come to trust one another. "I bet that
fine high yellow 'n you been shackin' up a regular storm."

"I don't know where that girl is, Oliver, that's the truth. I
wish to God I did."

"She was just in here, lookin' for you."

"Why, that scarce could be—" Dove reflected dully.

"Of course it scarce could," Finnerty admitted as fast as he'd learned all he needed to know. "Why should she come lookin' for you when she knows right where to find you? Dockery! Two shots here!"

"I don't drink so heavy as I used, Oliver."

"Make them doubles!"

A sawed-off crutch pried the big door wide, letting the street light glint on the wheels. In he swung and darkness like night closed in behind him and like night came rolling soundlessly. Schmidt muted his wheels when he didn't feel like balling.

Finnerty put out a foot. "Big Dad! A small celebration *in your very honor!* This here is an old-time fan of yours, seen you on the silver screen! Join us!"

"We've met," the cripple excused himself, "I'm not drinking with fans tonight." He put his hands to his wheels, then paused to look Dove up then down. Finnerty read the hesitation right. "One drink, Big Dad," the pander pleaded.

"*Bum,*" Schmidt told Dove directly, "you look like you've come into a roll. If you got gold on you, I'll get my share."

"And if you got none," little grinner Finnerty promised Dove, "he'll see you get some. We all got to live," he approved of both bullies at once, "Stoodint here was just asking was you actually on the road with the Strangler." And handed Schmidt his whiskey down.

"Why, there was nothing to that," Schmidt found a minute after all. "The Strangler'd get his lock on me 'n I'd let him keep it till I'd scaled the house, for I was workin' on percentage them days. Then I'd bust it and let him pin one shoulder and I'd flippety-flop for the yokels—they thought he surely had me. I'd let him try till I felt him tire. Then I'd get my scissors—" he crossed two fingers to indicate two locking thighs—"I'd work him off me 'n clamp *my* lock on him—" his crossed wrists trapped the Strangler's head—"You understand if I'd turned the pressure on I'd of been out of work. But he never did bust mine." And handed up his empty glass. "No, he never did bust mine."

"Drink up," Finnerty ordered without a flicker of expression. "He never did bust his."

"I wrassled a Mexican kid once back home," Dove volunteered, "but he threw me so durn hard I never did try *that* again."

Suddenly the cripple denied Dove and everyone—"No! He never did bust mine!" And brought both big fists down upon his stumps as if to deny himself as well—"Zybysko couldn't bust mine! Zybysko never did bust mine!"

"Easy now, Dad, easy," Finnerty calmed him to lead him on, "I venture the girlies put more than one head lock on you that you never even tried to bust—How about *that*, Big Dad? Referring," he added hurriedly, "to your screen career of course."

"Screen? Career?" Schmidt leaped to the bait like a starving bass, "Why yes, I *did* have a small part with Beery, but I didn't know I'd made mention of that."

"You've talked of little else the past twenty years," Finnerty thought, and added aloud, "It came to me through mutual friends of the silver screen. I understand it was a wrestling scene you done. May we hear more about it, firsthand as it were? Big Dad?"

"All past and done," Schmidt told him, "I met a woman who also had a bit part in the picture. We got engaged just before I went on the coast-to-coast tour with the Strangler. But the show broke up in the East and my coach ticket run out in Needles. I was in just such a hurry to get back to that girl that I didn't want to lose an hour. Instead of wiring her for money I spent my last buck on a bottle 'n climbed an empty instead. One minute of midnight, December thirty-first, nineteen hundred and thirteen.

"Next time I seen her was after the operation. Nursed me back to life with her own two hands. Begged me to go through

with the marriage just as if nothing had happened—that's a
woman for you. How was I to take advantage of unselfish-
ness such as that? Her with her whole career before her? Ruin
two careers because one had smashed on the rocks? I sent her
away and been taking care of myself ever since, better than
most with better luck than my own has been."

"But," Finnerty inquired coolly, "Didn't it take some time
to get used to being smaller than other people after you'd
been the biggest thing in sight for so long?"

Was it the question or the pander's tone? That Schmidt
didn't care for either was plain. "I don't see nobody around
here bigger than me," he looked right up at Finnerty as Dockery put three whiskies down and didn't pick up his own. "If
there's anything you can do I can't, now is your chance to
tell me."

"Don't be salty with *me*, Big Dad," Finnerty's tone was
serene. "I don't pretend to compete with you. But Sto*o*dint
here now is something else—he'll out-stud any man alive, Big
Dad."

Schmidt turned on Dove with a swerve of his wheels. "Can
you do anything I can't do better, bum?"

"I can't do lots of things even able-bodied men can do,
mister," Dove hurried to say; and even to his own ears that
didn't sound quite right.

"For example," Finnerty helped him, "he could never get
work as THE LIVING HALF."

So that was the bit. Out at last.

"I wish you both joy of your trade," Schmidt told both,
and wheeled off as noiselessly as he'd come.

Yet Finnerty called after, openly jeering, "If you aint
champ*een*ship material, might as well let the women get you
now!"

Then pressing his finger hard into Dove's chest—"You
know who he meant by that 'joy-of-your-trade' crack? *You*,
that's who. You don't have to take it, Tex. I'm back of you."

Dove emptied his own glass and Schmidt's too.

"I'm back of you, too, Oliver." And wished one of the glasses were full again.

"And when I back a man I back him all the way. For as you know, Finnerty don't fight. He just kills and drags out."

Sometimes one of his glasses was full, sometimes both. In the bar mirror faces of people watched him too steadily. Along the bar faces of dolls watched the people. Faces of people and faces of dolls and his glass was full again. He had come to find somebody whose name was right on the tip of his tongue but just at that moment the juke began playing something about saints marching in. The people began marching behind the saints and the dolls behind the people as Dove began marching too. Where bells were ringing, trains kept switching, saints were marching, time was passing and his glass was full again.

Till a voice came down through the whiskey-mist saying no Linkhorn could read.

"*Who* can't read?" he heard somebody asking ready to fight, who *sayz* I can't?"

"Nobody said you couldn't, son. Now be quiet or get out."

"Don't talk like that to me, Ol-i-ver," he warned Finnerty.

"This isn't Oliver."

"Who you?"

"Dockery, that's who."

"And this is Big Stingaree, that's who—*Who!*"

The floor tilted a little but he got hold of something and held, just held. Till the lights came up and there, with a small halo all around its edge, stood his own little whiskey glass filled again. For sheer love of whiskey, he began to cry. As dolls came marching, saints came marching, people were laughing. Through a kewpie-doll jungle that had no end.

"He'll be alright, Doc," somebody who was the best friend anyone ever had told someone who wasn't. He pulled

at Finnerty's sleeve to make him listen—"The people want me
to make 'em laugh again, Ol-i-ver."

"Read 'em a kiddy-story out of your book."

But the startled print leaped about like birds without brains,
so whoever said no Linkhorn could read had been right after
all, and everyone was so disappointed in him he began to cry
for everyone, dolls or anyone, who had been disappointed in
the end.

"I'll sing for the people! I'll dance 'n sing!" That was the
solution, he realized, to everything. And supporting himself
with one hand on the juke, he raised one big foot as if just
to raise a foot like that in itself was a feat. And peered all
around through the whiskey-mist to make sure the people
were watching this. After all standing on one foot was something not everyone could do. He was the only one who knew
exactly how it was done. They'd soon see that. Somebody applauded, now he had them. If he could just change to the
other foot he'd bring down the house.

And slowly began to change feet.

He came out with his hands hanging loose and head swaying, bending forward so far he tottered a bit. Someone else
clapped, then another and another. The dance went faster,
foot to foot. Some saw love in it, some despair. Through a
kewpie doll jungle the king of the elephants danced again.

He put his hands on his haunches and began a slow, obscene
grind. The music stopped but nobody applauded at all.

"Can that!" someone protested, "there's women here!"

"Let him show what he got!" Someone else saw things differently.

Then out of the whiskey mist nearer and nearer Dockery's
eyes like those of a bee bent deep, too deep into his own.

"Now you're overdoing things, son. If you can't behave,
get out. I won't tell you again."

"Who you?"

"Dockery, that's who." People began pushing this way

then that, he had come to find someone but where was she at? *Who?* he kept asking, "*Who-who-who?*" and pushed them all back—"Let me go. Who you?" he asked them.

"If we let you go you'll fall on your head."

"Fall on my head—*that's* what I want! I got a good header comin' to me!" And struggled madly to fall on his head.

But they wouldn't let him, he couldn't beg or buy them just to let him fall on his head. Bells began listening to their own fool tunes, trains to run right toward one another. Women were waiting in doorways for him. His glass was full again.

"If you aint champ*een*ship mater'l," he announced, "might as well let the women get you now!"

"He wants to let the women get him—let them *get* him then," all agreed.

"Get him out of here," Dockery had had enough, and out the door in the middle of a mob of laughing panders, the feather of his hat bobbing higher than any, Dove stumbled still trying to get in his header. But every time was held up again.

By the time they got him next door to Mama's his new suit-jacket was gone forever, one trouser was ripped from belt to knee, the shirt pocket hung by a single thread. Yet somehow he'd kept his hat, though its feather was broken.

"Here comes Big Stingaree, ready to ball!" one pimp called.

"Come to let the girls get him!" another explained.

"We don't want him," the girls seemed sure.

While in the doorway, faithful to himself, Oliver Finnerty stood and watched.

And felt his old nausea slowly subside.

When taxies wheel backward from the curbs and the darkness between the lights grows longer, when the whiskey in the glass before you is one whiskey you don't want and the sky holds a sort of criminal glow full of longing and full of loss,

then is that Come-here-and-tell-me-all-about-it, that Let-me-
just-talk-to-you-mister-twenty-cents-will-see-me-through,
that Hit-me-with-a-dime-and-I-sleep-under-blankets, that all-
night pleaders' hour. Then the pale lost ghosts of the girls in
the night's last doors—(how white their night-old hunger
leaves them!)—see there's no way left to keep the last of the
lights from going out and even the pimps begin giving up.

The legless man smoked the first bitter cigarette of the
coming day and watched the last of the two-leggers hurrying,
hurrying; hurrying home to love and to rest. And a pang like
a pang of utter defeat, like a wind off the flat ice plains of
death passed over his heart and shivered it like a leaf.

So what if they had had a bit of a laugh on him? Worse
things than that happened to people every day. A handicapped man had to learn to take the bitter with the sweet,
it was part of the game and all of that. Everyone knew they
were nothing but a pair of pimps of the cheaper sort while he
himself had never yet taken a cent off a woman.

But dropped his eyes in a brooding dream to where his
great thighs once had been.

And saw no way of getting his own life back, his own good
life gone too far, too far.

One at the hip and one at the knee.

Why give *them* a chance?

What chance had anyone given him?

Whatever it was Floralee had done to make her think God
could no longer bear her, it didn't of necessity follow that He
was the one who phoned for the Hurry-Up.

One moment the juke was beginning *Please Tell Me How
Many Times*, the next the parlor was full of the boys in blue
and someone smashed the glass of the juke—Now what was
the need of that? But the song came on louder for lack of glass
—*I'd feel bad if you'd kissed too many but I'd feel worse if
you hadn't kissed any.*

Where was Reba when the glass went out?

Praising the Chinese no doubt.

Where was Five when the box was smashed? Galloping from door to door in nothing more than her earrings and a bath-mat, hollering "Get them guys out!" And rushing three tricks down the hall with their pants in their hands in as much of a hurry not to be witnesses as Five was anxious to prevent them. She shoved one out a window, another walked past a nabber with a bill in his hand, and the same nab said to another—"Uncle Charlie!" And let him pass.

Where was Mama when the juke glass went? Studying a twenty-two-hundred-dollar receipt for down payment on a house and lot, six kennels and a pair of Doberman pinschers; and having her first misgivings.

Where was Finnerty when all this transpired? In a single-motor plane with two thousand two hundred in fives and tens, on his way to Miami to get his arm pits tanned. And gnawing his nail with burning regret, asking over and over, "Oh, why didn't I bury that crip?"

Where was Floralee all the while? Humbling herself in the sight of the Lord by supporting the length of a roaring drunk while other roarers encouraged him.

Where was Kitty Twist that lovable kid? Thinking of Finnerty and wishing she were dead. When she heard the crash she took a big swig of gin, tossed the bottle out the window and followed after it—right into the arms of two of them.

"I just don't have any luck, and that's all there is to it," said tough Kitty Twist.

"Your luck is as good as the next one's I'd guess," the nab said, "Up you go, sis."

And sure enough, up into the Hurry-Up went Kitty Twist. "Who's that?" she asked the paddy wagon gloom, "Who's else takin' this ride?"

"It aint Herbert Hoover," Frenchy's voice said.

"Officer," Kitty Twist told the nab guarding the door, "What are you waiting for? We're ready to roll."

"There may be others along in time," the officer said.

"You only got one wagon for the good sake of God?" Kitty scolded him.

"We're trying to make it in one trip, sis," he apologized, and a roar like a battle shout rocked the stars just then. The girls poked their sad fancy faces out and heard an iron clamor ring.

"Sure sounds like someone don't want to come along," Frenchy guessed.

Someone framed in a door-shaped light. Dove in an undershirt, nothing more, hollering "hands off me!" Slamming right and left with the flat of a book, raging with whiskey and terrible fright. Kitty saw one nab catch it across the cheek— "Hands *off* I said!"—another caught it smack in the eye. Then one of them clasped him by the nape of the neck, another caught his book hand. "Be a good boy like I was at your age," one said, and another yanked his legs right out from under. Then all three got a good firm hold—"One! Two! Three!—" Kitty and Frenchy had just time to get out of the way as the bare-assed body came flying—*Bawnk*—and Watkins' ex-representative lay on his stomach clutching an iron floor.

"At least this time you came along," Kitty congratulated him. And gave him a tentative dig with her toe.

The body never stirred.

Kitty found then she didn't care really whether he came along or not. She didn't care for anything or anyone, least of all herself. Anything that happens has a right to happen, so what does it matter who it happens to? That was how Kitty felt.

"I heard a sneeze in the closet," the nab informed the girls, "and when I open the door, there was this boy buck—naked but for hat and undershirt and a book under his arm."

"Just somebody who didn't have time to pull his pants on,"

Frenchy sounded out the law on how much he really knew.

"So long as he wasn't no inmate he aint in serious trouble," the nabber felt. "He don't look to me like no pimp."

"Myself, I never seen him before," and gave Kitty the nudge.

"I never did neither," Kitty Twist said.

Dove came to in a dungeon heat with something across his face.

Hello, pants.

He felt his head swell and subside, then try to swell again. By not so much as batting an eye it hurt a little less. When someone lifted the pants off his face he stared straight up. "I think the sonofabitch is dead," he heard an indifferent voice report and caught a whiff of cigar smoke.

"I don't see no blood, Harry."

"They bleed inside."

"Then we're both in this together."

"*Both?* Since when did Smitty get out of it?" The pants dropped back.

"Why, that's *right*. Oh, that Smitty, suppose to be watchin' the whore in the Hurry-Up, instead he's showin' off he's a tackle now for L.S.U."

"Remember the time he finished off the nigger with his open palm? That shows you what jiu-jitsu can do."

"No, but I was with him the time he lost his temper on the Spanish lad for pretendin' he can't talk good English. That's what pretendin' can do."

"Officer," some phony down the tier piped, "I can pay for aspering if it aint asking too much."

"It's asking too much. You'll get aspering at your destination," Harry promised the piper and belted Dove a crunchy kick in the side just for a crunchy little surprise.

"I been kicked lots harder than that," Dove reflected and

wished they'd stop smoking. It didn't seem respectful at a time like this.

"You know what, Jeff?" Harry asked softly.

"What?" Jeff was anxious to know.

"I think the sonofabitch really *is* dead."

Deep in Dove's throat a great tear trembled, making a bubble that tickled his neck. There wasn't a breath of air in the cell and if they didn't quit smoking he'd have to cough and come alive once more. He'd rather be dead, Dove thought, than *that*.

"Poor rummy. Between whiskey and women, his heart give out."

"Was that his heart clanged like a damned bell when he landed on iron? If you can't make sense don't say nothin'."

"Captain'll be on our side," Jeff kept trying, sense or no.

"*That* cracker? Are you sure you're feeling well? I'm sure he'd purely hate to see that cracker puss on the front page of the *Picayune* for cleaning roughnecks out of the department. *Sure* he would."

Then a silence bespoke an understanding reached. Dove felt one take his arms and the other his feet.

"People treat you better when you're dead," Dove realized as they bore him gently. "Now this is really something like it."

"Where we takin' him, Harry?"

"Where you think? Loew's State?"

A river-boat moaned like a weary cow abandoning hope between darkness and tide.

Dove felt the air clear suddenly and knew they were in the open night. Somewhere above him a window slammed.

"What are you silly bastards up to now?" Dove heard a new voice, more commanding than Harry's.

"Another one kicked off on us, Captain."

"How many times do I have to tell you that a man can die in jail just the same as in a hospital? Get him over to Charity and get a receipt. I'm getting sick of having to tell you every time." The window slammed. Dove hoped that they wouldn't drop him; he had a feeling he was hanging above concrete.

"What he mean, Harry, 'get a receipt'?"

"He means register the stiff with the hospital."

"Couldn't we just leave him on the steps and trust to the kindness of nurses?"

"I'd as soon be took inside *if* you don't mind," Dove requested politely.

Like statues of astonishment both nabs froze. In that second Dove realized that had been his own voice and leaping free, was off and running straight into a red brick wall.

Harry caught him on the rebound and led him by the hand back to Jeff.

"I knew he was faking all the while," Harry decided, "I was only waiting for him to make one false move. *See*, I made him give hisself away."

Dove folded his pants carefully into a pillow and tucking it neatly under his head, stretched out contentedly, waiting to be lifted again.

"You see," he excused himself to the Southern stars above the nabber's heads, "I really wouldn't want to leave this old world, for it's the only one I know anything about."

Jeff looked at Harry. Harry looked at Jeff.

"Son," Jeff broke the news at last, "we both been on duty this whole hard hot day, and it's been just one darned thing after another. Would you mind *walking* back to your cell?"

"Why," Dove leaped to his feet and began pulling on his pants, all eagerness, as though invited to a chicken dinner. "Why, I'd admire to do just that. A little walk in the night air would clear my head." Then looked slyly from one to the other. There *was* something in the air.

"You fellows mad at me about something?"

"Of course, not, son," Harry reassured him with good-natured gruffness. "You're a character. That's your turn and

we enjoy it. We want everyone in on the joke," and slammed
Dove so hard on the side of the head with his open palm that
he spun him almost clean about. Dove stood shaking his head
to let the night air make it even clearer. The nights were certainly getting cooler.

"Promise us you'll tell the court everything that happened,"
Harry threatened him with his big hand raised, "*Promise.*"

Dove stood rubbing the back of his head: a huge thought
was struggling to live in it.

"I tell you," he decided slowly, "I don't think I'd care to
bring up a thing like this in court at all. It might make me appear a bit of a fool."

"I *told* you this was a boy of good breeding," Jeff came to
his aid.

Harry studied him steadily, hand still high. "I've took an
awful lot off you, son," he announced, "I'm just not going
to take any more."

"Oh, put down your hand, Harry, the boy's had enough,"
Jeff decided. "He's a real smart lad and means just what he
says."

Harry let the hand fall. "God help him if he don't," he
said.

A minute later the big door closed behind Dove.

"I think I'll get a little rest," he decided, and groped in
the dark till he found a bench.

Each morning the tenants of Tank Ten took turns at the
tank's single window. It opened upon the courtyard of the
Animal Kingdom's Protectors, whose men in heavy gloves
busied themselves protecting the kingdom's little charges
from early morning till late at night.

BE KIND BEFORE IT'S TOO LATE was the kingdom's motto,
painted in hospital white. Sometimes a kindly looking woman
in a nurse's uniform came outside to help the work of kindness on. This was done by shooting each hound squarely be-

tween the eyes and shoveling the carcass into a cart. Cats were
less trouble, Dove saw right off, for they had only to be
swung by their tails and get their little skulls cracked against
an iron post. And didn't have to be shoveled at all. Straight
into the cart they went—*plop! plop! plop!*

For some reason the prisoners felt it had devolved upon
themselves to keep track of the number of dogs done in as
opposed to the number of cats. A C.C.C. deserter called Make-
Believe Murphy began making book, taking bets in Bull Durham on the day's totals. A non-betting man, neither pro-dog
nor pro-cat was required to keep a reliable count. Dove volunteered, and never left his post without reporting to his relief the exact numbers of each done in during his watch.

And sometimes wondered, that if the men and boys to
whom Tank Ten was home were outlaws, where the true
criminals were being kept.

"The best days of my life, my happiest time," a human
dishrag called Pinky would recall, "was doing close-order
drill in the evening with the national guard."

Pinky had stolen fifty feet of garden hose in lieu of back-
wages. That the back wages were largely imaginary didn't
make the hose less real, and Pinky still had five months to go.

His cell mate was a beetling, black-browed timberwolf
right out of the timber with a blood-red gash for a lolling
tongue and hands like claws to rend. A real baby-eater with
a spine-chilling record: he had lowered himself through a
greenhouse roof and come within inches of escaping with two
flower pots of African violets. Unluckily he had gone through
a pane and been trapped in a chrysanthemum-colored crash,
face-down in freshly planted ivy but still clutching his precious violets. The fall, apparently, had subdued the wilder side
of his nature, because now he seemed happy enough just being
permitted to wash and dry Pinky's spoon twice a day.

Another was an old sad lonesome lecher with a face that
had never been up from the cellar, who had nobody's sym-

pathy at all; not even his own. The turnkey had nicknamed
him "Raincoat"—which was kinder than what the prisoners
had named him.

This ancient simple satyr's offense had been nothing more
dreadful than the devising of a time-and-money-saving operation. Raincoat had discovered how to save time and money in
making love, and at the same time to protect the lover against
emotional entanglement. A pair of rubber bands and a raincoat with one loose button was all the self-sufficing lover
required.

So attired he had taken a stroll, one wanton April evening,
down Carondelet Street. Having, of course, taken the perfectly sensible precaution of severing his trousers at the knees
and binding the bottoms to his calves with the rubber bands;
lending an impression, to the casual passerby, that he was
fully clothed. Here and there, passing some woman who appeared deserving, he would fling the raincoat wide for her
amazement and delight, then modestly button himself and
modestly hurry on.

Talent can spring up anywhere.

"I'm not here for insulting a woman," he reproved society
gently, "I'm here for not insulting one. I put on my innocent
little show for her but instead of going on about her business
she looks back over her shoulder as much as to invite me to
follow her. She must have taken me for a moron, to think
I'd do a thing like that. For Heaven's sake, a man could catch
a disease that way.

"She started coming toward me—'Don't be afraid,' I heard
her say, 'I'm not going to hurt you.' Oh, no, not *much* she
wouldn't. I know *her* kind. But I hadn't expected one to *turn*
on me. She was getting closer by the second, I was rooted to
the spot, her hand reached for me—O *God*"—Raincoat buried
his face in his hands, the other criminals stood about. They
had all been to the Sex Bureau and back, they knew what the

man had been through. And waited politely till he had composed himself.

Raincoat dabbed at his eyes and went on—"Do you know what that *thing* had the brassbound gall to ask me?—'Would you like to sleep with a nice girl?'—that's just what she asked and not more than *three* feet away! The woman was sec-crazy, that was plain. But you know what I answered her? 'I'd rather go to bed with a wet shepherd dog!'—now that's *just* what I said. How did a notion like *that* come into my head? Then I ran.

"Before I could so much as say God with my mouth open there were half a dozen of them around me, I don't know where they came from yet. Hauling me this way then that, tearing my clothes, screaming 'sec fiend! sec fiend!' If I were a sec fiend I would of gone with the woman instead of trying to run, wouldn't I?"

There were always half a dozen in for drinking or distilling corn likker, and it wasn't surprising that those who bought too much and those who made too little should cell together. What wasn't so easy to understand was how men who could no longer communicate with the outside world, but could only sit and mutter, automatically fell together. Citizens of the Republic of Natural Bugs, they felt themselves trapped together in an alien land.

Raincoat's cell mate, for example, was a natural whose wife had had him locked up because he had made up his mind to have a baby by their fifteen-year-old daughter. Nobody could talk Natural Bug out of this. He couldn't be roasted or frozen out of it. He *knew* he was right in this. But Raincoat was the only one to whom he communicated his defense.

"He says the kid is a lot better-looking than his wife," Raincoat interpreted. "And not only that, but she's much younger."

And there was always, in one cell or another, the usual sexless, toothless queen of mezzanine, park bench and shrubbery. One of these was Wayback, who claimed to have been a saxophone player who had become addicted to something, he didn't yet know what. He was too far back for that.

"The doc wouldn't tell me and I can't read Latin," was his excuse, "but whatever the stuff was, someone kept raising the price of it on the doc so naturally he had to raise it on me."

The price had gone up until he'd had to hock his upper plate. Then he'd had to hock his sax to redeem the plate because he couldn't play without it. Then he was all set to go to work, but had no sax. Something had to be done. He was doing a year and a day.

"You see," he'd begin as though he couldn't get over it yet, "I couldn't blow a sax without a plate."

"We've heard it all before," Out-Front would interrupt him. "You're not way back, you're yet farther back than that," and there would be no word for a while out of the sexless, toothless, saxless, dopeless, hopeless queen of mezzanine, park bench and shrubbery.

Out-Front was way out front about what *he* was on. He was a rugged old hand who'd taken morphine for migraine headaches contracted in the red zinc mines of Oklahoma. He'd been at the Federal Hospital at Lexington, Kentucky, for healing of his habit and remembered that institution with genuine gratitude.

"The beauty part about Lex is that they take you off your habit by putting you on something new nobody ever heard of before because they don't have a name for it yet. Then all you got to do is kick two habits instead of one. I loved the joint. A man would be a fool not to trade off one little fleapowder habit for a real burning-down one, wouldn't he?"

Out-Front preferred to cell up with another user, but he could put up with a sex case if necessary—"You got a worse sickness than mine," he'd tell men like Wayback. What he really couldn't bear was a lush. In those whose weakness was whiskey he saw a hostile tribe undeservedly favored by the powers that be. Why was it that one little white pill was enough to put a man with marks on his arm to hard labor for months, while another, weaving on the corner with a pint of uncorked gin sticking out of his pocket, got a free ride home, if he could still give the nabbers his address?

"When you see a bum duck into the gutter for a butt," Out-Front challenged all corn-likker kukes, "you can be sure he's a wino or a gin-head. No self-respecting junkie ever falls that low."

Dundee claimed to have spent every weekend for thirteen years in the same cell. His wife had a brother on the force, and to keep Dundee from blowing his check on whiskey, brother picked him up on the job when the Saturday noon whistle blew and booked him for vag. Then he turned Dundee's check over to sister—"to protect you from yourself." Monday morning brother handed Dundee his lunch bucket and let him out in time to get back on the job without getting docked.

"One thing I've always insisted on," Dundee boasted wildly, "I never come along till I've finished my Saturday lunch."

Dundee's cell mate had also been strangely victimized. His name was Wren and he liked to buy Fords on Sunday, particularly in small towns. He'd pay a thousand dollars or so for one, by check, and show the dealer his bank balance for that amount. Then he'd drive it to the used-car agency across the street and sell it for six hundred. When the Ford dealer would have him picked up, to be held till the banks opened on Monday morning, Wren claimed he had always been sporting enough to warn the man, "You're making a big mistake, friend."

Morning would prove the check perfectly good, and Wren would sue for fifty thousand dollars for false arrest. The most he'd ever actually collected was thirty thousand.

"I must have made a million," he computed. But a sinister change had come over Ford dealers on Sunday; particularly in small towns. They had begun to trust him. He had had to act increasingly furtive and fly-by-night. He had even gone to the length of pasting a stage moustache onto his upper lip that looked ready to fall off any moment; and still they wouldn't arrest him. Wren had run into a solid wall of human faith. And every time he ran into it it cost him four hundred dollars. Finally he had such a vicious run of not getting arrested that he would have gone broke altogether but for a tiny drill, a length of wire and some colored crayon. Parish police had picked him up in a roadhouse for tampering with slot machines.

"I drill an eighth-inch hole in the side of the machine—it's only aluminum casting. When the three payoff bars come up I stop the works with the wire and she pays off. Then I plug the hole with crayon of matching color—usually blue, red or silver. When the chumps fill up the jackpot I come back again. Sometimes I got a buddy to cover for me while I drill, we concentrate on fraternal organizations. What can they do about it? Slot machines aint legal either."

It was true that the authorities were uneasy about their right to hold him. Yet it seemed that somebody ought to.

Cell doors to Tank Ten were left unlocked. Only the big door to the block, operated by air brake, barred the prisoners from the outside world. This permitted the area between the jail's wall and the cells to be used for prisoner recreation. And since this was left to the prisoners' own devising, all it came to in the morning was someone reporting casualties in the Animal Kingdom, or a spitting contest in the afternoon. But even the spitting contests lost interest, as the tobacco-chewers always won.

The men changed cells at will. When Wren wearied of Dundee's grievance against his brother-in-law he moved, simply for change of grievance, into the cell of a barnyard cretin called Feathers.

Feathers had been snatched redhanded in the act of chicken-spanking.

"I never heard tell of no such crime as that," Dove declined to accept chicken-spanking as a crime, "it must have been he tried to steal that hen."

"Feathers wasn't trying to steal nobody's hen," Make-Believe Murphy protested. "All Feathers done was set that leghorn on his lap and pat its bottom. Understand, I'm not saying the man was in his rights. After all, the bird hadn't done nothing to be spanked for."

"I *like* chickies," Feathers clucked from his cell.

"I'll represent him even if I don't care for the case," Murphy assured Dove. He seemed to have appointed himself a sort of Kangaroo Public Defender. Who was defending Murphy Dove didn't ask.

Gonzales vs. Gonzales was more to Murphy's taste than *Feathers vs. Louisiana*. Gonzales, a laborer six days a week, was resting on the seventh when Mrs. G. suggested idly that they go on a second honeymoon. This had upset Vicente, as they had never had a first. He had gone through the house methodically with a Number Five shovel, smashing holy images, pictures, glassware, chairs, pottery and a Victor gramophone and every time he'd brought the shovel down had cried out, "Call *this* a honeymoon!"

He had been prying the bathtub off the floor by its stubborn enamel claws when he'd heard Consuela run into the bedroom, snatch something and run out of the house again. He'd apprehended her trying to save their wedding photograph and pointed to the stove. She had always been an obedient wife, and she did what he ordered now: she threw the picture in.

Then they had stood, holding hands by side, until the flames had caught.

"Mister Gonzales," Consuela told him then, "that just did it." And had phoned the police, had him booked and now promised, every time she came visiting loaded with dainties, that she was going to get him ninety days for malicious mischief if it was the very last thing she did.

"Why you do that, Vicente?" Dove inquired with some concern.

"When I feel like going, I go," Vicente explained to his own satisfaction if nobody else's.

"You were in your rights," Murphy told him confidently, "you were remodeling your home. No court in the country can convict you."

"I'm just sorry he seen fit to remodel that photograph," Dove felt, "if you ask me that was pure meanness."

"I'm glad you brought that angle up," Murphy said, "I got that one whipped too. It was my client's intent to burn only *his* half the picture."

"It didn't do her half much good," Dove felt obliged to point out.

"I see," Murphy regarded him coldly, "you're the type would actually deprive a man of his freedom for the sake of an old photograph. What kind of man are you anyhow?"

"I'll tell you *just* what kind," Dove informed him, "I'm the kind that'd injunct that Mexican's shovel, if I were his wife, before I let him in my house again. *That's* what kind."

"Shovel no matter," Gonzales promised everyone cheerfully, "when I feel like going, I go."

"A little on the headstrong side," Make-Believe Murphy had to concede, squatting beside Dove. He was a lanky stray from nowhere who'd been lost in the shuffle along the way. A year or two older than Dove. Older prisoners tolerated his make-believe practice, knowing that was as close to practising law as Murphy was going to get.

"Great Hand of God," he marveled now, "for what it cost

this country to keep us criminals in here, we could send a navy to Mexico."

"What for?" Dove wondered. "We don't have no war with Mexico."

"Well, by God," the boy resolved. "By God, if we don't we'll send down 'n get us one."

The only true criminal in the whole tankful of fools, the only one who had soldiered honestly against law and order, was an old-timer named Cross-Country Kline, with a battered and seamed old round brown ball of a face that looked as if it had been lined into the grandstand and lined right back. They were having a hard time getting Country out.

"Blow wise to this, friend," he advised Dove, "it's always easier to convict a man of something he didn't do than it is to prove that what he actually was doing was a crime. That's why the nabbers are so much tougher on the man without a record than they are on the finished criminal product. They've got the finished product solved, they can nab him any time, so they can afford to be friendly. It's the bird who pops up on some corner they never seen him around there before, he claims he never been arrested, he got no needle marks, he don't act like a thief and they can't find a set of prints on him that worries them. They figure he must be some too-wise ghee. They got to find a crime to fit him. And if he's innocent that takes persuasion.

"Do you know that half the men serving time are serving it for somebody else? Shaking somebody else's jolt for copping somebody else's plea, playing culprit for a lesser crime than the one they actually done?

"What a young fellow like you got to think about, if you're going into crime serious, is what any young business man got to consider before he invests in anything—How can he wire himself so that, if he takes a fall, he falls the least distance instead of the longest? He got to wire himself to the courts, the state's attorney's office, the police department. He can't trust just any old lawyer, you don't learn the law by going to law school. He got to have someone who can operate behind the bench as well as in front of it, behind the public prosecutor as well as in front of him. Then if he takes a fall he got a choice—Should it be one to life for armed robbery or one-to-three for simple robbery?

"But blow wise to this, buddy, blow wise to this: Never play cards with a man called Doc. Never eat at a place called Mom's. Never sleep with a woman whose troubles are worse than your own. Never let nobody talk you into shaking another man's jolt. And never you cop another man's plea. I've tried 'em all and I know. They don't work.

"Life is hard by the yard, son. But you don't have to do it by the yard. By the inch it's a cinch. And money can't buy everything. For example: poverty.

"Take my own experience with money, for example. I was suppose to be a writer on the coast but all I ever wrote was phone numbers. I'd slip into a party like I was invited, spot some fluff who looked like she'd left her jewel case home, talk her out of her address and phone it to a couple fellas who were just setting around some hotel room talking religion. When she got home the jewel case would be empty. How should I know they were that kind fellas?

"We made so much I didn't have time to spend it. Still I felt them fellas were giving me a shellacking. I got out and went on my own. I lined up a most trim little number—you understand I passed for sharp myself them years. Husband had gold. Had her own car. One day she give me the key to it on a ring with her other keys, to drive around while she shopped. I wheeled eighty an hour out to her place, cleaned out every bit of her jewelry and the husband's too, and was waiting for her when she got through shopping.

"I was scoring like that every week, stuffing a suitcase for a trip to Chicago. There was a fence I trusted there. What tripped me was I figured it was my turn to give a party.

"The country had just gone dry. I was living in Catalina and went across to L.A., bought a second-hand suitcase and stuffed it with Canadian rye. I got off the boat with it and carried it up hill to my cottage. I had to go past the nab station. I knew all the nabs. I set the suitcase down and cut up jackpots with them a spell. One of them asked, 'What's in the keister, Kline?'

" 'Just what you're thinkin' is in it, MacElheny my boy,' I told him, 'booze.' We all had a laugh. I laughed too.

"I just got into the cottage when somebody knocked. Four nabs I'd never seen in my life before. 'What's in the keister, Kline?' Only this one meant it.

" 'Liquor,' I told him right out, 'Want a shot?'

" 'We'll have to take you to the station, we have a tip you're bootlegging.'

"I went along. What else? Some clown of a justice of the peace clapped a hundred-fifty-dollar fine on me. I didn't have that much on me, so they kept me in the clink. I played cards with the jailer and went to bed. I was still laughing but not so loud.

"About three in the morning a deputy sheriff came in and shook me awake, took me into the jail office and pointed.

"It was all spread out on a table. $120,000 in hot ice. They must have tore that cottage apart to find it.

"My head was spinning like a top the rest of that night, trying to figure how to get rid of the stuff. I'd never been fingered for burglary, if they didn't have the ice I was clean. In the morning the chief turned me over to a deputy, to take me on the boat to L.A.

"The deputy was skirt-crazy. As soon as the band started playing he made it to the dance floor, lugging the jewelry in a cardboard shoebox under his arm. Once he threw it to the drummer to keep while he dragged a broad around the floor.

"I wasn't handcuffed. Where could I go? Nowhere but overboard and I can't swim enough to bother. So I sat around gnawing my fingernails twenty-eight miles worth, waiting for a break. When we were almost in it came.

"The deputy got the shoebox back, and we went up on deck to watch the boat make the pier. I said I was getting seasick and made for the rail. We were in the channel, almost to Wilmington Harbor. The deputy came along with me—to hold my head I guess—and when we reached the rail I started one from the ankle and he took it big.

"He hit the deck on the back of his neck and I grabbed the shoebox and heaved it. It plopped into the propellor wash and burst like a bomb. It rained jewelry all over the muck in the channel.

"The nab went for his gun and I held out my hands so he wouldn't dare mow me down in front of all the passengers. He put the gun back and begun bawling, handcuffing me to the rail and crying like a baby, both at once, simply slobbering all over me. Then he ran for his box, still sobbing. He could have saved his sobs. They kept a gang of divers prowling that channel bottom ten days without bringing up a single piece. By the time we made the pier there were four cars from the bureau of identification. That nab stopped me three times on the way and *begged* me—begged like a kid for candy —to get out and run for it. 'Give me a chance,' was how he put it, 'You owe me that much.' I sat awful still.

"The B. of I. give me the business. For seventy-two hours they kept me in the blue room and the things a bunch of tough coppers can think to do to a guy who won't talk makes me shaky when I remember it yet. I could tell you things that'd make Uncle Sam's whiskers turn black.

"They jumped on my feet. They slapped my ears till I couldn't hear. They put the glare in my eyes and held the lids open till I thought I was going blind and all the time somebody I couldn't see kept hollering right into my ear at the top of his lungs. I got a pivot tooth now in place of one some ham-handed law cracked out, but I aced it out. Years

later in stir I used to wake up thinking they were starting on
me again, but I aced it. I aced it till one of my fluffs heard a
radio broadcast 'n sent me a lawyer. That was when my real
troubles begun.

"You should of seen the jobs they hung on me! A finger
for every jewel heist pulled in California since the earthquake.
I found I was the Hollywood Taxi Bandit, and also some
San Diego peterman who'd been out of range over a year.
They put me up in front of some goof in pinch-nose glasses
squealing I was the guy stuck him up in Pasadena and took
his portable typewriter. Now *would* I fool around like that
with all that ice in my kick?

"Still I wouldn't widen about the ice. I was framed was
all I'd say. I went back and talked to the stir-simple kukes in
the clink. They told me the only way to handle my case was
to get some broad-lawyer whose daddy was a judge—she'd
drag it into his court and get it white-washed.

"One old-timer warned me, 'Don't let no lawyer get you
to shake another man's jolt,' but I didn't heed him. I give the
broad-lawyer a large slice and for three months I lay in that
lousy jail when I should have been partying in Chicago. Then
she told me the best thing I could do was ask for probation.
I had no record, it should go through sweet. I listened and
pleaded guilty to two of them bum beefs, stuff somebody else
had pulled they had to have a culprit for, and threw myself
on the mercy of the court as a first-offender. Then up spoke
my broad-lawyer right beside me, 'Your Honor, this man has
had his chance'—*Wham!* Daddy give me 4½—1 CC—*two*
stretches, one for four and a half and the other for a year to
be served concurrently.

"There I was with my ice in Wilmington Harbor, clean of
my own jobs but tagged for two other guys' and on my way
to San Q.

I was still laughing. But for some reason I kept gagging.

"I don't mind getting roughed up, everybody gets roughed

up. Everybody, in jail or out, is shaking somebody else's jolt. The thorn that sticks my side to this day is the one time in my life I was innocent was the one time that I got it. You through with them funnies, buddy? Let's see 'em here. Maybe some of 'em's in trouble 'n I'll have to help 'em out."

Country Kline claimed it was because of his good behavior but it must have been bad bookkeeping—he had been released from Leavenworth nine days before his last sentence had expired officially. When he'd learned of the error, he was in the South and had raced all over Louisiana and Mississippi trying to get some local official to lock him up for nine days in a county jail, give him a receipt and thus square him away with Federal law. He was uneasy about surrendering directly to Leavenworth lest he have to go to bat again against the same judge who'd already sentenced him once. "He might just get mad and give me a year for contempt or something," was what Country still feared.

He'd driven for days, asking gas station attendants whether they thought he was a fugitive, but no local official would lock him up. "You don't owe us nothing down here, son," sheriffs and constables alike had told him. "You owe it to Broomface, not to us. Go on back to Kansas, son, we don't want you. They *got* to take you."

Now he waited for the feds with a mixture of hope and fear he could never clearly divide, his cap tilted cockily on the side of his head and a plug of Red Seal in his cheek. Dove studied that philosophical mug creased like a first-baseman's mitt and concluded he couldn't possibly have done better for a cell mate.

Whatever happened, it was Country's consolation, he had Broomface where it pinched. He owed so much time here and there that even were he to serve it concurrently, he was sure to die owing at least fifty years. They'd never be able to collect.

He saw new ways and means of beating the law even in devices invented by madmen. One day Natural Bug came up with a brand new one. When told by a turnkey, "I wouldn't do that if I were you," Bug replied quickly, "I wouldn't do that if I were you." When the doctor poked his head into his cell to ask "How you feeling?" Bug answered as fast, "How you feeling?" Every attempt at conversation with him whether about the weather, death or parole withered on the vine.

"One conversation with you is its own cure," his own cell mate abandoned him in disgust, and sure enough—"One conversation with you is its own cure," Natural Bug replied.

"He's no more bug than you or I," Country felt certain, "all he wants is privacy and I can't blame him. I don't even want to think of the trouble I could have saved myself if I'd thought of a thing as simple as that years ago."

All of the inmates of Tank Ten were white. At night they heard laughter from the Negro tier one flight above, and most of the trusties were short-term Negroes. Murphy insisted it was his influence that kept the tank lily white, but Dove suspected privately that the authorities had something to do with it.

These were neither the great gray wolves of the snowplain wilderness nor fanged cats treed and spitting; but only those small toothless foxes of summer someone had chased and someone had chained, barking at changes in the weather.

The tricked, the maimed, the tortured and the sly, doers of small deeds from the nation of furnished rooms, they came off streets half as old as time to buy a little and sell a little and take their adventure in penny arcades. Their lives had been bounded by those windows saying ROOM FOR TRANSIENT. SLEEPING ROOM. LIGHT HKSP., where across a book of a thousand names the clerk who profers the pen suggests, "Give me a phony, mister. We're both safer off that way."

Everybody is safer off that way.

They emerged from between those long green walls and those long spook-halls that are shadowed by fixtures of another day. That damp dull green the very hue of distrust; where every bed you rent makes you accessory to somebody else's shady past.

They were the ones who'd rather play a pinball machine than put in a claim to a desk in an ad agency. Above gutters that run with a dark life all their own or down cat-and-ashcan alleys too narrow for a Chrysler, they hid out in that littered hinterland behind the billboards' promises, evading the rat-race for fortune and fame. Their names were "Unemployed Talent Scout" and "Part-Time Fry Cook," "Part-Time Beautician" and "Self-Styled Heiress," "Water-Ski Instructor" and "Dance-Instructress." And they strolled as matter-of-factly through their part-time nightmares into a self-styled daylight no less terrible than all their dreams. Their names were the names of certain night-blue notions and they seldom lay down to rest.

Their crimes were sickness, idleness, high spirits, boredom and hard luck. They were those who had failed to wire themselves to courts, state attorney's office or police. Hardly a stone so small but was big enough to trip them up and when they fell they fell all the way.

Fell all the way and never got up. If life was a cinch by the inch, they did it by the yard. They always found someone named Doc to play cards with. They went out of their way to eat in a place called Mom's. They slept only with women whose troubles were worse than their own. In jail or out, they were forever shaking somebody else's jolt, copping somebody else's plea, serving somebody else's time. They were unwired to anything.

Lovers, sec-fiends, bugs in flight, the tricked, the maimed, the tortured, the terribly fallen and the sly. All those who are wired to nobody, and for whom nobody prays.

That the public defender defends by saying, "Your Honor, this man has had his chance."

Country Kline rolled a cigarette one-handed, drew the string of the sack with his teeth and lit it with a flint device cupped carefully in his palm, as though fearing Dove might divine its magic and patent it; it looked like Dove would see freedom first. "My glin-wheel," he explained cryptically, and handed Dove a cigarette already lit.

Dove took a deep drag. "I made a small errow myself," he admitted, "I figured it would work better the second time than the first, being as I'd already a bit of practice at it."

And he waited for Country to ask "Practice at what?"

"Practice at what?" Country at last obliged him.

"Practice at playin' dead. It seemed to me that was the coward's way out so I took it. I held my breath 'n stared straight up 'n never moved a muscle. All I fergot was not to talk. So whenever they didn't have anything else to do that week, they'd put me on a stretcher n' carry me in the police wagon over to another station 'n set me down 'n tell the other policemen, 'He's dead, you don't have to feed him,' 'n then they'd leave me there. When it came meal time all the other guys got bologna except me. 'Lay down, ghost,' they'd tell me. I wasn't suppose to get no bologna because I was dead, you see."

"I see," Country assured him, "go on."

"Well, all the other criminals caught on and they'd holler, 'How you feeling today, ghost?' 'I feel like hell is a mile away 'n the fences is all down' is what I'd tell them. Because I felt like hell was a mile away 'n all the fences was down."

"How long did that keep on?"

"Why them fellows acted like they now thought nothing could kill me. I was in five stations last week. Finally I told them if I didn't get something to eat pretty soon I really *would* die 'n then the joke would be on them. So they finally

give me something but I still don't know what it was. I guess
the joke begun to wear. You know another funny thing—not
eating like that loosed up every one of my choppers but except the very one I could best have spore?"

Dove waggled that chopper that would never come quite
all the way loose.

On the wall above his blanket someone who'd checked out
long ago had scratched: *Poor John Mendoza. He went East.
He went West. He went the way he thought was best. He
loved his girl but nobody believed him.*

In the weighted hours of the blue-moon night Dove
thought about Poor John Mendoza and wished that his girl
had believed in him.

He learned how to get an extra drag out of a cigarette by
wetting his lips when the snipe was too small to be held in
the fingers. He learned how to split a match four ways. And
every night, before turning in, pursued lice across his blanket
with burning matches. When a louse was caught he crackled
once, and died.

One morning Make-Believe Murphy suddenly appointed
himself meal distributor. Although all the tins were practically
identical, he began a pretense that each had been designated
for a particular prisoner. For some reason everyone sub-
mitted to this nonsense, while Murphy identified each with an
eye for minute differences in the way the cornbread had been
sliced.

"*Yo tengo hambre, Campañero,*" Gonzales complained
when he felt himself shorted.

"We're all hungry, buddy," Murphy assured him but keeping his left palm closed, "nobody's getting shorted."

"Then you can open your hand," Dove told Murphy, "so
we can see for sure nobody is getting shorted."

"I don't have to open my hand to nobody," Murphy

clenched his fingers so fast cornbread crumbs pinched out of
his fist, "Or do you figure you're big enough to make me?"

"I don't have to make you," Dove conceded, "if you don't
it'll just go to prove you *are* shortin' the man."

Murphy opened his fist slowly, as though hoping enough
of the bread had pinched out to make it look like a fair distribution after all. But at least half of Vicente's slice lay there
pleading guilty to everything. Dove picked it out of his palm
and tossed it to Vicente.

Murphy reddened but said nothing more.

"I wouldn't of done that if I were you," Country warned
Dove, "that was the Mexican's quarrel, not yours. What did
I tell you about shaking another man's jolt?"

"We're all shaking somebody else's jolt anyhow, Country,"
Dove decided.

Kline was the only one of the prisoners who didn't care
whether he got cornbread or not. "Eat mine," he sometimes
told Dove, extending his plate, and while Dove ate would
wail a cheerful dirge—

> *Like to go home but it aint no use*
> *Jailer-Man won't turn me loose.*

Great itching lumps formed below Dove's skin, and traveled so fast he could see them move. If he touched the cluster
above his knee and then touched his ankle, in a minute his
ankle was swollen and itching too. He waited till the turnkey
passed, then threw open his shirt—"These whelps give me a
terrible eetch, mister." The turnkey saw the nauseous lumps
and returned with a spray-gun filled with insecticide.

"All you got is the nettle hives," he told Dove, "this'll burn
your hide but it'll cure it."

Dove declined. "I'd ruther have my hide scrofuloed than
scalded," he voted to stick with the nettle hives.

That night he saw himself lying asleep in a bed two stories
over a murmurous street. Lights like fireflies went on and off,

a piano played in an unseen court. And under the music as he
slept and saw himself asleep, Dove heard a metal whirring as
of tiny wheels on stone.

And sidewise, hand over stump and stump over hand, heard
the hard ascent of the legless man up a gaslit stair begin.

Coming on as he'd been coming for years, by bar light, by
star light, by mist light by stair, breathing heavier with each
step, yet sure in his final hour to claim his own at last. There
was time, just barely time, to lock the door against him. The
key was in the lock but he lacked the strength to give it a
full turn. Dove saw the rubber point of the short-hand crutch,
that the cripple used to help him up stairwells, come through
the wood of the door like the door was dust and wakened
wishing he had never dreamt.

Bad air and boils—yet sometimes there came a day so blue
it caught at the heart like a sense of loss—all these days too
blue, all lost. Rainy days were melancholy but sunny ones
were worse. When it was raining out there he could sink
into a sullen half-dream where nothing could touch him. But
blue days recalled his every folly and he'd think, "So much
time gone! so little time left! Scarcely time left for a boy to
rise!"

Murphy sat in his own cell, bent above a small digest called
Guidance, which revealed, for one dollar a year, how to grow
rich through prayer.

"It don't do no good for a man to rise these days, son," was
Country Kline's curious philosophy, "for that can't be done
any longer except on the necks of others. And when you
make it that way, all the satisfaction is taken out of it. Son, I
hope you don't mind my saying so, but you got pimp wrote
large all over you—but that's the sorriest way of all to rise,
and the reason I'll tell you why—if God ever made anything
better than a hustling girl he's kept it to Himself. There's no
trick in not going down the drain if you don't live in the sink.

But you take a woman who makes her living where the water is sucking the weaker bugs down and she don't go down, she's twice the woman that one who never had to fight for her soul is."

One day the tank grew strangely still. Murphy came to lean too casually against his door. He and Dove hadn't been on speaking terms for a week.

"What's the extent of *your* education," he suddenly demanded of Dove.

"It don't extend nowheres, account I got none," Dove acknowledged.

"What's your excuse for being in here?" Murphy persisted.

"I was drinkin' heavy," Dove told him.

"Most you Injuns do."

Apparently Murphy had given some thought to this.

"I aint even part Injun, mister," Dove went along.

"If you aint, what you squattin' like one for?"

Dove, on his haunches with a blanket about his head, let smoke trail through his nostrils before he answered, knowing any answer had to be wrong.

"My folks always set this way, mister. I notice sometimes you do yourself." And flicked his cigarette through the bars.

That was it.

"Get up 'n put that snipe out," Murphy commanded. "You trying to burn the place down with all us white folks inside?"

"I wouldn't go throwin' fire around, mister. That snipe is put out."

"Put it out again."

"Mister," Dove called to the African-violet fiend lounging in the run-around pretending he had been promoted to trusty, "Would you mind puttin' out that put-out snipe for me?"

"I didn't give him the order," Murphy interrupted, "I give it to you."

"Then put it out yourself, mister."

"Deputy!" Murphy called parties unseen, "bring in the prisoner of the court!"

Somebody spun Dove about, shoved him through the open door and down the run-around into a cell full of prisoners. He had never seen all the tenants of Tank Ten assembled, and now he wished he hadn't till he felt stronger.

They looked like bulldogs, they looked like coyotes, they looked like real hard cases. The human dishrag with hair and brows so colorless he seemed more like something hung out to dry than anything actually living. His faithful timberwolf beside him, holding a spoon in event the rag should want it washed, shined or dipped in gravy. Wayback without a tooth in his head, standing beside Out-Front who had enough teeth for two. Wren, holding Dundee's lunch bucket to keep Feathers from laying an egg in it, and Chicken Spanker himself, looking as though he'd like to peck somebody. And Gonzales, without his shovel. But who was ready to go all the same.

Even Murphy was dismayed. "Just look at the material they're sending me. Who can do anything with material like that? Sec Fiend!"

Raincoat was late, he hadn't known court was convening. He hurried in apologizing for the way he was dressed. Only Cross-Country Kline was missing and Dove was grateful for that.

"Sec Fiend!" Murphy demanded. "Who's the judge of this here court?"

Several gave dull unseeing glances about: at walls, at bars, at windows, at doors, at faces in the winding air, for they didn't know which sec fiend was meant.

"*Raincoat* Sec Fiend!" Judge Murphy made it plain as possible, "the court asked you a question!"

"What was the question, Hon'r?"

His Honor had forgotten the question himself.

"It don't matter," he improvised cleverly, "Just tell the court who was it said he could whup you if he wanted and you *admitted* he could *if* he wanted."

"You could whup *me* any old time your Honor you wanted to whup me, your Honor." Timberwolf always wanted to be first.

"You whup me too!" They all got the idea at once, with envy, some even pretending that Murphy actually had so favored them.

"You whup me somethin' terrible," the Dishrag lied.

"You whup me even worse," the Wolf just wouldn't be outdone.

"Whup even worse," the Bug began his echoing.

"Get *that* one out of here," Judge Murphy decided.

"One out of here," Bug had just time to agree before he was rushed back to his cell and told to stay there, they'd tell him the verdict later.

"Tell you the verdict later," he agreed, being the most agreeable of bugs.

"What I whup you *with*, mighty fellows?" Murphy asked.

"Big fistes!" Sec Fiend shouted as though only now beginning to feel pain.

"Big fistes is *right*," Murphy agreed and poked his fist right under Dove's nose—"What it look like?" he demanded to know, "Is it look like a man's fist or don't it?"

"Wouldn't be surprised if that aint but what it is," Dove shrugged indifferently.

Murphy stepped back, pulled a crumpled sheet of notepaper from his pocket and read while all listened reverently:

"These are the rules of the Kangaroo Court. Any man found guilty of breaking into this jail without consent of the inmates will be fined two dollars or else spend forty days on the floor at rate of five cents per deem. Or else he could carry his Honor three times around the run-around piggyback if the jury recommended mercy.

"Every man entering this tank must keep cleaned and properly dressed. Each day of the week is wash day except Sunday. Every man must wash his face and hands before handling food even his own. Any man found guilty of spitting in ash tub or through window will voluntarily duck his head in slop bucket, else have it ducked. Each and every man using toilet must flush with bucket immediately afters. Man found guilty by jury of his peers gets head ducked in bucket else he wants to or not.

"Throw all paper in the coal tub. Don't draw dirty pictures on wall, somebody's sister might come visiting. When using dishrag keep it clean. Any man caught stealing off another criminal will have William Makepeace Murphy to reckon with.

"Every man upon entering this tank with ven'ral disease, lice, buboes, crabs or yello glanders will report same immediately. Any man found violating any of these rules will be punished according to the justice of the court and the jury of his peers and William Makepeace Murphy. Also Tank Treasurer."

William Makepeace Murphy batted his eye at Dove, proud as a frog eating fire. "Every time you open your mouth from here on out it will be used against you. No mercy is this court's motto."

"Then I won't talk."

"Prisoner in contemp'!" Dishrag chortled—"Boy, did you walk into *that*."

"He's right," the judge backed up the peer. "You're now in contemp' somethin' awful."

"Why?" Dove asked.

"Because I contemp' you, *that's* why, son." Murphy took a sympathetic tone, "I want to help you but you're not helping me. If I were you I'd make a clean breast of all the dirty crimes you done and throw yourself on the mercy of the court. I think you'd feel better spiritually."

"But you said the court's motto is no mercy."

"Using a legal loophold like that is even more contempt'-'ble. Now you're deeper contempted than before."

"Ataboy, Judge!" the Dishrag cheered, "walked right smack-dab into it again! Now he *got* to confess what he done!"

"Why, I never did *outrightly* crime," Dove had to defend himself.

"Of course not, because you're a holy angel," Murphy congratulated him, "only where are your wings?"

This flash of wit literally rocked the cell. "Where are your wings, Holy Angel?" "*That'll* learn *him* to crack wise."

Dove had to wait a minute before the court grew relatively quiet again.

"I just meant I weren't guilty of nothin' you read in them rules," he explained.

"Guilty of *nothin'* you say? Why then it naturally follow you're mighty innocent of *somethin'*. Let's see you deny *that* one."

"Of course I'm innocent of nothin'," Dove began to get angry as he grew confused.

"Then you're guilty of everythin', naturally."

"Guilty of everythin'!" the Dishrag bleated, the Timberwolf beetled, Sec Fiend giggled and Feathers crowed, "Guilty! Everyone guilty of everythin'!"

"Looks like you walked smack-dab into it again," Murphy mourned for him. "If you'd just own up the court *might* go lighter. What we call mightigating circumstance."

"I stand mute," Dove resolved suddenly.

"Too late," Murphy still sympathized, "you've already confessed."

"Confessed *nothin'*," Dove protested. "I didn't confess *nothin'!*"

"You said you were innocent of nothin', and if *that* aint confessin'—"

"Innocent of nothin'! Guilty of everythin'!"

"You've heard the verdict," Murphy informed him. "What are you standing *there* for? The slop bucket's in the corner."

"I don't duck my head in no slop bucket," Dove took a firm stand.

Country Kline came to lean in the door. "I suggest you recommend mercy, gentlemen," he told no particular gentleman.

"*Six* piggybacks! Call *that* mercy," Dishrag decided.

His Honor waited to see whether the prisoner would accept commutation. Dove looked at Country. Country nodded.

Dove stooped, hands on knees as though for leapfrog and His Honor clambered onto his back. Then it was up and down and around, Dove bowed nearly double with the lank youth's weight, while the jury of his peers raced from cell to cell, keeping count at every turn.

When the punishment was done and Murphy had dismounted he told Dove lightly, "It wouldn't do no great harm to spend a little tobacco on the boys to show you don't bear them no ill will."

Dove handed the court his *Picayunes*. His jealousy satisfied, Murphy lit one for Dove.

Peace reigned in Tank Ten once again.

And the bugs were back in their beds.

Early next morning the turnkey came up long before the meat tins were due.

"Kline! get dressed! Sheriff's waitin' on you. That's all I know."

But the tank knew more than that: the feds had come for Country at last. Yet Country took his own good time in getting ready, as though still unsure about what that judge might throw at him.

"I need time to think this over," he told the waiting turnkey as though he had a choice in the matter.

At last he shook hands all around, and last of all with Dove.

"See you a hundred stretches hence," he promised and Dove was sorry to see him go.

To go in a driving rain, when the Mardi Gras was done, but night bulbs still burned on.

The night bulb that usually dimmed at six was allowed to burn that morning till the courthouse chimes rang at nine. A minute after the bulb began fading. Slowly, as though burning out. And the cells were left shadowed by the night that had passed.

A dark and lost hour, the first Dove had spent in a cell all alone. When a faraway train called like a train going farther and farther from home and he thought, "That engineer sounds terrible lonesome."

Later, by standing at the run-around window, he saw they were at it again in the Animal Kingdom. But he had lost all desire to keep count. Someone was trying to get a spitting contest going for a sack of Bull Durham, but no one wanted to play. A green Lincoln wheeled around the yard, swaying a bit down the unpaved alley, its siren rising as it hit the open street with headlights fighting the fog.

"There go the nabs!" he announced to the tier, and everyone came crowding to see, but by then it was gone.

Still its siren rang on the iron faintly and he felt dead sick for home.

All that wintry afternoon the Southern rain never ceased. In the run-around the prisoners gathered together uneasily as dark came on, to read the rules of the Kangaroo Court like men reading Genesis on a raft at sea. Toward evening came a lull in the rain: in the lull they heard boots climbing stairs as though burdened.

It always took the sheriff longer to open the Tank Ten door than the outer doors because it was opened by the brake locked in a box on the outer wall and the key to the box, smaller than his other keys, always eluded him for a minute.

The men listened while he fumbled. "Somebody with him," everyone sensed.

The sheriff and a deputy with a badge on his cap, and between them Country Kline bent double, and all three soaking wet. He looked somehow smaller and his toes kept scraping the floor as they half-dragged and half-carried him.

Beneath the cocky red cap his face was so drained of blood it held no expression at all. Somebody bundled a blanket and stuffed it through the bars. Country sagged, mouth agape.

When he was stretched out he clutched his cap against his stomach and drank the rain running off his hair. The fingers began searching feebly for the wound.

"I knew I had him when I seen him vomick," the deputy explained. Country's face was more gray than Dove had ever seen a living face and his eyes kept dilating with shock.

"Shouldn't have turned rabbit on us, dad," the sheriff reproved him while the doc swabbed the belly with cotton batting.

"He jumped out of the car," the deputy seemed to feel he owed the men peering through the bars an explanation, "I hollered, but he just bent over and started zig-zagging. Not sure as I blame him. Ninety-nine years is a mighty long time."

Country's throat was the same dead-gray as his fingers; the color of the concrete that had held him so long; the color of his only home; as well as the hue of that new and untried shore to which for so long he had half-wished to go.

"We'll have to op-rate, dad. Say 'Okay,'" the sheriff asked.

Caught between the double disappointments of dying too soon or staying alive to no purpose whatsoever, his eyes looked inward to make a choice; unaware that the choice had been taken from him. Behind his eyes Dove saw the man racing like a fox in an ever-diminishing circle. It was so hard to go, it was so hard to stay, it was all so hard all the way. The fingers, wet with rain or sweat, twisted weakly on the cap, trying to keep hold; the eyes kept trying to understand.

The sheriff put one ear to his lips to hear the whisper of legalized consent. If it had been himself with the gun he would have gotten the man at the knees, he felt.

The fingers abandoned the cap and wandered about the wound's gray edge, tracing the torn tissue to make sure it was at last his own.

"Tell us we can op-rate, dad," he asked. "I ought to sew you now."

Outside the rain ceased a minute, as though it too listened for the whisper. The doctor looked up at the sheriff and the sheriff looked down at the doctor, his face a mask of impassivity. He'd been sued once; he wasn't getting sued again. The odor of iodine began filling the tank.

"Say yes," Dove urged him, "Say yes, Country."

The turnkey came up, trying to hurry and walk softly both at once. "They got some broad downstairs claims she used to be his old lady. Got papers to prove it, I didn't look too close. No, I didn't search her, I was afraid of what I'd find. Maybe she'll say yes for him."

"'Used-to-be' don't git it," the sheriff shook his head like a weary mastiff, "as I understand it, as long as he's conscious he's suppose to say it hisself. If he aint, it takes a legal relation, else I'm liable. First aid is as far as law give me the right to go."

Outside the rain began again, Dove heard the wind blowing between the wash of it, trying to say "Yes. Yes. Yes."

But no one heeded the brainless rain and nobody heard what the wind tried to tell. For the wind and the rain came every day and whispered like two unpaid lawyers together all night, fixing to say what, in the coming day, what everyone wished to hear said.

"It's awful when it's like this," Dove thought, "and it's like this now."

Out of the corner of his eye he felt he was being watched, yet did not turn his head. Something moved in the corner— that cat! Hallie's brindle again! She made a dash for it right across the floor and as she turned a corner invited him, by one whisk of her tail, to follow. He followed into a room where a virgin burned vaguely high above and, closer at hand, a woodstove cast a heartshaped flame the flowing hue of blood. A woman's black lace slip and a man's blue jeans were entangled on the floor and he could not tell where the cat had gone. A layer of dust had fallen, long ago, across the floor and the walls. The entangled slip and the jeans that had, but a moment before, been clothing, was a heap of dust. Panes, pictures, doorways, curtains; all were dust.

He touched a speck to his tongue and it was not dust, but salt. As the light of the virgin too high on the wall began burning too bright and he wakened with the night bulb shining right in his eyes.

And the taste of salt on his tongue.

"What's the word on Country?" he asked.

"Turned his face to the wall half an hour ago," the turnkey replied.

And heard Gonzales grieving—

> *"Toda le noche estoy, ay, nina*
> *Pensando en ti. Yo, do amores*
> *Me muero, desde que te vi*
> *Morena salada, desde que te vi"*

"I feel like I been everywhere God got land," Dove thought, "yet all I found was people with hard ways to go. All I found was troubles 'n degradation. All I found was that those with the hardest ways of all to go were quicker to help others than those with the easiest ways. All I found was two kinds of people. Them that would rather live on the loser's side of the street with the other losers than to win off by theirselves; and them who want to be one of the winners even though the only way left for them to win was over them who have already been whipped.

"All I found was men and women, and all the women were fallen. Sports of the world, poor bummies, poor tarts, all they were good for was to draw flies I was told. You could always treat one too good, it was said, but you never could treat one too bad. Yet I wouldn't trade off the worst of the lot for the best of the other kind. I think they were the real salt of the earth."

And his heart remembered the harlots' streets till it came to a rutted and unpaved road at the end of a little lost town. A town where time, going backward, had left great paving stones severed by wind and sand. And felt the wind still coming across the mesquite to where a single gas lamp at the end of town made a lonely fire. By midnight its faltering, flickering glow would lighten a legend across a dark pane:

LA FE EN DIOS
Bien venidas, todas ustedes

"Terasina," the boy asked in a small awed wonder of the woman who once had pitied his ignorance there, "Are you there? Are you there in your bed at the end of the world while I'm here in my bed at mine?"

On the morning that seven meal-tins came up instead of eight, an immediate clamor rose. A prisoner didn't get breakfast the morning of his release. All were willing to go hungry for freedom's sake. "Who's makin' it, Mr. Foster?" they had to know, "Who's makin' the big door?"

Dove, on his haunches and his blanket over his shoulders, answered instead for Mister Foster.

"All you crim'nals can quit worryin'. It's Linkhorn makin' it today." He had kept exact count of the days.

The Rag, the Timberwolf, Sec Fiend, Natural Bug, Wayback and Out-Front, Chicken Spanker and the Honorable

William Makepeace Murphy crowded about to wish him the worst.

"You'll be back tomorrow!" Wayback promised.

"Hell, he'll be back tonight," Out-Front was sure.

"Meanwhile, make this last you," Murphy said, and presented Dove with a sack of Bull Durham, neatly tied as a gift ought to be.

Dove hesitated. Gathered crumb by crumb from seven sacks, it was nearly three-quarters full. "*And* the papers," Murphy added proudly, holding out the pitiful gift.

Dove accepted. "I'll see you guys," he told them, then shook hands on that understood lie, knowing he would never see a man of them all again.

In the mixed-up April of '32 the numbers of jobless rose to eight millions, two hundred thousand steelworkers took a fifteen percent wage cut and it took a cardinal to perceive that the country's economic collapse was actually a wonderful piece of luck, for every day it brought thousands closer to the poverty of Christ, who had been nowhere near before. For thousands it was the chance of a lifetime to bring Jesus' simplicity, the cardinal said, right *into* the home. All over the country men and women and even small children began taking advantage of this spiritual opportunity. All manner of little goodies like that were lying about in the mixed-up April of '32.

The D.A.R. demanded that unemployed aliens be deported; a mob lynched a man at Atwood, Kansas; a detachment of the Nicaraguan National Guard killed its American commander; a crisis in unemployment relief was imminent; somebody shot the President of France; cotton was up slightly following wheat and Huey Long said the time had arrived to redistribute the wealth. Russ Columbo was still singing *Please*.

Cuban sugar was held to imperil our own; Mayor Walker announced that New York Had Kept The Faith. The search for the missing Lindbergh infant was extended to England;

Al Capone was on his way to Atlanta. Mayor Walker decried local pay reductions and Huey Long said he would vote Farmer-Labor before he'd vote with the "Baruch-Morgan-Rockefeller Democrats." Cotton was down again following wheat but the Congress decided not to redistribute the wealth after all.

In the curious April of '32 Mussolini wrote a play and Calvin Coolidge had to make public apology and pay a St. Louis insurance man twenty-five hundred dollars for calling insurance abstractors "twisters" in a radio speech. Max Schmeling was taking his forthcoming fight with Sharkey seriously; California refused to pardon Tom Mooney and people were still singing *I Surrender Dear*. Senator Borah demanded that arms be reduced and atoms of hydrogen were transmuted to atoms of helium. The president of the University of Wisconsin announced that statesmanship had come to a full stop; Herbert Hoover was having his portrait painted; the Congress was asked to unseat Senator Bankhead and the crisis in unemployment relief was more imminent than ever.

In curious, long-ago '32 so many people were saying that Prohibition was a failure that the New York Chamber of Commerce said it officially. Cotton was up again following wheat and domestic wine-growers demanded that domestic wines be made legal. A fragment of a human jawbone found near Lake Victoria was believed to be that of the earliest man. The Congress refused to unseat anybody. Kansas was the last state still voting dry and even Kansas was close to going wet. Sharkey was taking his forthcoming fight with Schmeling seriously and an ash-dust obscured the sun over Buenos Aires for forty hours.

"The darker the valley the more the spirit of Christ-like charity appears," said that same cardinal in that strange brief spring, and New Orleans began planning a beer parade.

There, in Dockery's Dollhouse while the juke played

Chinatown My Chinatown
When the lights are low—

a straight-haired flat-chested hard-of-eye hustler called Tough
Kitty was trying to get credit for just one little beer.

But the bartender, acting as oddly as Hoover, didn't seem
to hear.

"Did my husband leave owing you money or something?"
she wanted to know. "Is that what's making you so salty over
a simple deal like a glass of green beer?"

"If you're talking about a party name of Finnerty," Doc
advised the girl, "he surely did, for he's gone and he'll never
return."

"So long as I'm around you can be sure that sooner or later
he'll show up," Tough Kitty promised upon her word. "He
thinks too much of me to leave me stranded and broke."

"He thinks so much of you," the old man asked mildly,
"where is he now?"

"I'm not free to tell," the girl answered before he'd finished asking.

"And I'm not free to hand out free beers," Doc answered
almost as fast.

So she drew from the pocket of her faded blue jeans a small
change-purse and emptied it on the bar: twelve pennies and
one nickel.

"I got enough for a beer," she took count, "but not enough
to get drunk on." And looked left-out of everything.

The old man brought the beer and scooped up half her pennies. "I've got a little money put by," he recalled casually,
"I'd like to invest in a chicken farm. Do you know where I
can go for advice?"

"Why, that's exactly what my Oliver—" she cut herself
short, the shrewd hard girl as gullible at the last as any. And
the old man turned back to his dolls.

His dolls that were never drunken.

Someone pressed the buzzer just right and, peering out, he saw that bully, missing many days, that once had called himself Stingaree.

It was plain enough, the moment Dove came in, that if he wasn't just out of hospital he was just out of jail. But so many had been in and out since the old man had last seen this one he had lost track of who was in where and who was out. And didn't much care which.

"Stay as long as you got something to spend," he warned the fellow, "then get out. Don't let me catch you cadging others for drinks."

"I bought drinks for others a-plenty here and you never seemed to mind, old man," Dove reminded him.

"I don't mind yet," old Doc assured him. "Buy as many for others as you want. What are you having yourself?"

"Whiskey and wash," Dove told him. The old man waited till he'd put his money down.

Dove poured his whiskey into his beer, taking his time with the pouring. Then took it to a table by himself, saying hello to no one. In the dingy light the panders and their women moved like people under water. Overhead the slow fans beat like the beat of a ship's propellers heard on a deep sea floor. Though he had known everyone in the place by his or her first name only five months before, now they seemed people from some lost lifetime hardly known at all. When he asked a woman if she had seen Hallie, all he got was a shrug. Either the woman didn't know or was too careful too tell. Nobody was long remembered on Old Perdido Street.

The only one whose memory of himself seemed fresh was the very one by whom he wished to be unremembered, with her side-of-the-mouth wise grin. Kitty came up to him but before she could either beg for a drink or offer him one, he shook his head, No. He was having no part of her.

It was a quiet afternoon. Dockery looked out once or twice to see that nobody was sneaking his own bottle. Of course the slobs were littering his floor once more—but a kind of tittering delight took him when his slobs did that, for it promised him the later joy of making all spick and span again. It was one of the few joys the old man had left.

He noticed Legless Schmidt's platform leaning against a wall and Schmidt himself at a table, stumps sticking straight out before him, across from Tough Kitty. The old man approved of that: she wouldn't be with him if he weren't spending. He even thought of bringing them a couple shots, compliments of the house, to get them started, but then thought better of it. And took to dusting his dolls, giving Raggedy Ann special attention.

He never heard the first threat. There was only a sort of half-muted babble that rose for a moment above the fans' steady thudding, then curiously subsided. When he looked out the redhaired bully with the hospital pallor had his back planted against the wall and Schmidt was standing before him, stumps spread wide, the flat of his palm on the floor to brace himself.

"I got nothin' against you, mister," Doc heard the bully say.

"You deny you left with her? You deny living with her?"

"I left with her and we lived together too. I don't deny *that*, mister. But if I knew where she was I'd tell you. But I been away myself."

"Don't give me that camouflage. You know where she is, for she sent you here to find out what I'm doing. You came by God because she sent you." He seemed oddly sure of himself. Kitty Twist stood just behind him. "You'll say where she is, and you'll take me there. Or by God you'll take the consequences."

"Give the men room, boys," the outlaws and derelicts vied now like men of public spirit working for the welfare of all.

"If it's what they both want, let them have it out," Dockery took his stand, " 'n no interferin'—a square shake all around."

"Make 'em shake hands, Doc, that shows they're both good fellas."

"Then let's see which is best," Kitty Twist put her two cents in.

The panders pushed the women back, and as fast as they pushed them the women struggled up front again.

Then all felt the big hush come down.

"Back up," Dove waved an iron spittoon, "I don't want trouble," and took one step toward Schmidt.

Schmidt didn't back but merely stood, figuring his man. Then turned, the women and men making room as he knee-walked to his platform and carefully buckled himself in.

"Going home early, Big Dad?" somebody asked, but the cripple didn't answer that. His platform was his weapon as well as his armor, and they all knew that.

Dove began moving slowly along the wall toward where the late alley-light shown through a half-open door. If he got within one jump he'd make a run for that. And never come back.

But as he moved slowly Schmidt moved slowly, a ball-bearinged monster with his hands on the bearings, ready to swivel, charge or reverse. Without closing in, the platform kept pace. Behind him, pale with pleasured terror, faces of men and faces of women followed and paused and followed again. With no sound in the place but the thud of the fans and the quickening breath, like a caught rabbit's breathing, of one who was almost caught.

Dockery saw Schmidt's lips moving silently, like a man trying a combination mentally before executing it. He feinted Dove to left, to right, and each time Dove switched the spittoon, left to right. "I don't know where your wife"—at "wife" Schmidt gave his wheels one hard swift twist and thundered in, his forearm protecting his eyes.

Dove swung the heavy spittoon like a discus under the

protecting arm. Schmidt rocked like a loosened stump in a storm but the platform kept coming in. Dove swung again.

The force of that second blow swiveled Schmidt's wheels, he banged blindly in the wall and rebounded, wheels going this way then that.

"*Get* him," Dove heard the whisper from every side, "*Now. Now. Now. Brain him while he's blind.*" For Schmidt's head was so low that his bald-spot looked at Dove. "*Now. Now. Now.*"

Yet Dove stood with his weapon, gaping at that helpless head; and couldn't lift the hand.

The cripple's face, when he uncovered at last, was smeared by blood down the whole left side where the spittoon's edge had ripped above and below the eye. Dove held out his own bandanna, for no one else offered Schmidt help. And watched while the half-giant daubed the blood off his face till he could see again. Then he touched the bandanna's ends together as if to apologize for soiling it, and returned it to Dove. "Thank you son," he said.

Perhaps it was his tone that made Dove think that was it. For he pushed his way into the crowd. "The fight's done," he said.

The crowd closed ranks.

"The fight's only begun," he heard Schmidt behind him say. "Get your best hold, son."

And reached.

Dove leaped onto the small table at the bar's far end and crouched upon it, trembling in the legs like a panicking puppy up there. Schmidt hurled the table with a single twist, sending Dove sprawling comic-strip fashion, all arms and legs, while the spittoon went clanging like a clock gone insane. The cripple held Dove face down to the floor, steadying him as he floundered. Then lifting him between his great hands, gave his hands that twist of a coiling spring. Dove hit the floor on his side, one arm outflung and the other across his

eyes. Schmidt straddled the outflung arm by riding the platform over it and lifted the other off Dove's eyes. When he
let it go it fell loosely, as something unattached, an arm without a bone.

"He's had it," somebody said.

It was true: they crowded in to see. Whether stunned by
his fall or fogged by fright, he lay like some animal whose
final defense lies in complete helplessness, eyes bright and
unseeing, open to anyone's blows.

Schmidt looked down at the face suddenly like a child's.
Then he brought back his right arm till its knuckles touched
the floor behind him. There were two men standing who
could have put a foot upon it. But one stood looking down
at the way the knuckles stretched the sunburnt skin. And
the other said, "Cold as a frog," nothing more.

"Faking," was Schmidt's answer to that, and brought the
arm high in a full-swinging arch—and down.

It broke with a soft and sogging sound, the very bones
went *oof*.

"I like to get up close to accidents," Kitty Twist pushed in,
and put her ear down to Dove's broken mouth, that was
trying to speak though swallowing blood.

"If you let me go," Kitty Twist heard him say, and repeated it for those not so lucky as to be as close as herself, "he
says if you let him go—"

"I'll say a prayer for you—"

"—he'll say a prayer for you."

"Tell him to save his prayers," Schmidt told her, "I want to
know where my wife is." He looked down at Dove. "Don't
think you can scare me with a little blood," he said.

Dove's head wobbled weakly from side to side, still denying
all.

And though, when Schmidt's fist was raised again everyone
thought "relent"—panders and cripples and fallen girls, yet

when it fell all felt a heartbroken joy. As though each fresh blow redeemed that blow that his life had been to him.

Later, a woman who saw that the face on the floor was no longer a face but a mere paste of cartilage and blood through which a single sinister eye peered blindly, recalled: "When I seen him on the floor unable to rise and fight back, it went right through my mind—*Murdering. Murdering.* Why give *him* a chance?"

And when it was done Schmidt looked all around like a man in a lifting daze. He looked at them all as though there were something they knew he did not know. As if he did not understand the blood that was fouling his hands.

Kitty Twist knelt to put her thin arms around the cripple's neck, and her lips were almost on his before he pushed her off, his eyes glassed by disgust.

"Get this man help and open the doors," he commanded, and the doors were opened just in time to let the last of daylight in.

Schmidt saw the day and the open door. Yet he sat his platform without a move until Dockery said, "Get him out of here."

And eagerly then, its tension relieved and its contempt wakened, the crowd went for the half-giant as though he were just some sort of thing. One shoved him from behind. Another hauled him by his hair. While another began kicking the little wheels that only a minute before he had feared; but that now didn't move fast enough to please him. While that same poor bitchified prey, Kitty Twist, spat down the nape of his neck.

And he took it, Schmidt took it, he took it all. Like a statue of grief with a sorrowing air, as though he had done nothing more than their own work for them: a saint of the amputees.

Out of the speakeasy that had outlived its time, through the final door of a dead decade, they wheeled the deposed hero that once had been a man. Onto a downhill street.

Somebody gave the platform a shove. And waited a minute, with others who waited, to watch the thing reel from one side of the walk to the other, gathering speed as it lost control, making uphill trudgers dodge like dodging a drunken wrong-way driver—when it hit the telephone pole not one laughed. They merely stood watching to detect, from their distance, some movement from that crumpled lump, half on the curb and half on the street. But saw no movement at all.

Inside they heard the juke box begin—

You made a lot of money back in '22
But whiskey and women made a fool of you—

And returned inside with the executive air of men ready, if need be, to vie with one another for whatever was best for the public welfare.

On Saturday nights the backland squatters came into Arroyo by Model T and by cart, but most came by foot. Some had shoes and some had none. But booted or barefoot they all shambled; and the woman stayed just a step behind all the way. She would have her shawl drawn across her mouth to keep the dangerous night-damp out and he would be breathing into a handkerchief or bandanna; after the Mexican manner.

But when they got into town there was so much talking to be done they forgot all about the dangerous air, or perhaps the air inside the city limits was made of better stuff. For the women chattered through all the stores, pointed in the windows with other wives or went to see a movie starring Rod La Roque. They all tried to get the old man to the movie too, whether he would or no: that much less chance of his getting drunk was the point.

He seldom fell for that. He sent her in and shambled off to the courthouse steps to hear if the preacher had anything to say he hadn't said on a thousand other Saturdays.

An uneasy rumor was going around that the old man wasn't as strong against the Pope as he once had been. In fact he didn't seem as strong against anything as he once had been. The wrath and the fire that had been as good as a free shot of tequila seemed to have gone out of Fitz.

Was it whiskey or weariness that had caught up with him? Or just that, since Byron had been buried, there was nobody left to heckle him? Whatever it was, when he led them to the uttermost edge of Damnation now and forced them to look over the terrible rim, the fall they saw was no more than a foot or two into a coal yard of rain-wetted cinders with a few rusty beer cans lying about. Broken gin bottles lay among the dead slag that held promise of neither flame nor fire. They sniffed for the assurance of sulphur on the air: and smelled nothing but marigold that grows in old dumps.

Marigold mixed with the scent of blown dust that they knew so well it had no more scent than air. The old man had not really taken them anywhere.

Yet out of courtesy and having nowhere else to go, they still listened to the threats of his faded passion.

"The glory is gone from motherhood," he told them. "Women who smoke and drink and wear pants are unfit to be mothers of men. What a monster-osity is a cursing, drinking, smoking, painted, bobbed-haired mother! When the Pope says modern woman is an insult to her maker he got more backbone than our own protestant preachers. Didn't the *Lord* say, if a woman have long hair, it is a glory to her?

"More shameful things are worn by women on the open street these days than were worn in brothels a few years ago," the old man went on and on. And there was nobody to ask him how did he know what had been worn in brothels a few years ago.

"Even our little girls are turned out into the streets almost naked, inviting God's judgement on sin black as Sodom! *Are* we willing to pay the price?" he asked, and answered his own question, "When it comes to God dealing with a nation's sin, there are no dollar days. Are we willing to pay the price?"

They stared up at him indifferently. If they had the price of anything they would be in the movie or brothel, that look told.

Few noticed, in that dusky light, the man in the city suit, a broken feather in his cap, leaning against a tree in the shadows. Strangers came through town at all hours these days.

"He's lost the call, that's all," Dove realized, trailing his hand down the howitzer barrel to where he felt it narrowing. Then touching a tree to his left with his walking stick, touched his way to the street. "Not paved yet," he thought at the stick's first touch of the familiar dust.

Under the street lamp in front of the domino parlor two Mexicans saw him coming along the curb. One took a step toward him to guide him across the street, but the other held him back. "If he needs help he'll ask or it," he told his friend.

The man didn't need help, it appeared. He waited for a cart to pass, then went without haste but directly down that old road that had once led west.

This was in that hour that frogs begin, when the scent off the honey mesquite comes strongest.

Deep in the chaparral frogs were clamoring. As he came near they ceased, were quiet as he passed; then set up a clamor again. It was that hour that frogs begin, when the scent off the honey mesquite comes strongest.

Behind him a car, sounding more like a Chevie than a Ford, came banging by and pulled up a few yards ahead.

"Give you a lift, bud?" a man's voice asked. As he came to the car Dove caught the scent off a woman's clothes.

"Am I going the right way to the chili parlor?" he asked.

"You're standing fifty feet from it now," a girl's voice told him.

"Can you see if there's a light in it?"

He felt her bare arm as she leaned across him to see.

"There's a light upstairs," she reported. "Should I holler them down for you?"

"Thank you kindly, I'll find my own way now," he told her. He heard the little car go banging back and felt himself alone in the big Rio night.

And felt a strange content in that.

"If God made anything better than a girl," Dove thought, "He sure kept it to Himself."

That was all long ago in some brief lost spring, in a place that is no more. In that hour that frogs begin and the scent off the mesquite comes strongest.